WILLIE JOHN

To Penny, Amanda and Paul.
They were the ones who took the knocks and
shared the joys.

WILLIE JOHN

THE STORY OF MY LIFE

Willie John McBride
and Peter Bills

PORTRAIT

Visit the Portrait website!

PORTRAIT Portrait publishes a wide range of non-fiction, including biography, history, science, music, popular culture and sport.

Visit our website to:
- read descriptions of our popular titles
- buy our books over the internet
- take advantage of our special offers
- enter our monthly competition
- learn more about your favourite Portrait authors

VISIT OUR WEBSITE AT: www.portraitbooks.com

Copyright © 2004 by Willie John McBride and Peter Bills

First published in 2004 by **Portrait**
An imprint of Piatkus Books Ltd
5 Windmill Street, London W1T 2JA
email: info@piatkus.co.uk

Reprinted 2004

The moral right of the authors has been asserted

A catalogue record for this book is available from the British Library

ISBN 0 7499 5024 2
ISBN 0 7499 5028 5

Edited by Lisa Hughes and Krystyna Mayer
Text and plate design by Jerry Goldie
Picture credits: Inpho, Getty Images and Corbis

This book has been printed on paper manufactured
with respect for the environment using wood from
managed sustainable resources

Typeset by Phoenix Photosetting, Chatham, Kent
Printed and bound in Great Britain by
Mackays Ltd, Chatham, Kent

Contents

Acknowledgements

The authors wish to record their grateful thanks to several people for their most valid contributions to the entire process of this book. To Gill Bailey, Editorial Director at Piatkus, for all her efforts, to Anna Crago (Editor), Isabelle Almeida (project manager), Lisa Hughes and Krystyna Mayer (editors), Ken Leeder (cover design), Jerry Goldie (text design) and Lisa Footit (indexer). Also to the literary agent John Pawsey for his help before and during the project.

Thanks, too, to Penny McBride for supplying the authors with an endless stream of sustenance in the form of food, teas and coffees! Our grateful thanks to one and all.

CHAPTER 1

A Date with Destiny

My love for Northern Ireland and the people who inhabit our community has been the underlying theme of my whole life. Nowhere am I happier than among the rolling hills in and around my home; nowhere, I believe, would I find warmer, more down-to-earth folk than those who live on the little farms and homes of this region.

'Dark and true and tender is the north,' wrote Tennyson, and it is doubtful whether he could have provided more apt a phrase, had he been thinking of my homeland when he penned those words. But the highlight, indeed the climax, of my long sporting life occurred a very long way away from the hills of County Antrim or Belfast city centre. It took place on the African continent, at the southern tip of South Africa, on the coast where the rugged land meets the warm waters of the mighty Indian Ocean. The venue was Port Elizabeth and the date was 13 July 1974. Just five weeks earlier, I had celebrated my thirty-fourth birthday.

What was I doing, you may wonder, in far away South Africa, without my beloved wife, Penny, and my children, Amanda and Paul, as I approached my mid-thirties? I had asked myself the same question more than once or twice. I was participating in my fifth successive British Lions tour, my third to South Africa alone. The young boy of just twenty-one who had eagerly donned his Lions blazer, tied his first Lions tie with justifiable pride and set off for what he expected to be the adventure of a lifetime to South Africa back in 1962, had returned to that tremendous yet tortured land twelve years later, older and wiser. Alas, my earlier visits to this great land, in 1962 and 1968, had resulted in heavy defeats. The Lions had simply been unable to handle the power and purpose of the renowned Springboks. This time, however, I returned as captain of the 1974 Lions and 13 July was a date with destiny for my team and myself.

We led the mighty Springboks 2–0 in a 4-match Test series. No touring side, not even the feared New Zealand All Blacks, had yet beaten the South Africans in a Test series in their own country. History, destiny, call it what you will, beckoned us with a seductive smile. But first, we had to endure what we knew would be eighty minutes of cruel physical punishment. The South Africans were, and still are, proud people; rugby was the game of the white population, which completely dominated the sport. We expected that, their pride hurt and their reputations savaged, they would hurl the proverbial kitchen sink at us in that crucial third Test match. If only it had been a rusty old kitchen sink and nothing else.

Boots, fists, knees, heads and anything else within reach came at us straight from the kick-off that day. The late Welsh rugby man Clem Thomas, a British Lion himself in South Africa in 1955 and by then a reporter for the *Observer* newspaper, wrote later, 'The game became the most violent Test match I ever witnessed. I sat there in amazement as two massive fist fights broke out, one in each half.' But I knew the mettle of the men alongside me. We survived a frantic opening in which the ball became smeared with the blood of many players, to emerge 7–3 ahead at half-time. Then, in the second half, our technical superiority edged us clear. We held our nerve, began to play our rugby and, by the end, had won the Test match by 26–9. The series and the glory was ours: we had created history by doing what no other visiting rugby side in this great country had ever done before.

The reactions of men at momentous times such as this are myriad. Some simply sink to their knees, a combination of elation and exhaustion having hit them with the force of a boxer's punch. Others, their rigid focus on the game still locked onto their personal mindsets, simply shake hands and walk off the field. Others leap into the air, releasing their tension in a series of wild jumps and celebratory acts. But this time, there was a single act that epitomised for me what I had tried to inculcate into my men throughout the previous nine or ten weeks.

Without any prompting, once the immediate embraces had finished after the final whistle, the fifteen British Lions on the field cast their eyes up into the grandstand at Port Elizabeth's Boet Erasmus stadium. What we were looking for were our colleagues, those Lions who had been with us since the start of the adventure, the men who had played an equally fulsome part in what we had just achieved. We saw them, standing up and cheering, and we simply stood there and returned the gesture, applauding each and every one of them for the part they had played in the historic achievement.

You can imagine the noise, the fuss and the chaos that broke all around us at the end of that match. For twelve long years, through three hard, demanding tours, I had seen at first hand what was required for the Lions to win a Test series in South Africa. In 1962 and 1968 we had failed; now, six years later, led by myself, we had come back to the country and at last triumphed.

Yet strangely, in the aftermath of victory, the importance of what we had just achieved did not fill my mind. Thoughts of a long night's celebrations ahead were not at the forefront of my imagination. Instead, when I finally got back to our team hotel and could settle down in a corner that evening and quietly smoke my pipe, my mind drifted far from South Africa, back to the little farm in County

Antrim where I had been born. In the midst of my greatest sporting triumph, the memory of my own father came back vividly to me.

When my father died at the sadly early age of fifty-eight, I was only four years old, but I do have a few clear memories of him. For example, I remember sitting on his knee beside the fire and singing. These, by the way, were the days when we had open fires and the neighbours would come round in the evenings to sit, sing and tell stories. There would be bread baking on the griddle and someone would pick up a fiddle or play an accordion. It was what we called in Ireland a ceilidh, or social gathering, and the next evening it would move on to someone else's house.

I can remember the day my father died with absolute clarity. It was Halloween 1944. My mother was baking an apple pie and I remember him knocking on the window and asking, 'Is it finished? Can I taste it?' She said, 'Go on, go on. We'll have it at 6 o'clock,' so my father went off to the potato fields to catch a rabbit for the pot. Sadly, within minutes my brother had run in, shouting that my father had fallen down and wasn't breathing. They carried him into the house on a door, which they had unhooked from the shed. He had fallen off a horse some time before, and his death was put down to a blood clot that moved and suddenly killed him; whatever the reason, he was gone. I was too young to understand what it really meant, but I do recall crying and crying, and saying that maybe he would come back next week.

After my father died, my mother, who was still only in her forties, sat us all down. It was a sad and very poignant occasion and the younger ones among us were in tears. There were five of us children. The eldest, my sister, was thirteen; the youngest, my younger brother, eighteen months. We sat around the fire and my mother said, 'We will never have any money, but I will guarantee you one thing: there will always be food on the table.' The fact was, you didn't make money on a farm; you made a living, that was all, but if my mother set herself a goal she always achieved it. Those were tough years, but she made sure we all had a chance in life. She was a brave and strong woman and I think I inherited those qualities from her, as well as a propensity for hard work and helping others.

Memories of those times came back strongly as I reflected on what we had achieved in South Africa that day. I was certainly proud, proud for the memory of my father and proud for my mother, who was back home in Northern Ireland, but I was also delighted both for the great young rugby men who had accompanied me on this trip and for myself. It had been the climax of my entire playing career, something I had dedicated myself to achieving for more than a decade. When I finally achieved it, the feeling was sweet indeed.

CHAPTER 2

The Boy and the Bees in the Apple Trees

'd like to tell you that I played rugby throughout my years of childhood. Doubtless there were boys in most countries of the world kicking a football or rugby ball about near their home with their friends until it was dark. But the fact is that I didn't play rugby football at school until my last year, by which time I was seventeen. Father's early death meant that I couldn't; I had to come home and work on the farm throughout my school days.

I suppose that given what followed, in terms of how I was to make my modest mark upon this world, I should also be able to tell you that I was born at around 3 p.m., kick-off time, on a Saturday afternoon. Alas, the truth is less fanciful. I first appeared in this world on Thursday, 6 June 1940, although it was in the afternoon. I was a poor mite of a thing upon arrival, weighing twelve pounds at birth.

I came into a world literally exploding into conflict. At 4 a.m. on the previous day, the German forces on the Somme had started their assault on Paris. Indeed, those born on or around the same date as mine would share their birthdays with some momentous events during the course of the next few years. In 1944, for example, in the early hours of my birthday, not only was a small boy lying in his bed, dreaming of what gifts might await him upon daybreak. On the Normandy coast of France, gliders attached to the Sixth Airborne Division were quietly landing just behind the beaches; the precursor to that morning's D-Day landings.

I was still in the little place where I was born, though; on the family's farm at Ballymatoskerty Road, in the midst of a small farming community called Moneyglass, near Toomebridge in County Antrim, Northern Ireland, some thirty to thirty-five miles from Belfast. I was fourth in the family. Firstly, there was a girl, Sarah, or Sadie as she became known, who was born eleven years before me. Then came two boys, Robert who was born when Sadie was two, and John, born three years later. I was supposed to be another girl, although I don't know what would have happened if I had been a girl. Perhaps Northern Ireland's netball team might have beckoned? My given name wasn't Willie-John, but William James. My father was William James and my mother always called me William. Indeed, if there was a William or John in the family, the tradition was that it would be carried on from one generation to the next. Another brother, Tom, was born three years after me.

When Dad died, Sadie was thirteen, Robert eleven and John nine. Sadie went to the local grammar school, a privilege for which you had to pay money. My parents didn't have a lot of money even before Dad died, but afterwards things became extremely difficult for us financially. However, despite her own grief and undoubted concern at the magnitude of the task now confronting her, my mother knuckled down to bringing up five children on her own. She usually found some money somehow, probably by selling a few cattle, and she was an amazing woman in every sense, including budgeting. In fact, she should probably have been an accountant.

Robert, my eldest brother, whom we know as Bertie, left school within a couple of years of my father's death. He would probably have stayed on had my father lived, but as the eldest boy he was needed at home. We had a farm of about fifty acres, roughly a dozen milking cows, some other cattle and a few pigs, as well as the working horses, because there were no such things as machines on a small farm like ours. Of course, we didn't have electricity on our farm, and for lights we used oil lamps.

The name of our house was Park View and it looked over a big estate, which had been taken over by the army soon after hostilities broke out in 1939. The roads that they put through the estate in order to do exercises are still there to this day. There was an aerodrome and I remember the planes landing in Toomebridge, big army planes. There was a machine gun opposite our house, trained on this estate where they played these mock war games. I can still recall our old hay shed being full of American soldiers.

One of my earliest memories is of going out and watching these men in uniform, and I remember they had a big cauldron where they were cooking. I'll never forget this man with his sleeve rolled up, plunging the full length of his arm into the cauldron and stirring it, as though he'd dropped a ring into it and was trying to find it in the murky depths of the stew pot. I'd never seen that before. My mummy doesn't do that, I thought to myself, she has a big wooden spoon. Then, of course, when the war ended in 1945, the soldiers all disappeared within a few months, but for some of those war years, they had literally taken over the farms.

Then, at the age of five, it was time for my first experience of school, Duneane Primary School. To get there, we had to walk, which meant leaving the farm shortly after 8 a.m. It was three miles each way, with my brothers, and for a young boy of little more than five, I can tell you, it was some walk. My big brothers, like big brothers everywhere, took little account of a smaller member of the family in short trousers, his little legs pumping furiously in a bold bid to keep up with them. But I managed. When we got there, we would settle down into the two little classrooms at the primary school, a small partition that folded back separating the two.

Fifty-eight years later, in spring 2003, I went back to that school – by car, I am pleased to say, not walking – to open a small garden that had been made. That day, I met a teacher, Mr Jim Giffin, who had been there during my last year. I remembered that Mr Giffin had a cane, for of course there was corporal punishment then. He used to stand at the top of the room and flick the cane and we were scared stiff. He could use it, and did so from time to time.

Before Mr Giffin arrived, I remember there was one boy who always appeared to be tough, but one day he suddenly ran out of school to the two big beech trees that stood close by (even now they are still there). It transpired that he had had an altercation with a teacher and ran out to these trees. We had a lady principal at that time and she ran after him. He climbed up one of the trees and was perhaps fifteen feet up when she commanded, 'Come down here,' to which he replied, 'I'll not be down today.' He was as good as his word, and stayed there all day. She waited for a while, but eventually even she got fed up with waiting and went back to work. When she had gone home and the coast was clear, he came down. He must have been about ten, while I was around six years old at the time.

When I started school, I went into baby infants, with two teachers, and the rest of the children were in the room on the other side of the partition. There were about thirty or forty children altogether in this country school, but we lived far from the world of luxury. There was no central heating, so the teachers would send us out at lunchtime to get more wood from the hedgerows and they'd load some coal or turf on to the small fire in the schoolroom. You would move around desks during the day, rotating so that you kept reasonably warm and everybody got a turn near the fire. Like at home, we had oil lamps in school.

The younger ones finished at 2 p.m., the older ones at 3 p.m. That meant that I had an hour to wait for my elder brothers to come home with me. By the time we had walked the three miles back to our farm, it was always dark in the winter. We walked along the roads, because there were not the dangers in terms of the traffic that there are today. I remember vividly starting that long walk home, but sometimes there would be farmers from the big mill very near the school. That was a godsend, because you might get a lift on the horse and cart almost the whole way back. It was probably quicker walking, because the old horse would plod along slowly, but it was still a brilliant feeling if you saw a farmer coming along with a horse and cart, because you knew you'd get a lift and get a rest until you got home.

Like most people living in the country, we went to bed early at night, usually by 9 p.m. for the grown-ups and much earlier for the children. As we got older and all had our little jobs to do, we needed that sleep. By the end of a typical day, I was physically tired and ready for bed. We would wash before bed, of course, but again, there were none of the luxuries we take for granted in our modern-day lives. There was no mains water in our farmhouse. Our water was pumped from wells and, because there was no electricity, we had to pump this water by hand.

We had huge tanks and one of my jobs when I came back from school was to hand-pump the water into the tank so it would be gravity-fed to the cattle, the pigs and the rest. It was the same for the dwelling house. There were two wells; one for the house, one for the garden. Believe me, with hand pumps that meant an awful lot of hard work. There was nothing more boring, frustrating or soul destroying than to pump the water and fill up the tanks. It could take me more than an hour. I remember being in what they called the byre, where the cattle were, and I'd be pumping, and the cows would be drinking while I was pumping, and I used to think to myself, furiously, 'I'm losing ground here – they're drinking it faster than I'm pumping it.'

There were also no milking machines, so we had hand milking on the farm. We milked the cows before we went to school in the morning. Organising us to do these tasks was where my mother came in, and she was amazing. We all had our jobs. Someone's job was to feed the pigs; someone else's was to carry the bales. You didn't have balers on our farm. Without tractors, horses did all the heavy work, which meant you had to feed and water them, then carry the loose hay and feed the younger cattle. So my mother would line us all up and say, 'You feed the cows, you feed the pigs, you provide the water and then we'll all meet at 6 o'clock when we're going to milk the cows.' We all had our own cows, which we would milk by hand, and then all that stuff had to be washed and sterilised in the dairy, and all the milk put through. It was unbelievable. My mother would manage all this and she would work in the house as well.

Mother was a very religious woman and Sunday was a holy day. No work whatsoever was done on our farm on Sundays, except the necessary things like feeding cattle and milking the cows. She was very strict; nothing else could be done, such as work in the fields. Then one year we had a bad harvest through heavy rain. For all farmers, survival so often comes down to just one thing: a good or bad harvest. We grew crops like oats, grass seed and flax, all of which were susceptible to bad weather. The ground was so wet that we had to cut the oats with hand-held implements, scythes, which was terribly labour intensive, but this particular time we had no choice. Then we tied up the sheaves into what were called stooks. In farming language, a stook was four sheaves.

Then, amidst this awful wet summer, one Sunday morning dawned, bright and clear. Many of the farmers all over the hills and valleys of Northern Ireland, in countryside made a vivid green by the long wet weeks of the summer, were working, taking advantage of the sudden lull in the weather. Of course, we expected mother to do the same, but she wouldn't hear of such a thing. 'No, we're not working on a Sunday,' she told us. I suppose in a sense us boys were glad to have a day off, but we also knew a glorious opportunity had been lost. Or so we thought.

That night, we all went to bed as usual, but this time a little earlier. We four boys all slept in the one room, about the size of my current sitting room at home. We had all been asleep when we were suddenly woken up, at 2 a.m. on the Monday morning, by my mother. The Sabbath Day had ended. She came into the room with a lamp, roused each of us gently and said, 'Boys, I've been in the field and the corn is dry. The moon is shining and if we get up now and get to work, we can have this cut and stacked before dawn.' So the four of us got out of bed, dressed as quickly as we could and went out into the fields to work.

There was a beauty in the scene all around us; in the big, bright moon shining down upon the corn, the occasional haunting cry of a mammal or bird somewhere near the farm and the honest toil of each of us in the moonlight. But there was something else I saw and understood that night, something that I would take into my adult life and that would be a key element of what I set out to achieve on the rugby football fields of the world. It was a feeling of unity, a sense of coming together and working for each other, for the benefit of the whole group. Perhaps the finest example of this trait would come years later, on the sun-baked sports fields of South Africa, where the 1974 Lions, under my leadership, would demonstrate such qualities every day of our tour.

We four brothers worked throughout the night, with my mother there doing her bit all the while. We had the job finished by the morning. Then we went into the farmhouse and my mother cooked us breakfast, after which we all set off for school, that three-mile walk away. I suspect we probably slept rather well that night, once we'd walked the three miles back home again in the evening and then milked the cows before supper. My sister, by the way, was at nursing college by then, so she was no longer living at home.

There were endless other things that typified my mother: her budgeting, her planning and her management. I learned so much from that and yet the extraordinary thing was that she had had no experience of such things; these were just skills she had developed. But life must have been a nightmare for her at times, because we didn't always agree among ourselves and sometimes that would spill over into fights. Boys will be boys, remember.

We had not only a farm, but also an orchard with apples. Every autumn, we would all help to pick maybe ten tons of cooking apples, which had to be graded and washed before being put through.

Linen was a big thing, and on our farm flax was an important crop. We had about eight acres of it, but it was a very labour-intensive crop. You had to pull it by hand and the neighbours would come in to help. Then you put it into the dams and retted it there for about ten days. After all that, you had to bring it out of the dams, spread it on the land, dry it, tie it up and take it to the linen mill. This process was staggered, because while your crop would be in the dam retting, you would go and help pull your neighbour's. You had to spread it the same day it came out of the dam, when it was still wet. By the time you had finished doing this, your neighbour's crop was ready for taking out.

I can still see us today, involved in this labour-intensive business. Your hands ached and were sore for days afterwards. Today, too many synthetic fibres are produced for world trade and it is all much cheaper in Asia, where labour costs are far less, but with flax, you still had to go through those processes, whatever the modern technology available. That's why linen was so expensive; it cost so much in terms of time. My mother managed all that and she also found the time, God knows how, to bake every day.

All the family worked hard. I remember Robert, my elder brother, becoming our horse man. Now that meant a lot of work and responsibility. Horses aren't like tractors; you don't just drive them into a garage, turn them off and lock the door. Horses have got to be tended, groomed, fed and exercised, particularly in wintertime, and Robert did all that, even though he wasn't that big physically.

I remember one day, when I was about ten years old, my mother telling me to go and take Robert his snack lunch out in the fields. We churned every Thursday and were all brought up on buttermilk with bread. I took Robert this for him to eat. He was ploughing a large field one furrow at a time with our horse. I smile nowadays when I watch a field being furrowed by a farmer sitting up there in his modern machine. That machinery enables him to cover about eight furrows in one row. When I was growing up, our old horse managed just the one. Nor did I realise how difficult that was, until the day I took Robert his lunch.

'Look, I don't want to stop, so could you take the horse down the furrow and back again while I have my buttermilk and bread?' he asked me, wiping the sweat off his brow. I was only ten and looked in trepidation at what seemed to me to be this very big horse, but my mother's old creed of always trying to help out others got the better of me. 'Course I can.' I answered. But really, I wasn't big enough.

I started off OK and got the horse going, but then came trouble. The plough hit a big stone, the thing went right out of my hands and I went with it. I just didn't have the strength to hold it. Robert came to my rescue and hauled the horse and plough back into the desired line, but I remember watching and thinking he had to be very strong, and if it had happened to him he would have fought it and held on.

Perhaps it wasn't so surprising that Robert grew up to be one of the strongest men I've seen. He could lift a plough and put it on a trailer or do anything like that. One day, a fire broke out in a hay shed and inside it was a trailer with bags of fertiliser sitting on it. There must have been two tons of the stuff. Suddenly, the trailer with the fertiliser emerged from the shed, with Robert pushing it to safety all by himself. The bigger the challenge, the more he rose to the task. Many is the time I have thought that if he had played rugby, his strength would have ensured he'd have been tremendous.

The brother nearest to me in age, John, was different. John liked to be around the farmyard, tending the animals, looking after the pigs. It's funny, but some people seem to have a natural touch with animals and John has always been like that. He inherited from my father a love for bee keeping. Dad always liked to keep bees, it was really his hobby, and he could lift a handful of them without even wearing a veil. Indeed, one of my sadly few memories of my father is of him standing still near a beehive, the bees creeping around his neck and face. He would smile, perhaps even laugh gently, but the rest of us were scared stiff by this demonstration of manliness or whatever it was. I have since been told that there is something in the body – whether it is an acid or something in the skin, I don't know – that bees and other insects recognise and respect. Dad had that and he could lift the bees and look at them and examine them to see if there was any disease present. He was an amazing man.

My brother Robert didn't have that, because he wore a veil and still got stung despite this. I remember him once being in bed for a couple of days, with his eyes burning after being stung. Then one day I too got involved in the world of bees and it is a day I shall never forget.

The men were busy working in the fields and I was only about ten or twelve years old. I was in the kitchen with my mother, and noticed that she was looking out to where we kept the hives. It was a warm day and anybody who knows bees knows that when a new queen is born in the hive, one will have to go because two queens are not going to live side by side. So one of the queens goes and she takes some workers with her and they swarm in support as she flies out. It's like watching a dense cloud, for there can be that many bees.

On this particular day, the bees had swarmed and were hanging, like a rather large ice-cream cone, in an apple tree. There was always a spare hive, so that if they swarmed they could enter this empty one once the queen had been led in there. My mother noticed the bees in the apple tree and said to me, 'You know, they're up a bit high, but if you get a ladder and climb up there, you can perhaps help save them.' She was worried that they would literally take off and disappear into the countryside. Then they would be lost.

In vain, I looked around for support. My elder brothers were in the fields, working. All I could do was to try and grow up another six or seven years instantly and do a man's job. But the summer afternoon air was filled with just one sound, the humming and buzzing of bees. I didn't want to leave the kitchen, never mind climb up into the tree to where the swarm was.

Mother came out with me and we got the old ladder up against the tree. Gingerly, I climbed it, as carefully and as hesitantly as I could. My instructions from mother were to shake the branch gently into a bucket and put a cloth over it, hopefully trapping the queen among the other bees. Of course, if you get the queen, everything is great because the others follow. So I gradually got the white enamel bucket in place, all the while trying hard not to lose my footing on the ladder as I leaned across, I got the bucket over the bees, and when I gave the branch a shake, they virtually filled my bucket. I quickly pulled the cloth from over my shoulder, covered the bucket with it and gave a loud whoop of excitement. I'd done the job. I held the bucket, which was full of bees, and my mother said, 'Well done,' from below, on the ground.

Alas, barely had the words left her mouth when I started to step down the ladder. Now this wasn't one of the modern ladders that have strong metal struts on to which you can step safely. This was an old, rickety, wooden ladder that ought to have been thrown on to the garden bonfire years ago, because as I started to come down it, a rung suddenly snapped as it took my weight. The cloth went one way, the now open bucket went the other way and I went tumbling down to the bottom, where I lay at my mother's feet in a heap. But there was no time to reflect. The bees were loose and they were angry. They went buzzing and humming all around us, so Mum and I took off for the safety of the kitchen like a couple of Olympic sprinters in the making. I can tell you, I doubt whether I ever covered a hundred yards or so faster than I did that day, with hundreds of bees in hot pursuit. I was frightened out of my wits and felt a total failure.

I got a couple of stings and a few bruises for my trouble, but no bees. Not then, anyway. But the strange sequel to the story was that when the sun went down and all had calmed down outside, Mum and I went back to the old apple tree to get the bucket and saw that it was still there, and so was just about every bee, with the queen among them! It was unbelievable, for we thought we had lost the lot. By then my brothers were back at the farmhouse and they took the bucket with the bees and put it inside the spare hive.

To this day, John still keeps bees. One Sunday, when we went over to his home, we sat and watched the bees working away and it was fascinating. A beehive is divided into so many sections. You have the drones, which are the males and the guys who tend to keep guard and that sort of thing. You have the queen, who is, of course, the head of the house. And then there are the workers, who comprise the vast majority. They're like the forwards on a rugby field – they do all the real work.

The drones fertilise the queen at certain times of the year, but the bees are obviously not going to feed them all winter so they bring them out, cut their wings and drop them off. They store the honey for the winter and that's really the idea. We took the honey from the bees, but then we fed them candy to supplement their loss of the honey. It was intriguing to watch a beehive and see how it all worked. My mother, too, liked bees, and I suppose that part of the reason she kept them after my father's death was in his memory.

Both Robert and John carried on the family farming tradition and both of them have their sons working with them on their farms today. They have bought more land over the years and the farms have got bigger, but I like to see them there, working the land. This closeness between our family and the soil goes back a long way and, although I chose white-collar employment, to this day nothing gives me greater pleasure than to feel the soil in my hands.

Tom, my younger brother by three years, was brighter than me academically, but I had the pleasure of being what you might call his 'guardian' at school. We went to primary school and then I attended Ballymena Academy and Tom followed me to both. He was a good lad, but he had a bit of an asthma problem, what they called 'a bad chest' in the country areas. That meant he didn't really play rugby, although it didn't prevent him from trying other sports, such as golf, badminton and table tennis. Tom and I became closer as he grew up and we had similar interests in a lot of ways. Eventually, when the time came for him to leave school, he followed me into banking. That meant that two of the brothers became farmers, the other two bankers. Don't ask me about the genes that directed the latter course of life – I haven't a clue about them.

As for my only sister Sadie, she was eleven years older than me so she undoubtedly helped my mother bring me up. But she was busy with her schoolwork and quite quickly disappeared into nursing and the long years of study that precede qualification for that job. I still remember her doing her bit around the farm after my father died, though. She was a strong girl and would help with the milking and tasks like that. I don't think having four brothers was ever a problem. Sadie could give as good as she got and smaller brothers were by no means an insoluble problem for her. When it came to work, she never shirked a thing, a quality that was to serve her admirably when she did eventually qualify as a nurse.

There wasn't a lot of time for what my mother used to call 'kicking a football about'. We were too busy, and always had work to do – but we also had plenty of fun and laughs. One of the big days of our year was the local Sunday school outing to Portrush on the Antrim coast. Where my mother found the money I do not know, but she would give us half a crown for the day. Half a crown was a lot of money to us and we would go off, clutching this lovely big silver coin tightly. On our trips to Portrush, we would meet up with the children we went to school with and play games, often on the beach. It was a day out away from home and very simple, but very pleasant. We went by bus.

Then, around the start of the 1950s, the tractor came in and we got our first one. That was when it became a bit easier and, eventually, we got our first car. When the time came for me to move to a bigger school, I was sent to Ballymena Academy, a grammar school about ten miles away. But if I thought that meant I would be let off duties back home because of the journey by bus, I was to be disappointed. I still had to help milk the cows before I went to school in the mornings, after which I'd walk down to the main road and get the 8.10 a.m. bus to Ballymena. It was the same in the evenings. I could never be involved in activities after school, because I had to get home straightaway and do my jobs on the farm. It was like a code of honour, an accepted practice. There was always work to be done.

There was a church near the school and stables within the school grounds. People went to church by horse and trap. When we went into church, the horses were put in the stables. My mother always insisted we went to church on Sunday, sometimes twice in the day. I was also in the Boys Brigade and that required more time and commitment, but what it also meant was that we had no time to be idle, to get bored, as I fear so many modern-day youngsters appear to be. You just didn't have time to sit around and the idea of wasting any time was abhorrent. Today I confess I have let one thing that my mother taught me lapse: I am not a good churchgoer. Perhaps, or so I might hope, I did so much then that I don't need to do it as much now. At least, that is all I can plead. I just hope I am a good Christian, though.

There was no television, so we made our own amusements. We raced on our bicycles when we were ten or eleven. We might try to play soccer sometimes among ourselves, but only when we could get a pig's bladder and kick it around the yard. We killed the pigs on our farm, or at least my brothers did when they were old enough, and we'd sometimes have the bladder for a football. I learned how to kill them, too, when the time came. You always knew when a pig had been killed on our farm, because we'd be eating pig's liver for a week afterwards. There was a man brought in to kill the pigs in the early years, when the three of us were too young to do it, but eventually my eldest brother would do the job himself.

I certainly don't think you could have called it a humane act. Firstly, you had to hook the pig with a long pole and a rod attached to the end and you tried to pull it out of the pen to where you were going to kill it. Then, once you had it secured, you hit it on the head, stuck the knife in, twisted it inside the heart and bled it to death, trying to hang on to it all the while. Then you got some hot water, scraped the carcass to take all the bristles off, hung it up and gutted it, taking all the liver and insides out. So we did all that.

For those of you who have only ever lived in towns or cities and bought meat in nicely packaged wrappers from your local super-markets, I have bad news. I am afraid this very process is enacted, in one way or another, for you to buy your meat in the usual way. This was a way of life for country people rearing their own animals. You regarded the animals as your food and your livelihood. Getting sentimental about their deaths was never possible. You and your family were involved in your own struggle for survival.

There was never any waste with my mother and, of course, they didn't want the liver in the factory, where we would send the pig for money. So my mother would say, 'Take a bit of liver down to old Hugh, Paddy or Willie,' and we would send them a bit of liver to do for a meal or two. These were our neighbours. There were no fridges then. The food was fresh, so when you got it, you cooked it and ate it. I well remember setting off on the big bicycle, taking a part of the pig's liver around to the neighbours.

It is funny how busy people always have time and my mother was a good example of this. We kept hens, at one time 300 or 400 of them, and sold their eggs. At special times of the year, such as Christmas, Halloween and times like that, my mother would bake cakes for old Paddy or whoever; guys around us who perhaps lived on their own and had a struggle. She would say, 'Now take that to Hugh and this one to Paddy.' She was that sort of woman, but that was the way it was in the countryside. When Dad died, the neighbours came and helped us pick the potatoes and that was typical. The countryside worked together and helped each other.

Mum would also rear half a dozen geese, and they waddled around the yard. Then at Christmas, we would kill one and have a goose on the table. It was as traditional as the lines of the old song: 'Oh, Christmas is coming/The goose is getting fat/Please to put a penny in the old man's hat/If you haven't got a penny/A ha'penny will do/If you haven't got a ha'penny/Then God bless you.' We would eat the chickens, too, wringing the necks of any that we needed for the pot. I keep chickens myself today for free-range eggs, because I can be sure of what they have been fed and that they have had a good life, free to run around in the open and pecking wherever they wish.

I remember with great warmth and a big smile the sense of togetherness that we had among ourselves as a family and as members of the local community. I hope, too, I now have that feeling of community with my own neighbours. It is a sense that we are all on this earth together and have to come through it and help each other along the way. There was that feeling around us; the knowledge that when someone was encountering tough days, somebody would turn up and give them a hand. 'Let's go and help because we are in this together,' that sort of feeling. It saddens me that so many people in modern life have lost that sense of unity. I go back to the Church and the teaching and the message of the Good Samaritan, and I think to myself, we don't have that now. We walk past on the other side. If we see someone in trouble today, it's easier to walk away than to lend a helping hand. It wasn't like that when I was growing up.

Community is the one thing that has slipped in modern life. God forgive, I maybe don't do enough, but I am very aware of the people that live around me. There's one old boy who lives two doors away from me and I go and see him and take him half a dozen eggs. That's the greatest thing he could have, because he hasn't had the pleasures and the joys out of life that I have had. Half a dozen free-range eggs and a good chat. I do that every week, spending a little time with him and others like him. You can't put a value on that.

I suppose that many youngsters will recoil with horror at stories of the lifestyle we experienced. I don't suppose many can even comprehend what it all meant, but from our point of view, it was a wonderful life for us children. Many is the time I have quietly reflected on those years and on my mother's great influence upon me, and I know that those values she taught us set me on the right road in life. She also kept us together as a family and showed me the merits of a close-knit unit, a real community. That influence was always there, I suspect, when I grew up and had my own family.

After my father died, my mother had a full and busy life in one sense, but in another it must have been empty, for she never showed the slightest interest in other men, and I suppose that was fairly typical for her generation. She had five children and she was going to bring them up according to the right methods with the correct values. That was what she did. Things by no means always ran to plan, but she would invariably come up with a solution to any difficulty and emerge happy when she had overcome a problem.

I reflect now on my childhood as one of special times, surrounded by lovely people. It was a life of intermingled sadness and happiness. Sadness, at the early death of my father and the fact that I didn't grow up with a dad to play with and chat to, but happiness, too, at the close bonds that I forged with my own brothers and sister, as well as with friends, through my mother's tutelage. Above all, I always remember the love and the values that my mother gave me. I have never forgotten what she did and what she meant to me.

CHAPTER 3

The Boy with the Big Stick

The first and only serious athletic activity that I ever got involved in at school was not rugby football, but pole vaulting. Don't ask me why, but it was just something I liked. I picked it up from a visit to the school gymnasium one day. I saw a senior boy swinging from the ropes like some orangutan in the wild, and I asked him what he was doing. He told me he was practising for the pole vault. I thought, I must see this. I watched him and then told the master who was head of PE that I wouldn't mind having a go.

You had to learn to get the technique right, because you fell on to sand, not the foam mattresses used today. If you fell awkwardly, you were likely to know all about it, so I worked hard learning the technique. The teacher spent hours with me. He was super. Then, when I went outside, he gave me this huge, long alloy pole, which you had to be a strong man just to lift up. I might have looked skinny, but by the time I was fourteen years old I weighed thirteen stone, so I was tall and quite strong.

I became keen and made up my mind to practise at home, determined to surprise this guy at school. So I mocked up the apparatus, which basically involved getting the chicken roost out of the hen house. The roost was about nine feet long, but I thought I could use it as a pole, even though it was heavy. I used it until one day my mother discovered what was going on; she was furious when she found out.

In the end, though, I got quite good at it and won the school's sports day. In fact, I won the shot putt, javelin and pole vault. I went home with this cup, as pleased as pie, and my mother couldn't believe it. 'Oh, so you got a cup,' she said, and I smiled and replied, 'Yes, I was the best.' And you know, that's special, to be the best. She liked that.

Things went on from there, really. The next target for me was the Ulster Schools Sports competition at the Queen's University ground. The PE master told me I could win if I was willing to work on it, but just getting there was hilarious. I don't know whether anyone has ever tried to transport a great big long pole around a city on public transport, but believe me, it is no straightforward task.

You had to bring your own pole and mine was about twelve to fourteen feet long, but you couldn't get on the bus with it, so on the Saturday morning I went to Belfast by train, with the pole in the guard's van. I walked out of the train station with my fourteen-foot-long pole, into a city in which nobody seemed to have heard about the pole vault. They were all looking at me and me at them.

I had to get a trolley bus from the Midland station to the back of the City Hall. Then I had to get another from the Ravenhill Road to the Queen's University ground. The driver kindly strapped the pole to the top of the bus. All the housewives from St Georges Market were there, a character each and every one of them, and the driver climbed up the top to un-strap the pole. I remember all the women with their big, broad Belfast accents saying, 'Hey mister, where yer goin' with that big stick?' It was absolutely brilliant.

I was already determined to do well at anything I got involved in; shades of my mother's influence. Thus, I won that pole vault two years in a row at the Ulster Schools. My two medals represented a personal thing, a real achievement in my mind. I'd say to this day, that was one of the special things, one of the proudest moments in my life, mastering that pole vault and winning those medals. It was the thrill of it, the feel of the whole thing, the achievement. The first year I think I won it at nine feet nine inches, a distance which is laughable now, of course. The next year I won it at ten feet three inches.

The technique required for this discipline was to have wider values. Learning how to fall was something that I took on to the rugby field – from the very start of my rugby career I always knew how to fall properly. You go down like a rag doll, and if you do that, it doesn't matter who kicks you, because you don't feel it. It's very different for the guys today, because they're all tensed up.

So that was how I started in sport. As for rugby, however, I'd never even had a ball in my hands until one day the masters of my school house asked me to play in an inter-house rugby match. My house was Slemish, the name of the site where St Patrick tended his sheep outside Ballymena. We didn't have fifteen rugby players, but I was quite big and they'd seen me with the pole vault and said they needed me to play against the other houses. I was chosen as a No. 8 forward, at the back of the scrum, but I then quickly moved to second row. I was seventeen years of age and had never played rugby in my life. Worse still, I didn't know the first thing about the game. All of which were excellent qualifications for a future captain of Ireland and the British Lions.

It was probably a good thing my schoolmasters had not heard the story of another athlete, who was also drafted into a rugby game, much against his better judgement. He too was tall and at the first line-out he jumped up, caught the ball and promptly threw it straight back out of play again.

Anyway, I remember going home and telling my mother I was playing a game of rugby. Well, she didn't want that, but perhaps she was more influenced by the fact that it meant I would need a pair of rugby boots. More expense for my poor mum. I remember the first pair I had, with leather studs. Mother had never seen anything like them before and I hardly knew what to expect but, because I was much stronger than the rest of the boys, I threw a few guys around the place. After all, I'd been brought up on a farm and farm boys tend to be bigger at an earlier age than boys from less labour-intensive backgrounds. Another thing in my favour was that I had always been big for my age.

Then a teacher called Bob Mitchell came up to me and said that he wanted me to play for the thirds, or whichever side it was. I went home and told my mother this, because it meant having to go to school especially for the match on Saturday morning. She said it was all right, as long as I was back for the evening, because there would be work to be done as usual. I assured her I'd be back in the afternoon, because the game was in the morning. So I played and again I was OK.

I think in three weeks I played in the thirds, then the seconds and then the firsts. By the end of that season, I had got into the Ulster Schools team. I played one game for them against Munster Schools at Ravenhill and there was someone playing for the opposition called Tom Kiernan. There was another young player on our side who would also become rather well known. His name was Davie Hewitt and he, like Tom and myself, would go on to represent Ireland and the British Lions, Tom and myself eventually captained both Ireland and the Lions on tours to South Africa. Maybe a talent scout ambling up and down the touchline that day on that muddy sports field would have seen something to his benefit.

Alas, Munster beat us, but there we were (had we but known it), three future British Lions all in the same junior match. The following year I played in most matches for the school and all the Ulster games. I was eighteen and did my leaving certificate that year, but knew my life was changing. I had to make my own road. Frankly, I did not see rugby football as a very likely major part of my adult life, certainly not at that stage. I'd enjoyed playing a few games, but in terms of my future, I wasn't putting it very high up my list of priorities.

During my school life, I had never been what you might call an academic. I tried to listen to what I was told and do my best at all subjects, but I was no genius in the making, so the day I left school for the last time I had one lesson in my mind. It was that nobody owed me anything, but if I was prepared to put in the effort and do the work, there were a lot of people who were probably going to help me. Therefore, I said to myself, I was going to try to achieve what I could. I was determined to grasp every opportunity that came my way. Perhaps this was being what I suppose would be called naive today, but I did meet a lot of genuine, pleasant people who were only too willing to help a young man if they could.

Home life had been a wonderful experience for me. There had been years of fun, sadness, joy, dismay, hard work, the warmth of family and the satisfaction that unity and working together can bring. I knew, however, that it was all ending and I had to go out into the wide world and make my own way. There was no place for me on the farm, my mother told me, so I had to do something else. The trouble was, I had no other interests except farming. It was all I had really known throughout my childhood.

Still, quite quickly an opportunity arose. One weekend, a cousin of my mother's was visiting us at the farm and at some stage we talked about what I might do. He was in banking and told me I should try it, and that it was a good career. I said I'd quite like to continue playing a bit of social rugby and he told me that would work out fine, because I'd get the time to do that, too, if I joined a good bank. So I did my banking entrance exam, but although I passed, they couldn't take me in for a while, because they only accepted so many candidates per year. That meant I was at home for about eight months. I joined a little local rugby club, riding my bicycle there on Saturdays and cycling home afterwards with my dirty kit in a bag on the back. The club was called Randalstown. I played for its second team. To qualify for the first team, you needed a motor car, because otherwise you'd need lifts all around the place.

Then, after some months, I joined the bank, and for a while largely gave up rugby, because I was away in Belfast. The bank I joined was the Northern Bank, which was part of the big Midland Banking Group. After a month or so at head office, during which time I mainly learned the ropes, I was transferred to Ballymoney – rather a good name for a place where I would work in a bank, you might think.

Ballymoney is a provincial town in Northern Ireland, with a total population these days of around 15,000. It is a good market town and the centre for all the little farming villages in the hills around it. It is by no means a place shorn of interest. The surrounding countryside has archaeology from 7,000 years of human habitation, and at the Ballymoney Museum you can see things such as Bronze Age rings and weaponry, plus artefacts from the 1798 rebellion. The oldest building in the town is the Old Church Tower, which dates back to 1637. Sadly, the church was destroyed in 1642 during the Irish rebellion, with the rebel armies also burning the rest of the town. The tower visitors can still see today is all that remains of the church, which was rebuilt and used for worship until 1782.

In Ballymoney Old Church graveyard, the secrets from hundreds of years of history in this area can be traced. Alexander Gamble, a United Irishman, was one of two men executed on 25 June 1798 in the Diamond and buried at the foot of the gallows. Gamble had refused to reveal the names of his associates and paid the price. However, in 1883, his body was unearthed by workmen and his grandsons reburied his remains in the churchyard. Then there is the headstone remembering Thomas Stewart, who died on 16 February 1760, and his daughter-in-law and also seven of her children. From these old, often broken and scarred, headstones, it is possible to trace much of the vivid history of this region.

Farming is clearly a strong element of the local community and the banks that the farmers need to help them in business affairs dominate the centre of the main square. The Northern Bank is in the High Street, enjoying a prominent site. In summer, pretty flower baskets fill the central island at the heart of the town, providing pleasant colour. Opposite the bank there is a delightful little bow window on one of the buildings and close by stands Mulholland butchers, with its mouth-watering joints of rare beef from local farms. By complete contrast, a little further down the street you will find a shop called Big Willie's Pet Shop. Nothing to do with me, I might add.

Ballymoney is only twelve miles from the Giant's Causeway, the renowned tourist location on the County Antrim coast, and about twenty miles from Ballymena. All around the town you see green fields and rolling hills, dotted with hedgerows, and the small working farms are everywhere. In the distance, the Antrim hills are clearly visible and you come to other smaller towns close by, such as Ballybogey and Ballycastle.

I have already outlined the details of travel in this part of the world when I was a young man. Horse and cart were still the best way to get around until the motor car began to arrive in the early 1950s. There was, however, one motorised form of transport before that, and that was the railway. Today, Ballymoney station, at the bottom of the town, is something of an architectural gem. Clearly a creation of the Victorian era, it has a lovely, cosy snug bar opposite the ticket office, where travellers heading down to Belfast or up the coast to Portrush can relax and enjoy a glass of some comforting brew before their train arrives.

Also to be seen is some very pretty wrought-iron latticework on the small bridge over the tracks. In fact, the whole station looks like something out of a John Betjeman poem, and I wonder if any travellers today let their minds wander back to perhaps ninety or a hundred years ago, and imagine Ballymoney station as it might have been then. Ladies in long dresses carrying cloth umbrellas to keep off the summer sun; small boys scurrying around, smartly dressed in blazers with caps, fresh out of school, hurling each other's caps into the air; fathers in their Sunday best clothes and with smartly trimmed moustaches taking their families out for a day's adventure on the railway. It all seems a very long time ago from the viewpoint of the twenty-first century.

My new working life in Ballymoney meant happy times for me. Of course, I missed my family and the closeness we had established among ourselves on the farm. Perhaps, too, I had become familiar with the animals and for a while I missed my daily chores around the farm: the milking, the clearing out, moving the machinery and animals. But I had long grown accustomed to the realities of life. I knew it could be hard and painful, not just pleasurable and fun. Things changed, often very quickly, and circumstances dictated new trends.

I suppose nothing would have given me greater pleasure than to stay on at home, working on the farm like my brothers, but that wasn't possible and you were taught from an early age that you had to be a man, to accept disappointments and even tragic events. You had to go on, be strong and continue to thank the Almighty for each and every day. Each new morning, too, brought a fresh day and a fresh challenge. It was how you adapted and reacted to these challenges that would decide how far you got in life, and what you would achieve.

Early on in my time as a junior bank clerk, when I was spending those few weeks in Belfast learning the ropes, three men came to my home on the farm one weekend. They asked to see me. Their names were Hugh Allen, Robin Gregg and Jimmy White, and it transpired they were from the Ballymena Rugby Club. Presumably the club sent three of them so that one could watch the other two.

I invited them in and they asked me if I would like to join their club, which I was happy to do. Ballymena Rugby Club, founded in 1887, is known the world over for the great players who have come through its ranks. Ballymena is primarily a soccer town, and Ballymena United is in the 1st Division of the Irish League, yet even today, Ballymena Rugby Club still turns out six teams most weeks.

Walking through the gates of Eaton Park, the home of Ballymena Rugby Club, for the first time was to prove to be a big moment in my life. Eaton Park was named after a Ballymena grocery shop boy called Eaton who emigrated to Canada. He made his fortune over there, creating a chain of grocery stores, but he never forgot Ballymena and his roots. When the opportunity arose, he bought land here and bequeathed it to the people of Ballymena. Today, the site of Ballymena Rugby Football Club on the outskirts of the town covers twenty-three acres, which house five rugby pitches, two cricket squares and a training meadow.

When I first saw the ground, there was an old Nissan hut there masquerading as a changing room. Inside it was a gas boiler that had seen better days. To get washed after a match, you stood under two taps, which were fired up by the ailing old boiler. If someone forgot to check that the taps were working, or if the water was frozen, you went out of the back of the hut and washed your hands, face and whatever other parts of your body you could manage in the river that flows down from the Antrim hills, past the rear of the shed. Boy, was that water cold in the winter. Then you went home for a proper wash. Years later, after I had played my final game for the club, I was ceremoniously thrown into the river.

There was no clubhouse or bar at the ground in those early days. Gradually, over the years that followed, things improved. In 1960, the first part of the pavilion was opened, followed a few years later by the first extension. Other elements were added some years later, so that today, the Ballymena clubhouse is one of the finest in Northern Ireland. In 1974, one of the rooms was named The

Millar/McBride Room' in recognition of our services to the club. I joked that it was because we'd helped to dig the original foundations of the clubhouse.

To start off, they picked me in the second team, which was the usual carrot for young recruits, but as things turned out, I was never to play in the seconds. Someone cried off from the first team before my first match and so I went straight into the firsts and stayed there, with a single exception, until I retired from rugby in 1980, twenty years later. I encountered at once the characters that fill the Ballymena club, people like John O'Neill and John Burns. Then there was Mrs Owens, another of the real stalwarts, who was on the ladies' committee. I can remember her dulcet tones to this day: 'Come on Ballymena! McBride, you are USELESS!'

These were the people who were the lifeblood of the club. They'd hold jumble sales in the town and work all day to raise perhaps £100 for club funds. And they're still there today, some of them, or their successors, doing all the invaluable jobs that keep a club ticking over. They fulfil a vital role and I admire them all.

Rugby, however, was only for Saturday afternoons. Banking was my full-time occupation, and I was to spend five years at the Ballymoney branch of the bank, learning all I could about the many aspects of the banking business. I quickly came to understand that this was indeed a career that could last me all my life, if I worked hard at it and continued to improve my knowledge. Of course, I hoped that one day I might be in charge of my own bank branch somewhere, a challenge that I often looked ahead to with much anticipation, but I knew that this was some way off in the future. There was an enormous amount of information I needed to digest first, not just about finance, the actual working of the bank and the staff, but about customers, too. I watched, listened and learned a lot in those early days, and it was fascinating to hear about all the different people with their different requests, and to understand the needs of a local bank.

My life was becoming hectic in every sense. My working week was at the bank, but on at least two or three evenings I would be either training at the club or out running, doing personal fitness work to improve my stamina on the roads and fields. Twice a week, there was official training, and I had to make my way to the club after work. I didn't have a bicycle, never mind a car, so thumbing a lift was the only way to get there. Some winter nights I stood for half an hour beside that road, trying to keep cheerful in the pouring rain, as car after car whooshed by. Then when I got to the ground, we had a hard training session for a couple of hours.

When it was all over, I would set off sometime between 9.30 and 10 p.m. on the mile-long walk back to the main road, and hope against hope that I got a lift quickly that night. But on many an occasion I would have to walk a fair part of the way, heavy kit bag slung over my shoulder, before someone eventually stopped. On Saturdays I was always playing a match somewhere, and it wasn't long before I realised my good fortune in having joined this particular club. People were wonderful, so down to earth and friendly.

Ballymena has always produced international players, one of the most recent at that time being the prop forward Syd Millar, who had toured Australia and New Zealand with Ronnie Dawson's 1959 British Lions. But whether you were a young, nineteen-year-old kid trying to make the grade or a seasoned international, you were treated the same way, with kindness and courtesy. People smiled a lot, cracked jokes and you felt this warm blanket of friendship being wrapped right around you. I loved that about the Ballymena club and I loved it about rugby football in general. I knew that feeling throughout my entire career and I count myself fortunate indeed to have done so.

To be perfectly honest, I had little time in my life to pursue members of the opposite sex. When I wasn't working, I was training, and when I wasn't doing that, I was playing. When that ended, I was with my friends from the rugby team, and when that was over, I was sleeping, getting my rest. When that finished, I had to go back to work on a Monday morning. Now I know some young people today would say, 'But that was in the Dark Ages,' and it's true, the difference between the life of a rugby player then compared to now is extraordinary. Somehow, we just had to fit it all in, with the nagging thought in the backs of our minds all the while, 'Don't neglect your work. One injury could end your rugby career tomorrow. You must keep your job. It's the key to your whole future.'

Nevertheless, it was through rugby that I began to see a lot more of Ireland than I had ever managed before. Ballymena did not just play matches within the north of Ireland; frequently, the opposition would be from the Republic. That meant games against sides from places such as Dublin, Limerick and Galway. Inevitably, there was a lot of travelling involved and even further intrusion into the weekend, but for me, it was part of my brave new world and I lapped it up. Remember, there had been no schoolboy inter-nationals in places like London and Dublin for me, because I had never played the game at that age. So, as I got into my twenties, I enjoyed travelling and seeing different places around Ireland, and meeting different people, too.

Indeed, the first game I ever played for Ballymena's first XV was in Dublin against Monkstown, at their Sydney Parade ground, today not far along the DART railway line from Lansdowne Road, where Ireland play their internationals. My introduction to senior grade rugby was nothing less than shocking. I was nineteen, built like a bean stick and, although quite good in the line-outs because of my height, very vulnerable, a point the Monkstown boys were quick to spot and capitalise upon. They had a couple of lads in their side who were amateur wrestlers – and I'm not talking about the fly-half and inside-centre. Thus, at some stage when skulduggery could be easily concealed within the confines of the two packs, I was belted so hard I collapsed on to the ground. It was, if you like, a little greetings card with the unspoken words, 'Welcome to first XV-grade rugby, junior. How do you like it? Are you man enough for it?'

Through the fog of the punch and its after-effects, I vaguely made out a substantial figure looming above me and in a trice it had hauled me back to my feet by means of a huge hand that grabbed a fistful of jersey. For all I knew, it might have been a forklift truck picking me up, for I was still groggy, but Hugh Allen, one of our toughest players, said sternly, 'For Christ's sake, get on your feet and don't let the bastard see you're hurt.' This piece of advice seemed rather strange to me in my state at the time, for anyone could see I *was* hurt. From my point of view, you could say it was a fixture too far at that time. I found the pace far beyond anything I had previously known and the physicality altogether more concerted. Clearly, I wasn't fit enough either, and much hard, physical labour in terms of fitness work lay ahead of me if I were to survive at this elevated level.

It wasn't easy to put in the time to improve. Not only did I have work at the bank all day during the week, but the bank was also open until 12.30 p.m. on Saturdays. Consequently, there was usually a frantic dash, often involving thumbing a lift from a complete stranger, to get down to Ballymena in time for the Saturday afternoon match, which normally began at 2.30 p.m.

One week we had had a particularly difficult and busy Saturday morning and my job was to balance the books when the doors finally closed. Of course, you couldn't do that until the last customer had gone, and as I looked at the abundance of incoming business that morning I was more than aware that time was not on my side. I went through the totting up process but, try as I might, I couldn't make the books tally. There were always a few pence missing somewhere. At last, at around 1.15 p.m., I went into the manager's office feeling quite desperate.

36

I said to him, 'Manager, I just can't make the books balance but I am due to play for Ballymena in the Ulster Cup final rugby match starting at 3 p.m. at Ravenhill, Belfast. It's the big occasion of the year for my team. Is there any way I can leave the books now, but come straight back after the game and finish balancing?' My manager was a decent, kindly man, the best manager I have ever had. He looked at me, weighed up the request, which was, of course, strictly against all the bank's regulations, and said, 'As long as you promise to come back as soon as the game is over, then yes. Now off you go.'

I grabbed my kit bag, which I always took to work with me on Saturday mornings, and virtually flew out of the bank. I rushed down the main street, pleading with every car driver to stop and offer me a lift. In fairness, a couple did, but they were not going the way I wanted. Quite soon, however, I did get a lift, to Ballymena, which was quite good, but all the while the clock was ticking towards, and then past, 1.30 p.m., and I walked right through the town without getting another lift. Kick-off time was less than an hour and a half away and Belfast was a long way from Ballymena.

At almost 2 p.m. I was distraught because it was so late. I think you could say I'd hit the panic button. I thought that I was going to let down fourteen of my teammates and the whole club, but then a lady pulled up and asked if she could help. Was she going anywhere near Belfast, I asked weakly? Not going near it, she replied, but right into it. There was a danger my sigh of relief might be misinterpreted as some local beast in a field exhaling air. I jumped into her car, but then I realised that even when I got to Belfast I'd still have to wait for a bus out to Ravenhill. I was still in trouble. She seemed to be quite a pleasant woman and I put my cards on the table. Was there any chance that she could take me to Ravenhill first, before continuing her journey into Belfast? She smiled, and happily did so.

She dropped me right outside the gates of Ravenhill at 2.45 p.m. I had just fifteen minutes to spare. I never saw her again, but if she is still alive today and remembers the desperate, sweating, big rugby man who looked almost suicidal in the centre of Ballymoney all those years ago, I want to say a special thank you to her. Alas, the day didn't have a happy ending, though, and we lost that final to CIYMS (the Church of Ireland Young Men's Society, for those not familiar with Northern Ireland rugby teams of the time).

When the match was over and we'd showered and had a cup of tea, my day concluded back in the bank at Ballymoney, where, after more work, I finally balanced up satisfactorily. I well remember that lonely Saturday night when I returned to the bank to finish my week's work. By then, the biro pen had come into widespread used, but not in the Northern Bank. There, it was banned, with the instruction that we were to continue using only dip pens, nibs with inkwells. So when there were interest rates, when somebody had an overdraft or the like, you had to work out the interest by pen, on a ledger, for there were no statements or anything like that. In fact, I remember the first statement machine coming in, a while later.

There was no doubt in my mind at that time as to my number one preoccupation. It was the bank, not rugby football. My dedication to the job led to me being dropped from the Ballymena first XV for a match in the 1959–60 season. It was the only time in my life that I was ever dropped by the club. What happened was this. The general economic climate was in turmoil, with five changes of interest rate in a period of little more than a month. When interest rates altered, there was much work to do, but it had to be done after business for the day ended; in other words, in the evenings. It was very complicated work because you had to close up every account, turn the interest rate into the new one and make the appropriate changes. It was all done on the old decimal system and you had to work like hell. I remember going home at midnight once during this intense period, with my eyes literally red from the concentration.

What I couldn't do during this particular week was go training. I just couldn't get out of the bank in time each night. So I was dropped, but the club never knew the reason why I hadn't been training, and I wasn't going to tell them, because this was my job and it was more important than rugby football. But I thought to myself, 'You bastards. You bloody dropped me and I'm working like hell and I can't do both. You've dropped me because I can't do all my work and go training. But I'll show you.'

They chose me for the second XV, to play against CIYMS. I thought, 'I'll go and give this one hell of a bloody go on Saturday and show them what they're missing.' It wasn't arrogance, it was just that I was extremely annoyed. I remember someone once asking me, 'Why do you play rugby?' and I told them that when you worked in a bank, you had to go out and kick some bastard on a Saturday afternoon because you couldn't do it all week.

In fact, I was so angry about being dropped that, for a brief period, I thought about packing up rugby football. There seemed a conflict between my commitments to the bank and the time rugby required, and I felt that the club should have taken the trouble to find out the reasons why I had not attended training, rather than just drop me without asking for an explanation.

The truth was, I was fed up with things. I didn't have any money, and couldn't afford a car, or even a bicycle, yet I had to make that long trek to Ballymena three times a week. I was working and trying to build a career. I was only twenty and finding it all pretty tough. A growing young man, especially one of my dimensions, tends to need to eat rather a lot and I was no exception. Very quickly, I began to see the difficulties my mother had experienced in bringing up five children without her husband as the chief provider. I could only shake my head and wonder, as my very modest monthly pay packet seemed to vanish before my eyes. Either I was eating too much or someone was putting their hand into my back pocket on wages day, I thought.

By that time, there were six of us young men sharing a flat in Ballymoney. I was earning the grand sum of twenty pounds six shillings and eight pence per month; little more than five pounds a week. Out of that I had to pay for everything, and believe me, I wasn't finding it easy. Where I was living was costing me about twelve pounds a month, which left me two pounds a week to live on and feed myself. You will understand that I wasn't in the pub each night, buying rounds and ordering large steaks for supper. By the end of each month, I was on regular nodding terms with that mythical being known as the poverty line.

In the end, I played in that second team game and scored two tries which, for a second row forward, takes a bit of doing. I remember going through the front of a line-out and seeing the opposition wing in front of me, but I knew he wasn't going to stop me. I hit him with my shoulder and he must have done about three somersaults as I went on to score. It was a feeling of, 'I'm not going to have this. I am not going to be dropped.' Sheer bloody minded-ness, if you like. As my friends will tell you, I can be pretty determined about something when I make up my mind.

Gradually, I began to get to grips with the demands of senior grade rugby. I had been put at No. 8 for my first game, a position at the back of the scrum that requires the kind of strong physique I possessed, but also some pace off the mark, great stamina for covering in defence and ball-handling skills for the purposes of distribution. I had some of those qualities but by no means all, and it was quickly suggested that I might be better off playing at lock-forward, or in the second row of the scrum, as it is better known. There I settled, warm, cosy and contented, into what is called the engine room of the pack, where strong men push and grunt, sweat runs everywhere, the props are held in the most awkward of personal places and private punches are exchanged as a matter of traditional greeting. I had arrived in the position that would be my home for the remainder of my rugby-playing career.

My progress could be clearly charted after a period of time. I began to feel at home in the top grade. I could handle the greater pace, ride the blows, make the tackles and contribute around the field. I even found out how to handle the occasional 'bandit' in the opposition, who wanted to dish out punishment to the new boy on the block, but was surprised and dismayed when the kid gave him some back. In other words, I was also learning the laws of the rugby jungle, an essential qualification if I wanted to play at even higher levels.

Soon enough, my progress was marked by selection for Ulster, which gave me a sense of great pride and satisfaction. My first match was for an Ulster XV against the Duke of Wellington's Regiment, which was stationed at the Palace Barracks in Belfast. They had one or two key men, including the Scottish international second row forward Mike Campbell-Lamerton. They were too good for us on the day and won the game, but I felt reasonably satisfied with my own performance.

At the end of that year, I got into the full Ulster side and we had matches against the other provincial Irish teams. Those games against Leinster, Munster and Connact were highly competitive affairs, for within these four provinces lay Ireland's leading players, internationals and international hopefuls who, as the season progressed, built up towards the end of the year and the traditional Irish trials. But before that, in January 1961, I played in the biggest game of my life thus far, when the touring South Africans, led by their excellent captain Avril Malan, came to Belfast to meet Ulster at Ravenhill.

I was only twenty-one years of age and there I was, put up against some of the world's finest forwards in players like Frik du Preez, Johan Claassen and Malan himself. It was my first introduction to rugby at the very highest level. Once again, I found it faster, tougher and more intense. You could not let your concentration lapse for one moment. The South Africans, a very fine side that year, had us beaten by half-time, when they led 19–0. I suppose that in cricket terminology, they then declared and put us 'in'.

We scored six points in the second half without conceding any more, but there was no disputing their superiority, or mistaking the great class of their players. The difference was the pace, strength and speed at which everything happened. When you were tackled, it hurt. So when you hit somebody, you did so to hurt them, so that when they got up, they thought, 'I don't want any more of that.'

The South Africans, again many of them from farming backgrounds, were big men who played hard and handed out tough challenges all over the field. You either learned to handle all that and play in similar fashion or you bowed the knee to them. I don't think I've ever done the latter in my life and I certainly wasn't about to start then, just because it was South Africa. So I ended up bruised and battered, but pleased I had survived my introduction to rugby football at that level.

I was always one of those people who could get the bit between their teeth and take up a challenge. The bigger the challenge, the more you grow, and that was a heck of a challenge to me. But I thought, I'm going to go out there, I'm going to survive and if possible I'm going to do well. I was still like a beanpole, but I was tough. I had taken my knocks in life by that stage, too, and I could fight back. I'd say to myself, 'So you've made the Ballymena first team. Now you've got to play so well the Ulster selectors come and watch.' And when I was selected for Ulster, I thought to myself, 'Right, now there's a chance you might get an Irish trial at some stage, if you play your best in several games.' Then, when the trial came, I told myself I could handle the step-up in quality required and might even win an Irish cap if I was on top form. In other words, I kept driving myself onwards, and was never satisfied to sit back and reflect on what I had done.

There were always too many targets and ambitions for me to aim at to waste time patting myself on the back about something that was gone. I think you have to accept those challenges in life, because I believe that when opportunity knocks, you must grab it, since it might not come again. It's no good saying you will wait for the right moment for something to happen, because it often doesn't arise when you want it to.

I've taken my chances and plunged myself into all kinds of situations. I regret hardly any. I am now past sixty, but even nowadays, when I'm retired, I tend not to have too many spare moments. When I do, however, I sit and laugh to myself about the stupid things and the good times, because having a laugh is also extremely important, in my view.

Thus it was that later that year, in December 1961, I was chosen for another fixture down in Dublin, this time an Irish trial match on the famous Lansdowne Road ground. Here danced the ghosts of famous players long gone and, although trials rarely attracted huge crowds, there was a fair smattering of support and interest for this particular game. In the week before the match, I rang up my cousin, who was at Trinity College in the city, to tell him I was coming down for the weekend. 'Let's meet,' we said, almost simultaneously, but he had a surprise for me. 'I'll fix you up with a date after the game,' he said, confidently.

I went back to my banking and didn't think a lot more about it. However, when I got to the Shelbourne Hotel, right on St. Stephen's Green in Dublin, on the Saturday night after the game, lo and behold, he was as good as his word. He told me two girls were coming to meet us. That was the good news. The bad news was that it was a blind date, so neither of us had a clue whom we were looking for. 'Another fine mess you've got me into,' as Oliver Hardy, of Laurel and Hardy fame, would have said.

Well, after a time, two girls arrived and seemed to be looking for someone, so we introduced ourselves. Yes, we'd met up OK, but then my cousin and I made an excuse and left them for a moment. When we got out of sight around the corner of the lounge bar we blurted out virtually the same words: 'Which one do you want to go with?' Doubtless the girls were asking each other the exact same question behind another pillar nearby. Anyway, we decided to toss a coin for it, a bright sparkling half crown piece, I remember. I called heads and won, which meant that I got to know a very nice girl by the name of Penny Michael, who lived in the charming seaside village of Malahide, not far from Dublin. Penny was the daughter of the Irish rugby medical officer Harry Michael, so she'd grown up with rugby as part of her family. We had a nice evening together, all four of us, and Penny and I agreed to meet up again the next time I was down in Dublin.

Little did I imagine how fast events were about to move for me when it came to my involvement with rugby. The new year of 1962 was just around the corner and it would catapult me into the most extraordinary circumstances imaginable on the rugby fields of the world.

CHAPTER 4

The Man with No Neck

They say great things can come out of adversity. I've found that to be true at times during my life, but you'd have had a hard job to persuade me this was the case after a February afternoon rugby match in England, early in 1962. From the depths of dismay, I was to experience an extraordinary height of personal ambition within the course of no more than six or eight weeks. Life is strange in that respect; it can kick you in the teeth and then give you a great big helping hand to lift you back on to your feet and put you on the road to achievement. I suppose this is all part of life's rich tapestry, or something like that, but whatever it was in 1962, I was intrigued.

In those days, the idea of national rugby selectors picking up the telephone and giving you a call, whether you had just been chosen or dropped from a side, was fantasy. The player simply waited to hear in the same way as everyone else, either on the wireless or by reading about it in the newspaper. Favours for players? Please, get a life, as the youngsters say these days.

I was working in the bank at Ballymoney when I bought the *Belfast Telegraph* one day. There, on the back page, was the Irish team chosen to face England at Twickenham on Saturday, 10

February 1962. It was a good thing I was sitting down when I read about it. Ireland had chosen nine new caps for the game and I had been included. Now you have to have a sense of humour to choose nine new caps for any game, let alone when you go to Twickenham. To call it a bold decision would be a crass understatement.

The new Irish second row forward, a certain W.J. McBride, had never even been to London, let alone Twickenham. Thank goodness we were driven there by bus – I wouldn't have had a clue how to find the place. But when we got there, I found Twickenham to be quite an intimate ground, with its old stands on the east, west and north side of the ground and the big open terraces on the south side. All around the pitch ran a small wooden fence, and there was precious little yardage between the pitch and that fence. Indeed, some years later at the ground, an England player was to break his leg when he collided with the fence.

I liked Twickenham as it was, though. As soon as you got off the bus outside the west stand, a sense of history filled the air. Anyone who knew anything about rugby union understood this place was special, the spiritual home of the game where legends of the past had played in some memorable matches. I loved the atmosphere created by all that. You changed in big dressing rooms, with plenty of space in which to move around.

Except on the south side, because the big stands had all been erected with a steep incline, the noise was tremendous when an international match was being played. The spectators seemed to crowd right down upon you and you could hardly hear yourself think, let alone hear words from your teammates once the match got underway. Your nerve could quickly become unhinged, and that was what happened the day Ireland took her nine new caps, all hopeful, expectant and a little wet behind the ears, to face the cream of England. And if you knew anything about rugby in that era, you understood that England had some cream. Players like Dickie Jeeps,

Richard Sharp, Jim Roberts and John Currie were seasoned performers out of the top drawer, and the others could play a bit, too. Most of the Ireland side that stepped into what someone once called 'this cathedral of rugby', filled with 60,000 people, were totally naive. It was no wonder that our senses were as scrambled as the eggs we'd had for breakfast that morning.

Ray McLoughlin got his first cap that day. It was only a small detail, but his name was spelled 'McLaughlan' all through the Twickenham programme. That sort of thing happened; it didn't seem important because you were just happy to be in the team. Mind you, that wasn't in the class of the French programme blunder in 1980 at the Parc des Princes, when the Shannon flank forward C.C. Tucker was named 'C.C. . . . . . .' – well, I'd better leave the fine detail to your imagination.

Anyway, Ray and I are still very good friends and we both got our first and last caps together. Some years later, the two of us were at a function in Dublin and people were asking questions. Willie John McBride and Ray McLoughlin, they said, had their first and last caps together, but what else did they have in common? All sorts of answers were given, but none got the point. The guy on the microphone finally revealed the answer. It was that both matches ended in resounding defeats. We had a good laugh about that and Ray loves that story.

I had never even been to an international game when I made my debut for Ireland, so I didn't really know what to expect, but I realised it would be a huge experience. To play at Twickenham was something else again, so when we first walked out on to the ground, I was in awe of it all. I had been used to playing in front of twenty people and three dogs at Ballymena, and maybe a few more when Ulster played a match at Ravenhill, but there were people everywhere at Twickenham and you had this feeling that they were all looking at you. Daft really, I know, but that is what intense pressure can do to your mind.

Anyway, we were right to be a shade apprehensive about it all, because when we kicked off, Richard Sharp, the England fly-half, got the ball and side-stepped this way and that, and England scored under the posts. Just like that, as the late comedian Tommy Cooper might have said. Of course, you think it was your fault. You think 'Should I have tackled somebody? What did I do wrong?' But it all just seemed way beyond anything I had seen before.

We stood behind the posts waiting for the conversion attempt and I thought to myself, 'My God, what have I got myself into here? This was a huge mistake. I'm not ready for this. I won't be going through this ever again, because they won't pick me after today.' The more the game continued, however, the better I found myself able to get a hold on what was happening around me. This was a new level. It was happening harder and faster, people were more determined, there was a lot more at stake and you were playing for your country.

Eventually, I felt stronger in the game, though, and even began to feel good. It was just that they were a better team than us. I was six feet three inches tall and weighed fifteen stone eight pounds, which was a decent size for a twenty-one-year-old. Mind you, I didn't have anything like the experience of the England second row men lined up against me – John Currie and Vic Harding – but I was the biggest player in the Irish team and managed to get a fair bit of ball. I settled into it because I began to tell myself that if I was good enough for them to pick me, then I deserved to be there. It was therefore another challenge, to accept the step up in class and power and speed. Could I handle those things? Was I good enough to live and survive in the higher class? I didn't know, but I was determined to try and find out.

England scored three tries that day, through Roberts, Sharp and Wade. Sharp, an elegant, elusive runner at outside-half, converted two and kicked a penalty to inflict a 16–0 defeat upon us, which was quite a thrashing. Afterwards, someone wrote that 'a raw-boned young man from Ballymena made his debut for Ireland'. That was me.

We took tea, as you do in such circles, in one of Twickenham's pleasant little rooms, with family and close friends invited. I wouldn't say it was the most memorable night of my rugby life, not after a defeat like that, yet the sense of achievement at having experienced international rugby was something of which I was aware. I'd come a long way in rugby in a very short time and I wanted to take it all in and think about what I'd done. However, I knew that much hard work lay ahead of me if I were ever to hold down a place in the Irish team for any serious length of time.

We went home to Ireland and two weeks later met Scotland at Lansdowne Road, Dublin. To lose to England away at Twickenham was one thing, but losing at home is never something you want to get used to in international rugby. Somehow, the sense of having let down your own people is magnified when that happens. Ireland made six changes from the side beaten at Twickenham, a rapid turnover in personnel that would be alarming in any sporting circle. Another new cap appeared and there were positional changes, but the magic effect the selectors clearly hoped such alterations would have, remained missing. Scotland won, by 20–6, although strangely enough, as a report later confirmed, the Irish pack dominated for much of the match.

Nevertheless, I had no great expectations of remaining in the side that was to face Wales in the next match, also in Dublin. But then came news that the game had been called off because of an outbreak of smallpox in the Rhondda valley. This meant that Ireland had only one more match to play that season, against France in Paris on 14 April. This time the selectors made five changes and two more new caps were chosen. This season-long game of musical chairs might have been funny if we'd just been there to have a laugh and then go home at the end of the entertainment. As it was, the smiles on Irishmen's faces were wearing very thin and we duly lost 11–0 to the French, again conceding three tries to nil.

Those were the basic statistics from the match, but from my point of view, momentous events took place. At one stage of the game, as I broke from a maul, the French loose-head prop Amedee Domenech stuck out his leg and kicked me just above the ankle. It was a fearful blow and I knew instantly that I had suffered a serious injury. I came off the field – it was just about the only time in my entire career that I did so – to be examined by a French doctor on the touchline. He rubbed the leg a bit, sprayed something cold on it and pronounced me fit for action. There were, of course, no substitutes allowed in rugby then, but the medical man's advice was rather reminiscent of the way they treated the soldiers on the Somme – 'What, only lost part of your foot, my man? We'll have you right as rain in no time,' sort of stuff.

But I wasn't laughing. I played the last twenty-five to thirty minutes of that match in complete agony, walking virtually on one leg. When I got into the scrums and line-outs, I knew there was something very seriously wrong. There was, too – I had broken my leg. When the match finished and we got into the dressing room, I told the medical people I could feel something moving, so they sent me to hospital in Paris; not only was my leg broken, but the bone had been kicked out of place. They put me in plaster from the ankle to above the knee. I came home on crutches.

Now as a rugby player, the greatest thing you can do is to represent your country. There is no equal to the feeling of running out to play for your country and wearing the jersey, but a British Lions tour is unique and to be given the opportunity to play for the Lions is a natural peak in any player's career. That year, a British Lions squad was due to depart for a 25-match tour to South Africa and any man who played international rugby that season would have been lying if he'd said that the thought of going had never crossed his mind. It had mine, but I felt that Ireland's three defeats and my own uncertain first stumblings in the world of international rugby had almost certainly precluded me from winning a place. Thus, given my renowned lack of judgement in such things, within days of returning home from Paris, I heard I'd been chosen for the Lions tour. Such was the shock that a feather would have flattened me.

'Of course, you won't be able to go because of the injury,' most people said. I nodded vaguely and kept my own counsel. I decided to say nothing, except issue soothing noises to the effect that I'd be fit and ready. This was because, I reasoned, you don't get chosen for a Lions tour every day of the week and, who knows, this might well be my last ever opportunity to experience that esteemed level of rugby. I was not prepared to give it up without a fight.

In truth, the Lions were due to assemble at Eastbourne in early May and I knew I had no chance of being a hundred per cent fit by then. Every player chosen for the tour was sent a medical form, to be signed by their doctor, saying that the player was fit and able to tour. So, still on my crutches, I hobbled down to see my local doctor in Ballymena. He was sitting at his desk when I went through the door. 'Well, how are you?' he asked. I said, 'Doc, don't ask me any questions. I'm great. Now just sign this form.' He looked at me, looked at the crutches and the leg in plaster and reached for his pen. He'd have probably signed my plaster, too, if I'd asked him, but as I made my way to the door clutching the all-important piece of paper, I turned around. 'Doc, I won't let you down,' I said, before disappearing.

They took off the plaster four days before we were due to meet up in Eastbourne and I'd never seen a leg in such a state. It was literally just limp skin and bone, for the muscle had wasted away to virtually nothing. All I could do ninety-six hours later was limp heavily into the training camp and pray that the Lions management accepted my assurances that I'd be fine once I got to South Africa and did a bit of training there.

Of course, training on South Africa's rock-hard grounds was about the last thing my leg needed at that stage, as anyone with even a modicum of medical knowledge would have known. But preparations for Lions tours were so haphazard that, incredibly, my story passed muster. I was kitted out, proudly I might say, with my Lions blazer, tie, shirt and trousers, and one week later limped (as little as I could) on to the plane at London's Heathrow Airport. Talk of the great escape.

It is worth pointing out here and now that, but for the great generosity of my employers, the Northern Bank, I would not have been able to go on that tour, nor any subsequent Lions tours. They agreed to pay me for the time I was away and that enabled me to go on the trips. Otherwise, I simply would not have been able to afford it. Alas, that happy arrangement began to peter out in later years, giving all sorts of players problems when they were chosen for Lions tours, but at that time I think major organisations saw some kudos in having a famous sportsman on their staff.

So, in May 1962, we flew from London to a country we had only ever seen in the pages of history and geography books. Where they could avoid it, aeroplanes did not fly for long over the sea, so we flew south over Europe, North Africa and the equator, like some giant on a flying pogo stick. It seemed to take forever to reach Salisbury, Rhodesia's capital, and when we got there, I remember thinking, 'My God, how on earth are we going to play rugby in this terrible heat.' In fact, the temperatures were not too high during our matches, because it was, of course, South Africa's winter. What was a far greater problem was the altitude, especially as the naive Lions committee had sanctioned a schedule that saw us flying up and down from sea level to high altitude like a yo-yo. It was absurd.

We stayed at a lovely hotel in Salisbury. On my first morning in Africa I came down to breakfast, smelling bacon and eggs, and I thought to myself that perhaps this might be like home after all. It wasn't, but Rhodesia was so lovely, so British and so clean and efficient, that it breaks my heart to see the nightmare it has descended to today, under Robert Mugabe's tyranny. How so noble, so elegant a land could have come to this defies belief. It almost brings tears to my eyes when I think about it. The people then were wonderfully hospitable: they took us for drives in their private cars, welcomed us into their homes for dinners, and showed us parts of the land no normal tourist would ever have seen. We did our bit by visiting schools and hospitals, and by meeting people wherever we could, for we were ambassadors as well as rugby players.

Before we left Rhodesia, we saw the Victoria Falls on the mighty Zambezi River, a tumbling cascade of water some 108 metres (355 feet) high and 1,400 metres (4,500 feet) wide. It was an awesome sight. When we got to South Africa, we saw the wild herds in the game parks, plus animals like lions, cheetah, elephants and rhino. In the Cape, we marvelled at Plettenburg Bay and Table Bay, the beautiful maritime entry point to all of southern Africa.

One of the most remarkable sights I saw in Rhodesia was the tobacco sales. Of course, Rhodesia was then a major exporter of tobacco and I remember getting up early one morning and going along to the sales. You had these huge bales and guys were sniffing and smelling the different leaves. The auctioneer walked down a long row of bales, taking bids and answering and raising prices, but I could never actually see anyone bidding. It was fascinating.

In the event, I didn't play in any of the first six games on that tour, but I trained twice a day, biding my time and working hard to get my weakened leg back to somewhere near its normal strength. By the time we got to the third Test, in Cape Town, two things had happened. The Lions had drawn the first Test, 3–3, and lost the second, 3–0. That meant the third Test would be critical and the selectors were probably in the mood to make changes. One night early on in that tour we were sitting around in a hotel room and I felt completely fed up. I was training twice a day to build up my leg, but had not yet played a single game in a Lions shirt. The Lions were unbeaten in their first six matches and my chances of serious involvement had begun to look slim.

Keith Rowlands of Cardiff and Wales was one of the Test locks and he turned to me that particular evening and said, 'Why did you come on this tour?' I remember looking at him and saying, 'To get your place in the Test side. That's why I'm here.' I was only twenty-one years of age. Keith didn't like that comment at all and he liked me even less when I was chosen for the third Test instead of him. In fact, I don't think he ever forgave me, but I wasn't about to apologise. I'd been through physical hell to make that trip and I wasn't going to give up at that point. Anyone who knows me understands that I am a determined soul who never quits on a job, no matter how tough it may seem. I stick to tasks, refusing to let go.

In the end, I played more games on that tour than a lot of guys who had flown out from England one hundred per cent fit. When I finally got home after that long flight up over Africa and Europe, I went to see my doctor, the man who had made it all possible. 'So, you made it then,' he said, smiling conspiratorially. 'I told you I wouldn't let you down. I didn't,' I said.

Now I have to say that poring over records and memories of those days is not exactly my idea of an evening's entertainment. I don't want to bore the reader with every detail of each match I played, but I do want to share some general thoughts that I have had in subsequent years.

Perhaps those who saw me play only at the climax of my career, maybe with the 1974 Lions, might find it hard to believe, but in 1962, on that first Lions tour, I was extremely nervous, especially on the day of my Test debut as a Lions lock. The largest crowd in the history of the famous Newlands ground at Cape Town at that time, 54,843 people, had squeezed in for the Test match, with another 4,000 locked outside. It was the biggest day of my rugby life at that stage and you could have cut the atmosphere with a knife.

I sensed this immediately we left our dressing room and went out into the corridor, lining up opposite the Springboks but, infuriatingly, we had to stand there and wait while the band marched off the pitch. I was as nervous as hell. I'd never experienced anything like this before. I glanced across at the Springboks and saw this huge man with no neck and curly hair. His name was Mof Myburgh and he was a prop forward who made an angry bull rhino in a game park look friendly. For some reason, undoubtedly to do with my nervousness, I decided I ought to make conversation with this guy, to show I was friendly. So I looked out across the field from where we stood, to a pitch where they'd just played a series of curtain raisers, the minor matches traditionally held before a Test match in the southern hemisphere. What I saw horrified me. Great patches of the ground had no grass on them at all and, can you believe it, I decided this would be the ideal conversational topic for the Springbok with no neck.

I looked across at him and said, 'Mof, there's not a lot of grass out there.' He paid no attention to me whatsoever. I thought to myself, 'Gee, this bugger's deaf as well as having no neck.' So, twice as nervous by now, I said it again, but louder, 'Mof, there's very little grass on this pitch.' He continued to stare straight ahead, as though I was about as irrelevant as a fly on the wall. He never looked across at me, still less took my eye. He was scowling, and deep furrows criss-crossed his forehead, like railway tracks outside a mainline station. I thought for a moment that perhaps he didn't understand English, but when the man with no neck spoke, I was immediately disabused of that notion. Continuing to look straight ahead, he seemed to speak out of just the side of his mouth as he said, 'I didn't come here to fuckin' graze.'

That was my introduction to Test rugby with the Lions and in a sense it mirrored perfectly the different attitudes of the Springbok and British Lions rugby sides of that time. The Springboks had an intensity, a rigid focus on winning that the Lions had not yet come to understand. The Lions were there to represent the British Isles and Ireland and to enjoy the tour. The Springboks turned up only to win. In a nutshell, that was the difference between the two and Myburgh's attitude encapsulated it.

However, when the match started, we did quite well and would have held the South Africans had one of our players not missed a tackle late in the game with the score at 3–3. They converted the subsequent try and we lost 8–3. With one Test match remaining, we had lost the series. We then lost the final Test, too, 34–14 in Bloemfontein, to make the series 3–0 to South Africa, with one drawn.

In theory, we had travelled with much hope, because the Lions squad contained some powerful forwards and talented players behind the scrum. Yet what undermined us, just as it had done on too many other Lions tours of that time, was the general approach. The manager was no less than Instructor–Commander D.B. Vaughan RN, an Englishman with impeccable credentials for playing an ambassadorial role on a long Lions tour.

Managers were chosen on the basis of Buggin's turn; good chaps who had served the game nobly and also had a record in the services were especially popular. The fact that some of them knew little about the real workings of rugby football around the world was merely incidental. It was important to have the right man in charge, but sometimes you got the feeling that this mattered more than choosing the actual playing squad. Mind you, having said that, the Lions of 1955 and 1959 had carved out wonderful reputations for outstanding rugby. The 1955 Lions in South Africa had drawn the series 2–2 and the 1959 Lions were hard done by, losing the Tests 3–1, but only after outscoring the All Blacks by four tries to nil in the first Test.

Among the players in the not quite so successful 1962 side, Tom Kiernan was dogged by injuries and only played one Test. John Wilcox of England, the other full-back, was quite a good player, but

PLOUGHING. WAG 1921.

Above: **My grandfather, Robert McBride in 1920, ploughing on the family's farm at Moneyglass where I was brought up. Today, my brother John and his son Tom still farm there.**

Below: **An early school photo. I am standing in the back row, extreme right, next to our teacher, Mrs Wilson. My younger brother Tom, who was to die so tragically in his twenties, is on my right, at the back, just behind me.**

H. TEMPEST LTD

Mundella Road Works, Nottingham

Above: I bet future Olympic champions were worried when they heard about this! W.J. McBride, Ulster Schools pole vault champion 1956/57, at the top of his form.

Above: My younger brother Tom, who died so young.

Right: Early days at Ballymena R.F.C.

My family: Penny, Amanda and Paul.

Above: In 1976 Ireland became the first of the home countries to win a Test Match in the southern hemisphere. Pictured above is the Ireland team and officials on that tour. Tom Kiernan, third left in the second row, was captain.

Below: Ray McLoughlin and I toss up pre-match Ireland v. Ballinasloe as part of Ballinasloe centenary celebrations. Ray and I won our first and last caps together in 1962 and 1975 respectively.

he had trouble with the strong South African sunlight. John had eyesight problems, which meant he'd go to catch the ball and it would bounce yards away from him. It goes without saying that this caused his colleagues a certain amount of consternation.

In the three-quarter line, we had a marvellous little Welsh wing called Dewi Bebb, who gave it everything, every time he played. Nothing quelled Dewi's spirit and he was the epitome of all that was good about Welsh rugby. Never beaten, he was unwilling to accept second best and always prepared to dig deep for the benefit of his team and his playing pals. Sadly, another Welshman, Ken Jones of Llanelli, disappointed me. He showed so much promise early on in the tour, but then disappeared. Three Englishmen did well, including Richard Sharp, our fly-half, even though he had his cheekbone broken by a wild challenge in a tough match against Northern Transvaal. Mike Weston, who played centre or fly-half, was a good guy with the right attitude; both he and scrum-half Jeeps played well.

Then there was David Hewitt, a hugely talented Irish three-quarter whose talents knew no bounds. Trouble was, he pulled a hamstring very early on in the tour and only played in the last Test match, but in one provincial game he made a break downfield that split the entire defence. Very often, he would just set up the opportunity and then pass it on for someone else to finish it off, but this time, he kept running. His mazy run took him past defender after defender and he seemed to have beaten most of the opposing team before he crossed their line. But one last player had managed to cover across, preventing David touching down under the posts. Now dotting the ball down is normally the first thing you do when you cross the opposition line, but not Hewitt, not on this particular day. He ran back into the field of play, moved nearer the posts and the remaining opposition player, and duly beat him with a dazzling side-step before recrossing their line and finally touching down by the posts. That was David for you.

Bryn Meredith won the Test slot as hooker for all four internationals, and rightly so. He was the best hooker I ever played with, a man who was very strong, had a good attitude and was a great influence on that tour. Sam Hodgson, his intended back-up, was probably the fittest man among us when we began the tour. Unfortunately, he broke his leg in the first game, against Rhodesia.

Meredith's attitude was mirrored by Glyn Davidge, another great man of Newport and Wales. I remember in a match against the Orange Free State, he was carried off three times with a bad back, but kept jumping off the stretcher and running back on to the pitch. Believe me, when you are on a Lions tour far from home facing the physical excesses of the southern hemisphere rugby nations, you crave an attitude such as that and the company of men like Meredith and Davidge. Perhaps it was no accident, then, that the following year, Newport beat the mighty New Zealand All Blacks on their tour of the UK and Ireland. With men like Meredith and Davidge at their club, the Welsh had power and presence on the field.

Of the other Lions forwards in 1962, Syd Millar from my club, Ballymena, played well, Haydn Morgan of Wales and Bill Mulcahy of Ireland, quite well. Then there was David Nash of Wales, a great forward who sadly got some infection in his blood and had to come home. He never played a single Test match, which was a huge loss for the entire Lions squad, but another Welsh back row man, Alan Pask, came in and played three Tests, proving himself a super player. Tragically, Alan Pask died in a fire at his house not very long ago, after returning to the burning building to try and save his dog. He was a great forward and a good man of rugby football. Also in the back row, Budge Rogers of England always gave one hundred per cent, but overall, I would say that there weren't many what I would call characters on that tour.

1962 was a momentous year in the history of South Africa for another, very different reason. A young black activist named Nelson

Mandela was imprisoned, thereby setting in place a chain of events that would come to define that nation's entire history over the course of the next thirty years. It was a wonderful country to visit for a Lions squad. Even today, it would still be my favourite place to go and if I were making the decision, I would hold the World Cup there every time. There is so much to offer everyone – the climate, the beautiful, varied scenery in places like the Cape, the Garden Route, the mighty Drakensburg mountains, Kwa-Zulu Natal, the Gauteng region, the Game Parks and the wine estates. It is a magnificent country, filled with some great people. In rugby terms, they have both the stadiums and the fervour for the game that makes it so special, but in 1962, there was always this underlying political situation, which was sad.

A Lions tour to South Africa is the apotheosis. One of the great things about such a tour was the development of young men and the standards that they learned; standards that were so worthwhile in life. You met people, made friends and maintained contact with many of them for a lifetime. All those things came out of a rugby tour. We travelled endlessly, too, taking the game to every corner of the country. It meant that I saw so much of South Africa for I played almost everywhere on my tours there in 1962, 1968 and 1974.

The world was a much larger place then and when you said you were going on tour to South Africa, your words somehow hung in the air, all conversation temporarily stilled by the enormity of the enterprise and thoughts of the great adventure that lay before you. I loved all that, just as I loved turning up at all sorts of towns throughout South Africa; some hot and dusty, some cold and wet, but all filled with people who came out to welcome you and talked rugby football with a passion that made their faces light up. They were special people. For rugby football in those times was a community thing. It was about people and about setting standards for young men, but also about developing our abilities as people.

Sadly, all that has gone from modern-day Lions tours and I bitterly regret that fact.

It was tough, too; very tough at times. When you saw the squatter camps on the Cape flats area outside Cape Town, you could be under no misapprehensions. Apartheid was apartheid, a brutal regime. Black men could not sit in the same train or bus as white men; they could not even share a park bench on a summer's afternoon. Those Lions played 'whites only' sides. Those were the cruelties, the indignities and the hardships of apartheid for the black and coloured population. I saw all that evolve down the years during my frequent visits to the country. Today, I have to say, I still find it unbelievable that it literally flipped over to black majority rule with comparatively little hatred or violence. It is remarkable that the Afrikaaners accepted it. I didn't think it would change as dramatically as it did.

Anyway, after twenty-five rugby matches spanning more than three and a half months, the last against East Africa in Nairobi, we came home. We were physically tired, certainly, but mentally stimulated by all we had seen. And it was wonderful to catch up again with my family and friends, especially Penny, whom I used to drive down to Dublin to see from time to time in the little A30 car I bought after a while. The roads were poor and the car would only do about forty miles an hour flat out, but it was always lovely to see Penny and our friendship began to blossom.

In 1962, however, when I returned home from South Africa I was unaware that before I set out on another Lions tour, tragedy would engulf my family for the second time in my life. It was to be another salutary reminder of the peaks and troughs that life places before us.

CHAPTER 5

Old Jack's Hellish Fingers

When I returned from that first Lions tour, I must admit it took me a while to get back into the normal routine of life. Ballymoney was a town I liked, but you would have to say that working there in a bank from nine to five each day and on a Saturday morning hardly compared with touring South Africa. It was a bit of a culture change when I got home.

Rugby was a big part of my life but it was by no means the only part. Unlike today, when the modern professional player eats, sleeps and drinks the game, I gave what time I could to rugby, but my work always came first. If people asked me something about rugby while I was at work, I would reply politely, but I would never get involved in lengthy conversations or discussions. Rugby was something I did at the weekends; that was the way it was and that was the way it had to stay.

So gradually I readapted to my old ways. Life was simple and humble. Tough, too. I would go to the bank each morning, spend my entire day there and then go home to the flat I shared in the town. There were usually six of us staying there, although I suppose during my time I would have had ten or eleven companions. But don't go running away with the idea that the place was a mansion and we each had our own room. You must be joking. There were always mattresses strewn around the floor, and only two or three of us were lucky enough to get beds. One evening I came home from work at around 5 p.m. and was getting changed to go out for a training run. The place was usually a mess and seeing mattresses, blankets and sheets strewn around was nothing unusual, but on this particular afternoon I was astonished to see this pile of sheets and blankets suddenly move.

The next thing was, one of my flatmates, Fred, poked his head out from underneath the blanket, I said, 'Fred, what's happened, are you ill?' He replied, 'No, I'm fine.' I said, 'How long have you been here?' to which he replied, 'All day.' 'What on earth for?' was my response. He sat up on his mattress and lifted his arm out from the sheet. He held up two pennies in his hand and said, 'That's all the money I have in this world. If I don't get out of bed, I don't need money and we don't get paid until tomorrow.'

Now Fred was no down and out – like me, he was a bank employee, but with the Ulster Bank – but he'd run out of money that month and come up a day short before his pay packet was due, so he simply stayed at home in bed all day. That was how it was then. When you worked for a bank, you weren't allowed to have an overdraft because the bank felt that if you couldn't look after your own finances properly, then you shouldn't be working for a bank. This, I suppose, had some kind of logic, however cruel, and there was no point thinking about going out to steal or rob, because no one else around you then had much money, either.

After a period of rest, I started playing rugby again, for my club, my province and then, in the New Year, for Ireland. Truth to tell, 1963 and 1964 were not years I recall with a great deal of fondness, for on Whit Monday, June 1963, tragedy again struck our family. My brother Tom had by now immersed himself in the world of banking and had been transferred to a place called Castlewellan, near Newcastle, County Down. Tom followed a variety of pursuits, such as drama and sports like golf. I remember it well, because he and I had arranged to play golf together on a special bank golf day, in which they would pay the green fees.

Tom and I liked our golf and we thought a day on a nice course on a bank holiday would be ideal relaxation. However, a couple of days before, he rang me up and said, 'Look, I'm sorry, but I've just been transferred down here and there's two or three guys in the bank who would like to stay here and go to the beach on Monday, so do you mind if I miss the golf?' I understood exactly what it was like when you went to a new branch. You wanted to integrate and mix well, and besides, I knew I'd have no problem finding someone else for the golf. So on the Monday, Tom went off to the beach and I headed for the Malone golf course near Belfast.

The next thing I knew was that the manager of the course and his assistant were suddenly seen running across the fairways towards me and the group with whom I was playing. I had a feeling at once that something was seriously wrong, but of course no one knew what the story was until they reached us, panting for breath. When they blurted out what had happened, I just went numb. You cannot know about such things unless you have experienced them.

Tom was not a strong swimmer – none of us was in the family – but he'd gone into the water at a rather peculiar place, near Newcastle, on the wrong tide, an ebb tide. They had to go out quite a long way even to get into the water properly, but when he and his pals got there, Tom suddenly disappeared below the water. He had been sucked down by one of the whirlpools. By the time his pals realised what had happened and that Tom was nowhere to be seen, it was too late. They did their best and got him out, but sand had got into his lungs and he died within half an hour. There was just no way back. It was two days before his birthday, three days before mine.

As I hurried off the golf course, the first thing I could think about was my poor mother. To this day, I don't remember a single thing about the drive from the golf course to our home. I knew my mother would be in a hell of a state. It was another of those knocks in her life. She had lost her husband, yet she was younger then and could fight back, as she had, but this was later in her life and I knew she would be devastated, which of course she was. We were all in a daze. I don't know how other people cope with that sort of thing. We drew together as best we could, the rest of us in the family. Collectively, we shed tears for Tom and our hearts ached at his loss.

The memories do not leave you. When it comes to my birthday each year, I still think of Tom and feel that he should be here, celebrating his as well. I think of him a lot throughout the year, too. It is amazing how that kind of experience sticks with you, but you know, life is hard sometimes. There are no families that don't have their tough days and indeed their harsh years. It comes to every family and, sadly, some seem to suffer more than others.

Tom was a kind, caring, decent human being. He was industrious, believed in living a good, proper life and, like all of us, had his ambitions. That he should be taken from us at such an early age was something with which I found it hard to come to terms. Many is the time I have sat quietly and pondered the fun and the good times we could have shared together had he lived. But many times in my life, I have had to face the cruel fact that life must go on. It had to this time, too, whatever the personal feelings you hid from the outside world.

On the rugby front, I hurt a knee in one Five Nations Championship match against Scotland around that time, and was not very effective, but the strangest things can emerge out of adversity, as I was soon to discover.

When I couldn't get my knee right, Hugh Allen from the Ballymena club took me to see an old medical expert he used. I was introduced to an old chap who was deaf, or at least clearly struggling to hear much, given that he had a hearing aid in each ear, and I thought to myself, 'This looks like the guy who needs medical help, not me.' His name was Jack Nixon and he was actually a chemist, but because of his hearing difficulties he'd had problems in that branch of medicine. I told him I had no money to spare, which was true, but he said he wanted to look after me and wasn't bothered about money. He was self-taught and a real character, and talked to me about a lot of things.

He asked me what was wrong with me and I told him I'd damaged a knee. His reply sounded stupid: 'Take off your shirt.' I thought he hadn't heard me, so I shouted a bit this time, 'Jack, it's my knee that's the problem.' So he just said again, 'Take off your shirt.' If this scenario had been played out a few years later, it would surely have made excellent material for a *Fawlty Towers* episode or something out of *Monty Python*. I just assumed the old chap was virtually stone deaf, so this time I really shouted, 'Jack, it's my bloody knee that's troubling me.' To which he replied like a shot, 'D'yer want to make me completely deaf with yer shouting?' He went on, 'Are you still in the bank?' and I nodded, so he said, 'Well, you stick at that, son, and leave me to the medical stuff. Now, take off your shirt.'

I lay down on the couch and he moved his fingers up my back, up the bones on the spine, and pressed his finger on a particular spot. He might as well have hit the ejector button in an aircraft and sent me hurtling upwards into the great unknown, because for a moment I completely lost my senses, such was the pain. He just said, 'It's nothing to do with your knee, it's coming from your back.' He said, 'You've been training and scrummaging on Lions tours, through international matches and provincial games and club matches. That's where your problem is and it's in the weakest part of your back.'

I began to listen. He told me that the human body works on balance. Most of us are one-handed or one-footed. You kick with the same foot, you go to lift something always with the same hand or the same side of your body leading. What we are doing is pulling the body out of balance, all the time. He told me my body was totally imbalanced at that time, that something had had to give and it just happened to be a knee. He said when I had been under pressure during the match against Scotland, my knee was the weakest point and it gave way because my back couldn't take the strain.

Well, Jack gave me some treatment and the knee problem disappeared within three or four days. I thought to myself, 'This guy knows what he's talking about.' He told me he wanted to see me after every international, so I visited him regularly. His surgery finished at about 9 p.m. and he'd always see me after that, but he'd give me some shocking stick about the match we'd just played, wherever it was. He'd tell me we'd been bloody awful and made all the wrong decisions and mistakes, but I figured that was the least I could do, sit and take that criticism, because he did so much for my body.

He had hellish fingers and thumbs. He went all over my back with them and he'd say, 'Am I hurting you, son?' I'd say, 'No, no,' but I was nearly dying with the pain. Then he'd dig in a bit further, a bit harder, but he was great at his job. That went on for about twenty years and for ages he never charged me anything. Old Jack kept me going for years and I have a lot to thank him for. Sadly, we have now lost him, but today I go and visit his son, because I still do quite a lot of physical work. He was an army physio and talks the same language as his father. Quite recently I'd done too much work, cutting a big hedge in double-quick time, because I had another pressing engagement. I'd also been digging a fair bit in the garden and my back was giving me hell. So I went along to see him and told him the truth. 'My old dad was right – you're just bloody daft, you are, and there's no denying it,' he laughed. Like I said, he talks the same language as his father. And now I have to take it from the son, too.

When I think about the fact that there are so many injuries in the modern game, I remember some of the things old Jack Nixon used to tell me. You see, the modern game may seem harder, but too many of the players can't take all the knocks because they didn't have the physically tough upbringing which players like myself and Colin Meads, the New Zealander, had. You only had to look at so many of those great former New Zealand forwards to know that they were farmers. In Wales, some of the players had grown up on farms, like Clem Thomas, the former Swansea and Wales back row forward, but others had worked down the mines or in steelworks, work locations where physical might was one of the essential requirements of the job.

Believe me, working in environments such as these instilled not only a physical toughness, but also a fierce mental attitude. In many respects it was hard as much mentally as physically. To be in those environments taught you how to steel your mind as much as your body. Although the game has changed so much, the value of possessing greater mental strength than your opponent remains a key ingredient.

Modern players think, or at least are told, that they can become strong men by spending hours in the gymnasium, but that establishes a different type of strength. When I was young, I would often work ten to twelve hours a day at home on the farm in holiday time, and I can still do that today. Such physical labour builds a strong mind, too. I think you'll find that evidence shows most injuries to modern-day players occur in training. This is because their bodies can't take what is asked of them, day after day. They run like robots; they are stiff, not supple. If you look at any good athlete you can see his muscles shaking, but our rugby players today think they're tough because they're big in terms of muscles.

Jack Nixon used to talk to me about my muscles. He'd say, 'You're too tense, son. That muscle is sitting there like a big lump. Your muscles and hamstrings should be so soft they're like jelly, so that when they're asked to take the strain, they can react immediately by tightening up and taking that strain.'

I came to know Jack quite well. I developed a healthy respect for him and enjoyed spending time in his company. I think sometimes in life you meet a particular person and the chemistry between the two of you just works. No one quite knows why, but it certainly happened in this case.

Jack owned a peat bog and I used to go there with him to cut the peat. We'd go for the day, and be out in the wilds and very often in the wind and the rain, but that never bothered us. We enjoyed each other's company and I think he was, like me, never so happy as when we were out working on the land, feeling the cold soil in our hands, the wind in our hair and often the rain falling down our faces. We were close to nature and it felt good.

Jack was a wonderful character and he told marvellous stories. He'd played rugby a long time before, but his hearing wasn't good. Trouble was, he rarely heard the whistle so he just played on. His proudest claim to fame was that he had probably injured more players after the whistle had gone than any other living player. Apparently, he was a hard nut on the field; not the most coordinated man, to be sure, but a real menace.

We'd take a couple of bottles of Guinness with us on our days out and put them in the bog water to keep them cool if it was summer and warm. When we'd have a break from work, Jack would say, 'Take off your shoes, son, and get in there. Bog water is great for your feet, and the body, too.' So sometimes I'd stand in this cold bog water for hours and cut the peat. I found that any cuts or bruises would heal so much quicker if they'd been in that water for an hour or two. If you immersed your hands in it they would feel as smooth as soap afterwards.

Then there would be the days when my kids would come with us and play around in the heather or the river. We'd take some food, light a fire and have a fry up, so there would be sizzling sausages and rashers of bacon on the grill and we would be surrounded by open spaces, with the sound of the wind and perhaps the cries of birds. It was a scene I loved. They were brilliant days and, I am sad to say, they were more than thirty years ago, but as I said, I realised long ago that life is just a short stroll through the fields and hills. Enjoy it while you can, for it doesn't last for long.

Ireland's 1963 Five Nations Championship season was un-distinguished. We won only one of our four games, which was often the case. Mind you, there were occasional times when Ireland were pretty special. In 1963, we played Wales at Cardiff and the front five of the Irish pack was probably as good as any they've ever put out on an international field. Certainly it was as good as, or better than, any with which I ever played. Ray McLoughlin, Ronnie Dawson and Syd Millar formed as good a front row as there's been anywhere in Europe for the last forty years. Bill Mulcahy and myself made up the second row. Perhaps it was no surprise that we won 14–6 in Cardiff that day, especially with the likes of Kiernan, O'Reilly, Walsh, Brophy and English outside the scrum, too.

Ireland usually had six or so world-class players, but struggled to make up the remainder of the team with sufficient class to beat all the other countries. But we enjoyed our rugby, we were competitive and I like to think we helped nurture and develop the game throughout Ireland. It has always been my firm belief that you should try to enhance whatever field you embrace in life, whether it is rugby football, gardening, architecture or anything else, so that when you pass on, you have left that profession or pursuit enriched by your presence. It may be a simple wish, but it is one I have always had.

Late in 1963, Ireland had a most important international match, against the touring New Zealanders. Towards the end of the tour, in early January 1964, Wilson Whineray's wonderful team would go to Twickenham and topple England 14–0, and they would also beat Wales and play out a 0–0 draw with Scotland. We knew we faced a tough test of our abilities. The reality was that we were not likely to beat the mighty All Blacks, but just being out on the same field competing against them was a fierce examination of each Irish player's physical and mental powers. If you went on to the rugby field against New Zealand teams less than a hundred per cent committed or not believing in yourself, then you were in serious trouble. Throughout the 1960s, the All Blacks were probably the best side in the world, an unbelievably good series of teams filled with strong men, physically and mentally, who possessed tremendous skills. They took on and conquered just about every team in the world. True, they couldn't win a Test series in South Africa, but they beat just about everyone else.

Ireland did not have a bad team, nor was it the worst pack of forwards ever seen in the green jersey. Bill Mulcahy was captain by then, the strong man of the pack alongside me in the second row. He was not especially tall, but he was as strong as titanium, never bending in any respect. He was an excellent rucking, mauling, scrummaging type of player. I was very much the junior partner, but we also had around us good men like Ray McLoughlin and Ronnie Dawson who would not be cowed or frightened by the sight of the All Black jerseys lining up opposite. Tom Kiernan, our full-back, shared such qualities.

Our team had been chosen when injury struck and the selectors brought in a guy called Johnny Fortune, from the Clontarf club in Dublin, on the wing. He was twenty-three years of age and reasonably experienced. Inside Johnny was a player named Jerry Walsh, a hard-tackling centre from the Sunday's Well club, who would cheerfully knock down walls for you. We may not have had loads of skill in our back line, but we certainly had buckets full of courage and determination – essential qualities when you confront a New Zealand side. You dig deep when you play the All Blacks or you do not play them at all.

I was the tallest forward in the Irish pack and was inevitably seen as the main source of line-out possession. Alas, the New Zealanders had obviously come to the same conclusion. So the nonsense began.

I went up for an early line-out ball and was pushed out of the line. We played on and came to another line-out and the same thing happened, so when I got to my feet, I had already decided I wasn't going to put up with this for eighty minutes.

At the next line-out, I arranged for our line-out thrower to call for me and prepared as though the ball was coming straight for me. It did, but I didn't jump. Didn't move a foot off the ground, as a matter of fact, but what I did do as the New Zealander opposite me jumped for the ball was swing my whole body around to face him, leading the movement with my fist. It struck him deep in the solar plexus as he was in the air, catching the ball. There was a loud sound like 'uuuuuhhhhh', a deep groan and the player sank to the ground. He went down so fast he made the *Titanic* look tardy by comparison. Play went on for a while, but when there was an infringement and the referee blew the whistle, I glanced back upfield. There I saw the player I had hit still on his knees, his head dropped down, but with the All Blacks captain trying to drag him to his feet.

The next thing was our captain, Bill Mulcahy, said to me, 'Jaysus, McBride, d'yer realise who yer just hit?' I said, 'I don't know but I'm not having that treatment at every line-out.' Mulcahy said, 'Christ, you hit Meads – now there's going to be trouble.' Anyway, Meads was helped to his feet and he was groaning and holding his ribs area. He wasn't very well. Mulcahy's advice was, 'Just be careful for a minute or two.' Within those couple of minutes there was a ruck, and to this day I don't know who or what hit me, but I got it, smack, full in the face and I was dazed. I went down and I knew why I had got it. I could hear voices echoing around in my sub-conscious for a few moments, and I wasn't very well for a time. But I got up and I survived. When it came to the next line-out, no one pushed me out of the line and I won our ball.

Soon after that, Johnny Fortune, who was virtually blind and could rarely even catch the ball, somehow held on to a pass and got clear through to score a try. We converted it and suddenly were leading the All Blacks 5–0. The excitement in the Lansdowne Road crowd was growing volubly. Before too long, however, Kel Tremain, one of the greatest New Zealand forwards of any generation, got a try for them to make it 5–3. But with the line-out nonsense sorted out by now, we got our fair share of ball and, with the crowd continuing to lift us, we hung on to our slender lead. We had reacted as Irish sides can; the dog in us had emerged, the sheer refusal to lie down and accept the inevitable was obvious. Not even the All Blacks looked as though they could shake us out of our stride.

We were ahead until midway through the second half. It was hard, unrelenting and you knew you could not allow your concentration to lapse, even for a moment. But then came disaster. We were penalised for some offence and, from a long way out, New Zealand's champion goal kicker Don Clarke lined up a penalty attempt. Everyone sensed that if he kicked it, New Zealand would win, but if he missed, victory might well be ours. I was standing near to where he placed the ball and I studied him closely. He was a big man, heavily built with large feet. Clarke was no great player, but his kicking, out of hand or to goal, was phenomenal. He approached the ball for this kick at goal and the ball flew off his boot like an Exocet missile. When I saw it soar away, I sensed it would go over. Which it did, and New Zealand went on to win the game 6–5. One of the biggest upsets in world rugby history had been narrowly averted, but it was an injustice, because we had given everything.

We lost, yet I believe that was the day I became a man on the rugby field. In rugby, as in life, you are faced with difficulties that require a solution. It is how you handle those problems and whether you are prepared to stand up and confront them like a man that defines your future path. I went on to that field not knowing who on earth Colin Meads was. By the end, I had a healthy respect for him and, I knew subsequently, he for me.

That day, and that moment, taught me a lesson. Never be afraid to do what you believe in, if you think it's right. Don't be distracted or side-tracked from what you seek to achieve; confront the obstacles in your path and overcome them. I knew I had to take on a player who was prepared to stop me doing my job for the Irish team. He might not have anticipated such a strong reaction so early, but he surely knew that if I was worth anything at all, I had to act in some way. I was never a dirty player, but I've done things and regretted them. However, when I hit someone, I did it with the intention of hurting them, so they would be dissuaded from continuing in such a way. I was not a handbag man, someone who dished out a light tap. With my physique, I knew I had the capacity to inflict some punishment upon opponents, if they deserved it because of their own actions.

In international sport, you must earn respect; it is not a gift of selection. Only when you go on to the field and confront the best, the most powerful opponents in the game, can you know whether you have what it takes to become a good player in that company. You dig deep for the qualities you require in such circumstances – courage, determination, strong will and refusal to buckle. Some cannot find such traits, but I knew Colin Meads had them in abundance. He was one of those players whom I called an honest-to-God rugby man; no matter how hard you hit him, knocked him down or whatever, he was always back up and in your face again. I loved that sort of player. Give me eight of that type of person and my team would beat the world.

The name of Colin Meads remains eminent in the game even today, long after his retirement. That is a testimony to the man and the player he was. He forged a reputation as one of the strongest, most powerful forwards who had ever played. I think he was a wonderful player even though, sadly, he might have done the occasional thing on the field that he had no need to do, because he was far too good a player to act in the way he did on some occasions. I think he knows that now, but that is just the way it is. From that day on, I never had another problem with him and we had some tremendous battles against each other. They were hard, competitive, but above all fair. We went on to face each other many times on a rugby pitch and the respect which was forged out of that first meeting in 1963 has remained to this day. We have stayed good friends long after our respective retirements from the game and I always enjoy meeting Colin socially.

That All Black match came at an early stage in my rugby career, but it was truly a defining moment. I am one of those people who believes that if you can wake up the following morning, look at yourself in the mirror and say, 'I didn't let anyone down yesterday, I couldn't have given any more than I did,' then no one can ask any more of you. I never wanted to come off a rugby field thinking to myself, 'If only I'd made that tackle. If I'd dived on that ball they would never have scored that crucial try,' or something like that. If you do that, you are a failure in my view.

When New Zealand came to the British Isles and Ireland to play, or when the Lions went down to the southern hemisphere to meet the All Blacks or the South Africans, the difference in attitude was marked. The countries on one side of the world were taking the game seriously, preparing diligently and playing it hard. On the other side, the game was viewed largely as a recreational pursuit, a sport that was supposed to inculcate and nurture qualities that would serve young men well throughout their lives. Or at least that was the thinking in official circles. I can tell you that when you were being belted by strong men from the southern hemisphere you didn't get up off the ground with a smile on your face, telling yourself that this was jolly good preparation for life and you should be grateful for the experience. You could see that the only way to handle such power on the sporting field was to return it in kind, thereby, hopefully, gaining respect from your opponents and levelling the playing field somewhat. But officialdom would have frowned upon such a viewpoint.

When I think back to those days, I remember my own early experiences. For my first game against France at Lansdowne Road, Bill Mulcahy was captain. It was January 1963 and I was winning only my fifth cap. Bill was a medical student, so he looked after our welfare as well, because no substitutions were allowed. You just couldn't go off. If you were dead, you stayed on to help clutter up the field a bit. Furthermore, you only met up twenty-four hours before the game and Mulcahy arrived to take the team meeting the evening before. 'Right,' he said, 'tomorrow we're going to play France. How do you think we should go about it?'

This invited all sorts of stupid suggestions. One of them came from a so-called senior player who said, 'Lads, I've played against the French a bit and I think tomorrow, for the first fifteen or twenty minutes, we should go out there and try and upset as many of them as we can. If they fall out among themselves, we'll maybe get a penalty or two or perhaps even score a try. That's the way to beat them.' Mulcahy promptly slapped his thigh and said, 'Jaysus, we've got it.' Ireland, everyone felt, were always at their most dangerous when the tactics were simple. Otherwise we got confused.

So the next day, we trooped into the old wooden shack in a corner of Lansdowne Road where the teams used to change. That hour before kick-off in an Irish dressing room was unbelievable. There were guys knocking their heads against the wall, while others were kicking at benches and doors and working themselves up into a right old frenzy. I'd never seen anything like it. Someone else was running around, saying to anyone who'd listen, 'Has anyone got a spare lace?' It was all highly professional, seriously thought-out preparation for the main event.

Those were the days when you provided everything yourself, apart from the jersey that the Irish Rugby Football Union gave you for the game, so there were guys polishing their boots, putting studs in and smearing vaseline across their faces to try and look as fit as possible. There was a wee little guy called Charlie McCorry and he was a jack of all trades. If you needed a sponge, a wrench to change your studs, a new lace or whatever, he had everything. The referee knocked on our door about ten minutes before kick-off, wanting to look at our studs. However, someone shouted, 'Don't let the bastard in,' so the ref banging on the door added to the racket and, quite honestly, I couldn't wait to get out of that hell hole. I reckoned the French would be a piece of cake after surviving in that lunatic asylum for the past hour. Besides, we had our secret tactical weapon to upset the French and put us on the road to victory.

Eventually, the referee came back and was admitted. Briefly and grudgingly. Now, with the French already out on the field and the crowd roaring and waiting for our arrival, things had really hotted up in the Irish dressing room. There were guys foaming at the mouth, the sweat was lashing off them, and any stranger wandering into the midst of this horror scene would think he'd stumbled through the back door of a madhouse. The boots trampled anything in their path and we ran out to face the fearsome French.

We get out on to the field and someone blows a whistle. It is a signal, no, an invitation, for all hell to be let loose. Mayhem ensues. I can't remember seeing a ball and, besides, it is irrelevant. You just join the nearest melee of players, grabbing, wrestling, swearing, punching and buffeting as you go. Then there is a scrummage and we know we're quite good at that. We've got a good few hard guys and we're looking forward to that first scrum. It's the traditional test of a team's manhood, whether their forwards can take on and eventually subdue the opposition pack. We stand back, yards apart as you did at that time, and simply charge at the French pack, like rutting stags. No holds barred, not a thought for personal survival or potential injury. This is our first real eyeball-to-eyeball confrontation with the horrible, garlic-smelling, unshaven French forwards and one thing is for sure – we're not going backwards, not by a single inch. There is nothing more humiliating for a forward than to go backwards in a scrum.

Anyway, we crash into each other, French arms grappling with Irish shoulders and vice versa. And then there's the explosion, as if someone has tossed a can of petrol into the midst of this sweating collection of humanity and thrown a match in after it. The whole thing goes up. Irish fists crash into French chins; sometimes Irish fists crash mistakenly into Irish chins. French fingers search out Irish eyes to gouge, a trick to which some French rugby men are as partial as to frogs' legs for dinner. There is widespread shoving, punches whistle past heads that have ducked out of the way and boots connect with shins. Then there's the verbal abuse. 'Ah yer feckin' French pig,' can just about be heard above a stream of Gallic invective, which I don't think is enquiring as to the health of our dear mothers back home. And the referee watches this passable imitation of life and times on the Parisian streets during the French Revolution and does . . . nothing. He never interferes. It's obvious his policy is to enjoy the show and let them sort it out. They'll come to their senses in a moment. Which is a dangerous assumption to make when Ireland plays a game of rugby football.

But in time we do come to our senses, mainly because we're so tired. Hurling punches at people, trying to kick lumps out of them, attempting to wrestle them into submission on the ground is pretty exhausting stuff. In the end, it all comes down to a lot of noise and threats more than anything specific. No one is trying to put back on his missing leg, but there is still one scene of chaos. An Irish forward is lying on the ground, pinned down by a couple of Frenchmen. Eventually, Bill Mulcahy, our brave leader, strides across to him and asks him what's wrong. They manage to drag the two Frenchmen off him, who seem like a couple of hound dogs who've scented the fox and don't intend to quit, and Mulcahy leans over the body of this prostrate Irish colleague. It is Syd Millar, our tight-head prop forward.

'What the matter, Syd?' asks Mulcahy. 'That bastard's bitten me on the arm,' is the response. And sure enough, Mulcahy rolls up Millar's sleeve and there they are – a couple of fang marks, as though Dracula has been visiting the night before. We're all standing around, shocked, appalled. Mulcahy gives him some medical attention. After all, he's a medical student and should know what he's doing. It involves spitting on his own hand and then wiping it across the bitten part of Millar's arm. But his advice is the key point. 'Now Syd, when we go into the next scrum, get hold of yer man's ear and give it a bite.' Millar looks shattered by this pearl of wisdom. Here he is, a proud rugby man of Ireland, and he's been humiliated by this Frenchman, biting his arm and pinning him on the ground at Lansdowne Road in front of 50,000 of his fellow countrymen. Millar looks at his captain with an anguished expression, and says, 'Sure I can't. Me feckin' teeth are in the dressing room.'

Oh, and the master plan that day? Sure, we worked the French up all right. So much so, they won 24–5, by four tries to one. It was their highest score and biggest ever winning points margin in matches against Ireland in Ireland, up to that time. Some match. Some tactic. Some experience.

In France, they played the game hard. Club matches down in the south-west could be as tough and sometimes even more violent than an international game. Rivalry between respective towns was at stake and the French did not believe in holding back. Ears were bitten, testicles grabbed and squeezed, eyes gouged. By comparison, the rugby in a country like England was kindergarten stuff, except in a few regions such as the West Country and the north, where they played a meaningful version and saw the value of being a winner.

The trouble was, England's national selectors of that era generally preferred to choose good chaps with the right background – decent Oxbridge men, for example – rather than some rough, tough forward from the Gloucester, Bristol or Bath clubs. Therefore, England's international form was at best varied and more usually a failure. England always had the players, but what they lacked was the right attitude and a better selection process.

There was a haughtiness in the air whenever we arrived at Twickenham to play England. The whole attitude around the place seemed to say to us, 'Oh, we're having the Irish over this weekend. I hope they do well.' That was why to win at Twickenham was always so special, because, really, given the lop-sided aspect in terms of the numbers who played the game in England compared to Ireland, we should never ever have won at Twickenham. But we did manage it occasionally. In fact, of the seven matches Ireland played at Twickenham during my time in international rugby, from 1962 to 1975, we won three and drew two more. That was a remarkable record for us.

Ireland had shown on rare occasions that they were capable of some stirring performances. The 1963 match against the All Blacks was one example and another came later that same winter when we played England, who had been Five Nations Champions the previous season, at Twickenham. England had started the 1964 championship with a 6–6 draw at home to Wales, but this was our first game of the Five Nations season. I don't think even we anticipated the kind of performance we gave, nor the result we got. We won 18–5, much of it due to a young outside-half who was making his international debut for us. His name was C.M.H. Gibson and he was to become one of the greatest backs seen not only in Ireland but anywhere in the British Isles or indeed the world.

Mike inspired our victory that day in which we beat England by four tries to one, with some of those tries outstanding. It was, of course, the first time I had been back to Twickenham since my disastrous debut there two years earlier, and to see this quite different Ireland team take England apart on their own ground was immensely encouraging. Alas, the dawn proved illusory; we went on to lose every other game of that championship, culminating in a

27–6 hiding by France in Paris at the end of the season. The moral of it all was that if things ever changed in Irish rugby, they changed back again to where they'd come from almost immediately. Or at least I think that's what I mean.

Ireland improved in 1965 – we won two of our four games that season in the Five Nations. But I think 1966 was the turning point, not just for Ireland but in British and Irish rugby as a whole. By then, Ray McLoughlin was captain of Ireland and there was a noticeably stronger streak of steel throughout the team. We drew at Twickenham, lost – although only just, 11–6 – in Paris, beat Wales in Dublin, but lost to Scotland at Lansdowne Road.

McLoughlin was a highly intelligent man, a deep thinker about the game who brought special qualities to the Irish teams of that time. I would say that under him was the first time we looked a properly organised, disciplined side who understood what was required to be successful. First of all, you had to be fitter and stronger. Ray believed that it all started with the scrummage; get that right and then you could think about developing from there. Without a power scrum, you have little chance in rugby. That holds true even to this day. If your scrummage is right, the whole game is right. The back row can break and roam, in either attack or defence, and your scrum-half has options, too. For some reason, it even seemed that your line-out worked better if you had a tight, strong scrummage. Perhaps the one phase invoked discipline and better organisation in the other.

So, 1963 had been a year of deep personal tragedy for me, and, although I had learned from them, 1964 had seen some disappointments on the rugby field. In 1965 I felt I began to see a flicker of light at the end of what had been a long, dark tunnel, and in 1966 Penny and I decided to get married. This meant she had to move from Malahide to Northern Ireland, which was a big step for her. In fact, I remember joking to her very early on in our marriage, 'You and I had better agree on things in this marriage, because it's a hell of a long walk back to Dublin.' We've been wed thirty-seven years now, but then I've been away a lot and haven't hung around too much, which is probably why she hasn't had the chance to get fed up with me.

CHAPTER 6

The Battle of the Albions

The diversity of approach in terms of selection and attitude was again emphasised when the 1966 British Lions went to Australia and New Zealand. Frankly, the tour was undermined before the squad had even met up because, plainly, there were players included who simply were not up to the task of taking on the All Blacks in their own backyard.

For a start, we had an extremely nice man who was chosen as Lions captain. Michael Campbell-Lamerton was an officer in the British Army and, in the eyes of the selectors, the ideal sort of chap to lead such a tour. I don't want to be unkind to Mike, because I liked him as a person and, after all, it was the selectors who had placed him in a position for which he really was not qualified, but I always felt he was a compromise captain. It should have been Ray McLoughlin of Ireland or Alan Pask of Wales.

In terms of the world game, Australia was really a backwater at that time. Furthermore, it was really only played in two states, Queensland and New South Wales, and standards even there were variable. Rugby league was a far bigger game in both regions and it duly plucked the brightest and best players from union. At one stage, the Australian Rugby Union was losing its best players almost faster than it could replace them and the game there appeared doomed. That was one reason why we stopped off on the way to New Zealand. The idea was that the Lions could play a few warm-up matches and make some money for the Australian Rugby Union to help boost their coffers.

It was no more than a kind of aperitif to the real business of the tour, the trip to New Zealand, and the results did not greatly concern us. We played eight games in Australia to help raise the profile of the sport. In fact, we were given quite a tough match in the first Test, getting home only 11–8 in Sydney, but we then thrashed them 31–0 in the second Test in Brisbane. However, the Australians did have a few very good players, chief among them a superb scrum-half named Ken Catchpole. If we'd been able to take him on to New Zealand as a Lion, we might have fared a lot better.

For the fact was, once we got to New Zealand the writing was plainly on the wall. We went to Invercargill, which is not a place, in a rugby sense, where you'd expect a picnic. We didn't get one, either, losing 8–14 to Southland. It was a bad start to our 25-match tour in a country where any sportsmen lacking mental strength are quickly exposed. We struggled past the combined South Canterbury, North Otago and Mid-Canterbury side, 20–12, and beat New Zealand Universities 24–11, but in between we went down 9–17 to Otago and 6–20 to Wellington, giving us three defeats in our first five games. The die was cast.

What happened subsequently was therefore hardly unexpected. We got a hell of a thrashing, losing every one of the four Test matches to suffer the ignominy of a whitewash, but it was no surprise because in my view, the whole composition of the touring party and also the attitude was wrong. Des O'Brien had been a wonderful back row forward for Ireland at the end of the 1940s and was one of the nicest men you could ever meet in life. He was courteous, charming and delightful company, and hardly ever uttered a cross word in anyone's direction. Once again, the Lions selectors could not have chosen a better diplomat to represent the public face of the Lions, but if you wanted a man who was a winner, who would crack the whip and make sure every player in the squad was determined never to take a backward step, then O'Brien was never going to be your man. Besides, he was totally divorced from rugby football in that he hadn't been involved with the game for years. His assistant was an Englishman, John Robins, but he was like O'Brien, lacking the iron resolve to knock his men into a hungry, fiercely determined unit. He tried to coach us a bit, but he and Campbell-Lamerton were not in tune and it didn't work. Then he damaged an Achilles tendon and couldn't do very much.

Campbell-Lamerton was under heavy pressure from the start, not just because of his responsibilities as captain, but also in terms of his own playing form, which was poor. Indeed, he was to miss two of the four Test matches because even he acknowledged that he was not playing well enough to merit a place. This was a shattering blow for a Lions captain, but it was a mark of the man that Mike did not shirk the decision and was prepared to leave himself out. He earned my respect for that.

Sadly, though, Mike began to lose a lot of weight due to all his duties and worries. His weight went down by two or three stone and he became a shadow of the player he might have been. Worse still, some people were starting to laugh behind his back, which was sad because he was a decent, honest man. However, it was obvious that he was losing control of it all and he lacked the right management to help him get through it. When it became clear to everyone that he wasn't playing well enough to get into the Test team, it had to be put to him that he ought to stand down – always a sad moment on any tour. But he then exacerbated the situation by coming up with a stupid idea that he could play prop forward instead. Now Mike was a second row man who had also played No. 8, because he was tall, but it was blindingly obvious to everyone, apart from the man himself, that he would never make a prop forward.

Ray McLoughlin, the Irish prop forward, received this idea with the comment, 'I don't think that would be a good idea, Mike,' but Campbell-Lamerton suggested we could try it out. So I had a chat with Ray and told him Campbell-Lamerton could get hurt if we weren't careful. No matter, we tried the idea. We went down in a scrum, with Ray on the other side, opposite Mike, who was trying to see if he could survive as a loose head prop. Ray was an extremely strong man on the rugby field and I knew what to expect when he confronted you. I was behind Mike, in the second row, and one thing I could do was scrummage. Rare was the occasion when I went backwards in a scrum. So I said to Mike, 'Now remember, I never move back, so you've got to keep your back straight because if you don't it'll bloody break in two.'

I got in behind him and just locked my feet in place. Then the pressure came on and Campbell-Lamerton went straight up into the sky, like a cork from a bottle. I was locked behind him and he was sitting up in the air. Ray came through underneath Mike, so that his face was right in front of mine, and he gave me a big wink and said in a loud voice, 'I think, Mike, we'll have to let yer down.' The fact was, Campbell-Lamerton was all right, but he could have been seriously hurt. The decision was made there and then that maybe it wasn't such a good idea for Mike to play prop forward after all.

Unfortunately, Campbell-Lamerton was by no means the only player who was not really good enough to be there and who was unable to handle what the New Zealanders threw at us. They played the game hard, with a single ambition – to win. Nothing else mattered. Hands were stood on, limbs broken, fists smashed into Lions' faces; it was all seen as part of the game. I knew from my own experiences in facing the All Blacks in 1963 what to expect, but some of my Lions colleagues seemed surprised and dismayed.

Worse still, they began to disappear when the rough stuff started and the punishment was being dished out.

I got a thoroughly unpleasant reminder of what it was like for a visiting rugby player in New Zealand on the tour in the provincial match against Canterbury. The local team kicked off and I caught the ball. Suddenly, I was surrounded by the physical hurricane of their pack, which started punching, kicking and assaulting me, because I'd had the temerity to hang on to the ball. They got hold of me and took me thirty or forty yards downfield towards my own line, the blows raining down upon me as we went. It was their way of saying, 'Welcome to New Zealand and proper rugby. This is what it's like here.' The more the blows came in, the bloody sight harder I held on to that ball. There was no way I was going to let go of it to those bastards, but it wasn't that which upset me most.

What maddened me was that not one of my fellow Lions players came to my aid, to help me hold on to the ball and give the New Zealanders some of their own treatment back. When the referee eventually blew the whistle to end this spell of physical torment, I was bloodied and bruised and bloody angry, but when I looked up the nearest Lions forward was about twenty yards away. 'Where the hell were you bastards when I needed you?' I shouted at them. And their reaction? Well, they laughed and one of them said, 'Why the hell didn't you let go of the ball, you bloody fool?'

I knew then that we had no hope of winning the series. I wasn't prepared to give the bastards an inch, but it was obvious our players weren't prepared to take the pain. That's the first rule of life, though; you have to take the pain if you are going to achieve anything. Only a few of the players felt like I did. We were prepared to go through fire to topple the All Blacks. Sadly, however, we didn't have enough like-minded players on the trip. Those of us who did feel that way were very frustrated at how events turned out.

Crazy things happened during that tour. The first Test match was to be played in Dunedin, in the far south of the south island, a cold, inhospitable place in mid-winter. New Zealand chose their Test match venues carefully; it is all part of the psychological pressure that they put on visiting rugby teams. They call Carisbrook, the Dunedin Test match ground, the House of Pain and it's a fair description of the place. It is usually raining, freezing or snowing and, much as I liked the hospitality of the New Zealanders off the field, I could not pretend that places like Dunedin were ever my favourites in a rugby sense.

So, in 1966, it was decided that when the Lions' Test match team was chosen, they would go up to Queenstown for some special pre-Test training. Now if it had been the height of summer you couldn't imagine a better place to train. Trouble was, this was winter and Queenstown is right in the middle of New Zealand's south island ski fields. I wasn't playing in the Test – Campbell-Lamerton and Brian Price of Wales had been chosen at lock – but I went with them as a reserve. The rest of the Lions squad went straight on to Dunedin, but don't ask me why, because I haven't got a clue.

For want of a better way of putting it, I farted about for four or five days. I knew I wasn't going to play in the Test and I wasn't taking it easy with the other boys, but at least I was in pole position to see the utter folly of how they arranged those British Lions tours. The nominated 'leader' of the Lions squad that headed straight to Dunedin was my great pal McLoughlin, a man with a terrific sense of humour. He wasn't in the Test team, because he'd pulled a hamstring playing in goal during a football match after training. That somehow summed up the chaotic nature of this tour.

Anyway, Ray would call us from Dunedin, at our hotel up in the mountains where everything and everyone was frozen stiff. There was about as much chance of getting any serious training done in the ice and snow as there was having a snowball fight in hell. So Ray's mischievous Irish voice would come on the line and he'd enquire, all innocence in his tone, 'How's yer tour goin', up there?'

Then he'd say, 'Jaysus, we had a hell of a party last night. We've got to do a bit of training around lunchtime today to run it off.' Of course, he knew full well that we couldn't find a ground anywhere near Queenstown where meaningful training could take place. It was too dangerous to run anywhere on the frozen ground, so instead Mike Campbell-Lamerton was taking us for walks every morning. We would walk up a hill and down again, slithering some of the way and trying to avoid injury. It was farcical, absolutely ludicrous.

Then, like a bolt from the blue, came important news. A location had been found where we could train properly. Better still, it was out of doors, so we made our way to this new training ground which somehow had miraculously escaped all the snow and ice that lay everywhere else. The sceptical among us smelled a rat and we were not to be disappointed. When we got there, though, there was a good covering of grass and it looked OK. So we started to loosen up and then began kicking balls around and doing a bit of running. Alas, this sudden burst of activity was halted when someone shouted, 'Watch out, aeroplane!' Yes, you guessed it – the 1966 British Lions training programme for the first Test was to be conducted on the grass runway at Queenstown airport.

When someone shouted out, 'Plane, plane!' we would all run off the runway and rush to a hangar until the plane taxied in. Then we went out and did some more work. I wasn't really part of it all. As a reserve, my role was to gather up the balls and that sort of thing – preferably before a plane landed on them. I remember running into this hangar three or four times while planes came in or took off. In the end, I thought 'bugger this', and I went in and had a smoke with my pipe beside the hangar. When we eventually rejoined the rest of the squad at Dunedin, it was obvious we were in no real shape to face the All Blacks. We duly lost the Test match, 20–3 – a real hiding.

I got bloody annoyed at the lack of desire and determination to stand up to the All Blacks on the field. One of the players who epitomised our failure was Brian Price, the lock forward from Newport and Wales. Now Price ought to have been a man the New Zealanders respected. He had played in Newport's winning team against the 1963 All Blacks when a single drop goal by John Uzzell was enough to win the match at Rodney Parade and inflict upon Wilson Whineray's 1963–4 team the only defeat of their 34-match tour. Price had also played for Wales since 1961 and should have been one of the rocks of the Lions pack in 1966. He was a great line-out forward, a far better jumper than me, but he couldn't take the rough and tumble. So when he got to New Zealand, he found that players like Colin Meads targeted him, just as Meads had done myself in Dublin three years earlier. Trouble was, Price was not like me; he was not prepared to belt Meads and stop the nonsense that went on. So, of course, Meads simply rode roughshod over the Welshman, who seemed content to melt into the background and lose his Test place. He didn't play for some time and I suspect much of it was because Meads had got to him.

Yet Price was big and strong enough to have done something about it. He was perfectly willing to be the hard man when he got home and played in the Five Nations Championship. Indeed, when Ireland played Wales at Cardiff in 1969, he punched Noel Murphy so hard that Noel had to retire and never came back. Price could do that in his own backyard, but when it came to giving it back to the best in the business, someone like Colin Meads, he wasn't so good. That disappointed me immensely and I saw it quite a lot. Peter Stagg of Scotland was another second row man of that era who never really had the toughness you needed, mentally and physically, to play the game successfully in the southern hemisphere.

There were a few real characters around in that Lions squad, the sort of men you need on such a long, difficult tour. One was Ronnie Lamont, the back row forward from the Instonians club in Northern Ireland. Lamont was one of those guys who would be the first one there if you said, 'Right, Ronnie, we're going to knock this wall down.' He would cheerfully run into it and half kill himself. Well, we ran out for the first Test match and Ronnie came up to me and said, 'Where's this bastard Tremain? Which one is he?' Kel Tremain was regarded as something of a god, a player who was crucial to the All Blacks. He scored tries, made tackles, won the ball, helped in passing movements. There wasn't a lot Kel Tremain couldn't do, but Ronnie Lamont was no mean performer. In fact, he was to become the forward of the tour, from the Lions' point of view.

So when Lamont asked me, I pointed out Tremain to him. David Watkins of Newport & Wales kicked off for us and the ball went roughly in the direction of Tremain. It would be totally false to say it went to him, but he might have been within six or seven yards of it, when he was hit by an express train named R.A. Lamont. Now, at the start of an international rugby match, each player has one hell of a lot of adrenalin pumped up within his frame, ready for release. Ronnie Lamont had it coming out of his ears at kick-off time in this particular match. The fact that the ball flew over Tremain's head made not a jot of difference to Ronnie; he hit Tremain amidships, with the ball nowhere in sight. Of course, Tremain was not expecting such a blow and when he was hit so hard, he went down like a log. Initially, I thought Ronnie had killed him.

As Tremain lay motionless on the ground like an innocent passer-by in the street who had been taken out by a sniper, 40,000 New Zealanders began baying for our blood. There was no sin-bin, of course, and although Mr Murphy, the referee, lectured Ronnie, he did not send him off. After his warning Lamont walked back, hands on hips, between myself and Noel Murphy, the Irish flank-forward. I looked across at Lamont and said, 'Ronnie, that was bloody stupid.' But I'll never forget Murphy, known as Noisy by his friends, looking at Lamont saying, 'Of course, it was bloody stupid. Now they're going to do us all. We're all for it!'

You needed men like Ronnie Lamont on a tour of that nature, though. I just wish we'd had a few more. Sadly, we were deficient in that department, in terms of character, fight and a willingness to dish it out to the opposition. If we'd had a few more, we might have done better in the Test series. But then again, things were going on off the field that were constantly undermining what we sought to achieve on it.

Terry Price of Wales came out as a replacement when England full-back Don Rutherford broke his arm, but it was obvious from the start that Price was not fit and should never have been allowed to come. He'd had a knee rebuilt and was nowhere near fit enough for so arduous a tour. In fact, he could hardly walk. Who put him through a fitness test, I don't know, but it was a disgrace. A bit like the one I'd taken in 1962 before the tour to South Africa, you might say.

The other full-back, Stewart Wilson of Scotland, played in all four Test matches and was a good little player, but he wasn't ruthless enough to stand up to a rugby tour of New Zealand. You must take the buffeting, the illegal blows, the punches and hard hits. People make me laugh today by talking about the 'hits' in the modern game, rather than the tackles, as though what they endure today is a hundred per cent tougher than anything we ever knew. I'd like to tell these modern players that when you toured New Zealand in the 1960s and 1970s, you got 'hits' like you'd never felt before. They came on the ball, off the ball and worst of all, when you were least expecting them. The New Zealanders were no pussy cats; they hit you hard and painfully. It was just as tough then as it is now.

The match we played against Auckland at Eden Park was another crazy affair. I was playing alongside Delme Thomas of Wales in the second row and Delme was cleaning up the line-outs quite well, which the locals certainly didn't like. Delme was shorter than me, but by God he was strong, and he could leap like a salmon at times. So they got at him and also at Ronnie Lamont at the back of the line-out. I remember leaving one line-out and crossing the field, only to hear the crowd roar. When I looked back, there was this shermozzle on the ground. Delme eventually arrived from the scene of the trouble and I asked him what all that had been about. 'Oh, I was having a lot of trouble so I had to give one of those boyos a tap with one of my size 14s,' he said, looking down. Delme had these huge boots that were specially made for him. One 'tap' from those and you'd have been black and blue for a month.

It was a stupid game, with guys running all over the field trying to fight or exact revenge. The referee had no proper control. At the end, as we came off the field, there was a big woman with large arms standing near us and she suddenly belted Lamont across his back with an umbrella, shouting, 'You dirty Irish bastard.' I grabbed the umbrella and broke it over my knee, so it wasn't much good after that. Then came the Canterbury game, a match for which Jim Telfer of Scotland was Lions captain. It was a similar sort of game to the Auckland match, but Jim's comment at the after-match press conference made it more memorable. He was asked whether he thought it had been a dirty game, to which he replied, 'Not particularly. Every game in New Zealand is a dirty game.' Then he added, slowly, 'I would just like to wish the referee a good trip home.'

On that tour, Dewi Bebb again demonstrated his bravery and quality, and another Welshman, Stuart Watkins, who was a wing, played quite well. However, the Irish centre, Jerry Walsh, unfortunately had to go home when his father was taken seriously ill. We missed Jerry, badly. Then you had Mike Gibson, who was a great player, and Alan Lewis and David Watkins, who were super guys, but our biggest problem on that tour was the forwards. There were too many who were simply not up to the job. Derek Grant, the Scottish breakaway, was one who certainly was; a hard man who would have died for you. Ken Kennedy and Frank Laidlaw, the two hookers, also played well, but the forward of the tour was Lamont.

He was simply tremendous. Sadly, he damaged a nerve in his arm on that tour and today, all these years later, he has a withered arm. It killed the nerve and the muscle just wasted away.

That's one of the things that annoys me about rugby football and the people who run it. The game never follows up that sort of thing. When you're gone, you're gone. Today, Ronnie, who is a big man in every sense, cannot lift up a chair with that arm, but after the injury on that tour they made a harness for him and he was given a medical certificate stating that he should wear it in subsequent matches. Nowadays, in my retirement, I do a bit of DIY and quite recently Ronnie, who lives close by, asked if I could help him with a job. I went round to his house and had to climb up into the loft to get something. Lo and behold, there I found the old harness, forty years after he had used it on the tour. I told him it was a museum piece.

Then there was McLoughlin, the man who went on two Lions tours and only played in one Test, because he mucked up his hamstring in 1966 and then broke his thumb before the first Test in 1971 and had to go home. Of course, he would have walked into the Test side had he been fit. He was potentially a very important man on that tour. Noel Murphy was another good man, a tourist who took no nonsense. He played his guts out and would never lie down.

Jim Telfer of Scotland was also a hard man who stood up to everything. He had no great skills, but would give it all he had. He was fit and had a great attitude. Alan Pask of Wales was another in that mould; a good player and a lovely man, too. Then there was Delme Thomas of Llanelli. He hadn't even played in a single Test match when the Lions chose him for that tour, but he came through so strongly that he won a place in the side for the second and third Test matches. He and I got in when Price didn't want to play anymore. He even played prop in the third Test, an unbelievable achievement that was testimony to his enormous heart and commitment. Unlike Campbell-Lamerton, he was strong enough to survive there.

By contrast, Gary Prothero of Bridgend and Wales was another of those who just couldn't handle all the demands of the game at this level. Prothero was a very good player technically, but he just couldn't cope. It was not that he wasn't good enough, but he got homesick. In fact, he was in such a state that he really should have gone home.

So the 1966 Lions followed a similar course to their 1962 predecessors. We enjoyed seeing a great country of the southern hemisphere, met some wonderful people and experienced marvellous hospitality – until we got anywhere near a rugby field. Oh, and we also had a lot of fun. Like the time in Greymouth when we were in town to play the local combined team. Some of the midweek matches in New Zealand were tough, but this one was not especially so. When you got to these small provincial towns in New Zealand, though, you often found that the motels were not big enough to take the full Lions party of around thirty-five people. Therefore in this particular venue we were split up, half the party staying at a motel named the New Albion, the rest of us being accommodated in the Old Albion.

Now rugby players on a long tour can get up to all kinds of mischief. Boredom can set in once you have finished your training for the day, and with fit, strong young men hanging around simply trying to kill a bit of time, things can occasionally get out of hand. Far be it from me to suggest that I ever did anything on long, boring, winter nights in New Zealand other than ordering a glass of steaming hot milk and going up to bed nice and early, ready for another training session the next morning. However, on this particular occasion, we were sitting in the Old Albion and there was just nothing to do.

It was wet outside and the town was so small that I think we'd seen it twice over on our first morning there. So, for a bit of fun, I asked who it was who'd suggested certain Lions players go to the Old Albion and some to the New Albion. I said I'd love to know, because it didn't seem to me very fair that some of us had to put up with the Old Albion, while the others lived it up in the New Albion, which was only a hundred yards down the road. Of course, my tongue was nearly coming through my cheek during this discussion, but anyway, I pressed on.

There seemed a general consensus that the other Lions were complete renegades for enjoying the facilities of the new place while we languished in the old one. Then someone said, 'Sure, you're right; why should those bastards be there?' So I suggested we go down to the other place and wreck it. You see, there was so little to do you had to find your own amusement. So we went outside and it was decided that our raiding party would consist of two men: Ronnie Lamont and yours truly. I always got nominated for the most important jobs during my rugby career. Around the corner from our hotel we found a bicycle, and on a stretch of grass right outside was a horse. I got on the bike, and Ronnie Lamont climbed up on to the horse and went clop-clopping down the high street of Greymouth. It was like a scene out of *Butch Cassidy*.

When we got to the hotel, we tied up both horse and bicycle outside and crept into the New Albion. It was pretty quiet, but we could hear the Lions in the bar. So Ronnie and I crept up these wooden stairs, went into all their rooms, emptied bags of kit and turned over beds, threw stuff out of the windows and totally wrecked the place. When we'd finished, we crept back downstairs and went out through the front door, where there was still no one around. Ronnie remounted the horse, I got back on to the bike and we rode and clip-clopped our way back up the street to the Old Albion, where we rejoined our pals and had a riotous time recounting the story of our raid.

Well, the next day, the storm broke. It was big, big news in Greymouth. Bandits had broken into the Lions hotel and turned over all their stuff, wrecked the rooms and hurled their gear out of the windows. The local paper was writing about it all, it was on the radio and the occupants of the Old Albion nearly needed hospital treatment from the split sides they were suffering. I don't think I've ever laughed so much, and I'll never forget the sight of Ronnie riding down Greymouth's main street like some latter-day outlaw. We had some huge laughs and the amazing thing was that the other Lions never found out that it was us.

CHAPTER 7

The Lady Who Donated Her Knickers

Ever since I had started my international rugby career, the countries of the southern hemisphere had held sway over their northern counterparts almost every time they met. I was a proud Northern Irishman and I had become sick of this seemingly endless hegemony. What had happened on the 1966 Lions tour, where we had been whitewashed 4–0 in the Test series, had typified events during the first half of the 1960s. Yet then, gradually, came signs that the oppressed were stirring; that it might one day be different.

In Ireland, much of the gradual change in rugby attitudes can be attributed to two men. Ronnie Dawson was a no-nonsense, uncomplicated sort of man, who was neat, tidy and organised in his own life and demonstrated he could have a real influence in the game at large in this part of the world. Dawson had led the 1959 Lions in New Zealand and had, virtually single-handedly, because there were no coaches, come within a couple of whiskers of not just holding the All Blacks in their own backyard, but actually beating them. His Lions would have done so had they not been penalised, in very dubious circumstances, twice in the final minutes of the first Test, after they had scored four tries against none by the All Blacks. But Don Clarke's lethal boot rescued the Blacks that day in Dunedin and they escaped, 18–17. That marvellous New Zealand rugby writer T.P. McLean called it 'undoubtedly the worst day in the All Blacks' history'.

Then at Wellington in the second Test, the Lions were leading 8–6 with only a couple of minutes to go, but missed touch from a penalty. The New Zealanders ran it back at them and ended up scoring a try, which Clarke converted to snatch an 11–8 win. Dawson had done just about everything someone could to win a Test series and he was a man who thought about the game. He felt the British sides could beat the likes of New Zealand and South Africa if they were prepared to cast aside the absurdly amateurish approach that had dogged their every tour to date.

Ray McLoughlin thought along similar lines. McLoughlin came from a classical rugby background in the south of Ireland, Blackrock College and UC Dublin. Like Dawson, he was a tough, front row forward who only knew one way to play the game, and that was hard and to win. He had little time for shirkers, people who wasted their ability and failed to realise that you could only hope to match the likes of New Zealand and South Africa by dedicating yourself completely to the task on a long tour. Certainly, Ray made sure there was some fun along the way, as events before the first Test on the 1966 tour in New Zealand's south island showed, but when the fun stopped, Ray became one of the most deadly serious men of world rugby. He understood implicitly that you couldn't beat the All Blacks by fooling around all the time.

A few of us felt the same way; we'd had enough of these continual beatings. By this time I'd been on two Lions tours and of the eight Test matches played in South Africa and New Zealand, the Lions had won none. In fact, they'd only drawn one, losing the other seven. That was a record to make you sick and for sure, those of us who were hard enough and cared enough were sufficiently fed up with it to try and change it.

It's like in life, you get sick of losing. We knew we were better than this, had players capable of better things, so it became obvious that the key element that had to change was the attitude.

In Ireland, as I've said, strong men like Dawson, off the field as a coach, and McLoughlin, on it as a player, led the change. In Wales, Ray Williams, who had seen the need for proper coaching, was another to grasp the nettle. In England, the old committee still ruled, which meant there was scant likelihood of a radical change in attitudes there. The good old chaps syndrome and gin and tonics at the bar afterwards still seemed to me more important there than the actual game, and particularly the winning of it, which I found very strange. But then, I was never a potential Oxford or Cambridge man and always preferred a pint of beer to a G & T.

Apart from the wrong attitude, where we really fell down in New Zealand in 1966 was rucking, securing the loose ball once it had gone onto the ground. The New Zealand forwards were altogether better disciplined, more adept and more powerful in this phase than the Lions' forwards. By securing a stream of quality possession from this phase of play, they set up opportunities for their backs, who enjoyed space and time to attack us outside the scrum. It all worked like clockwork, although I vividly remember that all the New Zealand players were fitter than us. Their whole attitude was different from ours, too. However, there was one enormous benefit that arose from that tour. Ray McLoughlin watched, listened and learned, and when he got home to Ireland he began to spell out to those who mattered just what had to be done to alter the balance of power in the world game.

I believe I'm right in saying that the eight-man scrummage, where all eight forwards push like hell and the hooker does not actually strike for the ball, was developed by Ray. I remember us stealing the ball from teams like England with this tactic, on their put-in to the scrum. In some cases, we would destroy opposing packs through our power. But McLoughlin was responsible for more than just that. He brought thinking and planning into the game by saying that we had to know in the forwards what we were going to do. We needed to be aware where the next play would be, whether we were going to move the ball left or right, whether a move was planned between the half-backs or whether we were going to spread it wide. In other words, some proper preparation was at last going into our rugby, whereas before we had just played it off-the-cuff, doing whatever came into any one individual's head at a given moment. But world sport was changing; you couldn't get away with that any more.

I have often wondered in subsequent years how the 1966 Lions would have fared had Ray McLoughlin been given the captaincy. It is one of those imponderables, but I think it is fair to say that there would have been a different attitude entirely.

Another Irish player of that era with the right attitude was Mick Molloy, an unsung type of second row forward who quietly went about his business in the engine room of the scrum, who I would say was one of the best partners I had in my time in the Irish side. He was strong in the rucks and mauls, had superb strength, scrummaged soundly and worked hard in the line-outs. There wasn't a lot Molloy didn't do on the field for his team.

There's another thing about rugby football. It's the 50–50 balls that generally decree the outcome of the game. If one side is consistently winning them, then they are likely to succeed in the long run. Mick Molloy was one of those players who seemed to come up with the 50–50 balls, time and again. He could win the ball when, by all rights, it should have been lost. He would grab the ball on the ground or wrestle it off some opponent when you thought there was no chance of getting it. Maybe those kinds of challenges are not seen too much from the grandstand but, believe me, Mick's colleagues saw him do that time and again and we had an enormous respect for him and his value to the Irish sides in which he played.

In 1967 and 1968, during the course of little more than twelve months, Ireland played Australia three times and won every game. The Wallabies were touring the UK, Ireland and France in 1966–7 and played thirty-four matches in all. However, unlike the New Zealand All Blacks three years earlier, who had made the same trip and lost just once, the Australians lost fourteen times and drew another three. This underlined the weakness of the game in that country. They beat England and Wales, but lost to Scotland, and when they came to Dublin, we enjoyed a rousing 15–8 win.

Just a few months later, we made a short tour to Australia at the end of our season, playing six matches, including a single Test, which we won in Sydney, 11–5. Another great character in the Irish team was S.A. Hutton of Malone, who today lives outside Durban. He was never the greatest prop in the world, but he won four caps in 1967 and did all right. He used to have these strange sayings, which he used on his team-mates, such as, 'Come on babes, come on babes.' But the funniest thing of all concerning Hutton happened on that tour of Australia in 1967.

We were playing against a New South Wales Country XV in a place called Wollongong. We weren't doing particularly well, for they were a rough, tough side. We had a weakened team due to injuries and most of our guys probably had hangovers from the night before. It was sometimes like that. Anyway, there was a line-out, Sam Hutton ran around from the front of it to tidy up possession and promptly dropped a goal. You wouldn't normally even attempt to drop a goal from that position, because nine times out of ten you would send the ball crashing into the face of someone standing right in front of you. I doubt whether Sam Hutton had ever attempted to drop a goal in all his life, so what possessed him to try it then I have no idea.

The ball took off, certainly did not rise any higher than the bar at any stage, and seemed to take a course way out to the right of the posts. At one point the corner flag looked a more likely target than the goalposts, but then it suddenly swung violently to the left before going to the right again and finally clearing the crossbar between the uprights by about half an inch. As it limped painfully over, Sam started a sort of war dance of delight. He was jumping up and down with two hands in the air. Yet it was three points we badly needed at the time.

Now short tours such as this were supposed to be about having a bit of fun. The night of our Test win was predictably a happy time which, like most such nights, eventually got out of control. I don't know why, but when Irish people get drunk, they fight. Anyway, one of the people doing the drinking with us in this bar turned out to be the owner, and boy, could he take a drink. At one stage, with general mayhem descending upon this place somewhere in Sydney, the police were called. But when they appeared, the owner got up, stood unsteadily on his feet and roared out, 'I built this bloody hotel and I'll pull it down if I want to.' A great roar and half a dozen flying glasses hurled against the wall celebrated this brave statement and the party continued.

The manager of the tour was a lovely man named Eugene Davy. It's funny, but in Ireland if you're a Catholic you are called devout and if you're a Protestant you are known as staunch. Isn't that brilliant? Anyway, I would say Davy was a very devout Catholic, who never took a drink, and went and said prayers for us all. That night after the Test match win we never got to bed and the following morning, when the first shafts of sunlight lit up Sydney Harbour and our hotel near Bondi Beach, you could see the human flotsam and remnants of the celebrations from the previous night. Sadly, I must confess I was among them. Eugene came cheerily through the door the next morning, seeking the breakfast room, looked at us and said, 'Aren't you boys marvellous you're up so early.' He was that sort of man; someone who never saw wrong in anyone. He thought his boys had been sleeping soundly the night through.

The following year the Aussies came to the UK once again, to play just in Ireland and Scotland, and we beat them again in Dublin, 10–3. However, we were more than aware that this wasn't the same as our games against New Zealand or South Africa. For us, Five Nations Championship games were much more important than matches against Australia.

I believe the message as far as changing our approach goes began to be understood as we came into the last years of the 1960s. The Lions were to set off once again for South Africa in 1968, and the appointment of Ronnie Dawson as assistant manager/coach raised eyebrows among a few of my fellow Irishmen. We knew that Dawson was serious about his rugby and that therefore there might be a chance that this tour would be different. Another factor in our favour was that Wales had just unearthed some extremely talented young players, among them a scrum-half named Gareth Edwards, an outside-half named Barry John and a wing named Gerald Davies. This trio looked like the real deal, as they say in America, and I was intrigued to see how they would fare if they were chosen for the tour. Another young Welshman who had had an extraordinary impact in a Five Nations Championship game and looked likely to make the tour was a full-back named Keith Jarrett. He had scored 19 points on his debut, against England in Cardiff in 1967, and he seemed to be another of a very bright crop of talented young Welsh players for the future.

In the event, all four Welsh boys made the tour. The squad was captained by my fellow countryman Tom Kiernan, who was the fourth Irishman to lead a Lions tour since 1950. In all, just twenty-six men have led touring British Isles teams to the southern hemisphere since the first one set off, way back in 1888. Astonishingly, Ireland, a small rugby-playing country in anyone's language, have had the honour of providing most captains in that time. Eight Irishmen, from Tom Smythe of Malone in 1910, to Ciaran Fitzgerald of St Mary's College in 1983, have led the Lions. In between, the other Irishmen chosen to lead have been Sammy Walker in 1938, Karl Mullen in 1950, Robin Thompson in 1955, Ronnie Dawson in 1959, Tom Kiernan in 1968 and myself in 1974. Speaking personally, but also speaking, I am sure, on behalf of all those men, I would say that to lead a British Lions tour was the greatest sporting honour ever bestowed upon me in my lifetime.

I think one of the reasons why so many Irishmen have been selected as leaders is that we have always had a very good balance in our rugby in this land. We have never got too carried away when we have won, or plumbed too many depths when beaten. We tend to take knocks on the chin and get up for another go the next time – which is an essential quality when you are on a Lions tour. When we lost, we would sit down in a calm frame of mind. Also, I believe the Irish temperament within the four nations was a good one. Our boys were popular, they had a laugh and were always comfortable with other people. They were personable and could see the funny side of a situation. And, by God, you needed that from time to time on those tours.

For those interested in the statistics, then, Ireland have provided eight Lions captains, England and Scotland seven each and Wales, just three. But I should point out that one Englishman, Martin Johnson, was twice chosen as captain, in 1997 and 2001, a unique achievement.

As before, it is not my intention to recount details of every game on this trip; that has been documented in minute detail elsewhere. What I want to do is provide an overview, some reflective thoughts from the distance of thirty-six years later. That tour was renowned for the fun we had off the field and the characters who filled the squad. I suppose I should concede that at times the nonsense that went on socially during the tour detracted from the rugby, but this was about the last Lions tour when that did happen. Nor do I believe we lost because we were too intent on having a good time, for a more professional approach was emerging and Ronnie Dawson certainly exuded that.

However, the manager, an Englishman from the Harlequins club named David Brooks, was an extraordinary man. He believed that he had been born to enjoy life and share fun and pleasure with his fellow men. Don't get me wrong; Brooksie, as he came to be known, was also a winner who cared passionately about the Lions and wanted to see us triumph. I thought that the parties and amusement seemed to get in the way of those aspirations and, in my opinion, you can't really do both if you want to be successful.

David loved a party more than anything, but he was a good manager, because he seemed able to spot any player who was a bit down and needed lifting from a long way off. There were often some during the course of those long tours. David's party trick was to knock the bottom off a wine glass by giving just a gentle tap on the weak spot of the glass. He would go quietly around receptions and then, a while later, you'd go to put your glass down and find it had no bottom. Brooks had spooked you. Some receptions ended with twenty-five or thirty people holding glasses with no bottoms. Childish, I know, when I look back, but at the time, in the company of a lot of other young men, it seemed great fun.

The trouble was, some parties got out of hand. The most famous occasion was on the night sleeper train up to the Kruger Park. The tour itinerary permitted a few days break, which was a splendid idea, but I'm not sure the Lions behaviour on the journey was so commendable. On the train, Brooks kept saying, 'We're off on our holidays,' which was true. He announced he would do a version of his wine glass trick and, at the appointed hour, a pile of glasses was lined up. He had carefully stacked them up, one on top of the other, and promised he'd then remove the tablecloth beneath them without disturbing the glasses. By this stage we were all half pissed. He built up twenty glasses and duly pulled the tablecloth. Twenty glasses went up in the air and came crashing down in pieces. Brooks surveyed the carpet of broken glass, sniffed with an air of disappointment and said, 'Didn't fuckin' work. Bring me more glasses.' The whole episode was then repeated.

A lot of drink had been spilled and eventually Syd Millar and I said, 'Let's get out of here,' and rushed down the train to our cabins. The next thing we heard was the beat of war drums, crying, 'The wreckers are coming, the wreckers are coming.' This was the group of Lions who had joined the wrecking contingent, as opposed to another group known as the kippers who preferred to get some sleep. The noise got nearer and nearer, with the cry 'We're going to get you' heard quite distinctly. Syd and I were hiding in the corner of our compartment and somehow they missed us. Inadvertently, they launched a raid on the next door compartment, which was occupied by an old lady and gentleman. Both were turned out into the corridor by the mob before the blunder was realised.

That somewhat punctured the commotion and we went off to sleep. The next thing was, I woke up some hours later and thought, 'This train is remarkably smooth and quiet.' There was a good reason for that – it wasn't moving. The commotion during the night had caused such a fuss that the train authorities had unhooked our two carriages and dumped them into a siding while the rest of the train proceeded on its way. There was one hell of a mess in those carriages, but eventually it was all sorted out and we were able to go on our way.

It was David Brooks who started the traditional 'happy hour' for touring Lions squads after matches. It was only for the team, a chance to come together and spend time with each other without any outsiders allowed in. I thought it was a brilliant idea. After all, we'd trained together, played together and taken some fierce physical punishment together. This helped create the strong unity you need on such tours. The only trouble with happy hours under Brooks was that they turned into precisely that – hours. Sometimes they went on for four or five hours. One night, at one venue, a lot of things got broken: tables, chairs, glasses . . . all manner of things. The bill was presented the next morning by an understanding manager who almost certainly had halved it and then reduced it some more. Brooks looked at the sheet of paper with the amount to pay, drew his pen elegantly from his inside jacket pocket to sign the cheque and exclaimed, 'Pooh! Couldn't have been much of a party.'

On reflection, I admit now that there were times when it would have been better if David had withdrawn. Clearly he felt it was better to be involved, but I'm not sure it did the reputation of the touring party too much good to have the manager present and sometimes involved in the shenanigans. One night in particular has gone down into Lions folklore history – and that night there was much damage. It happened at the New Fairmead Hotel at Rondebosch in Cape Town, which was owned by a former Lion, Jeff Reynolds, who had himself toured in 1938 and played for the English club Old Cranleighans and the Army, as well as the English national side.

We decided at the start of the party that we would have a fire, and everyone that came into the hotel had to donate a piece of clothing to keep it going. All the Lions stripped off their shirts, ties or trousers. It was stupid really, but Brooks felt this was brilliant. Then a woman arrived outside the hotel and was informed of the situation. To be allowed entry she had to donate an item of clothing. Cool as you like, she promptly removed her knickers, which were flung onto the bonfire to the accompaniment of roars of laughter. It was, as I say, pretty stupid stuff.

However, there was some rugby played in the midst of this mayhem. Ronnie Dawson, the coach, never took a drink, so he was always up early and in fresh condition to give us hell on the training ground. Some days we needed it, too. That reckoning the following morning was essential after the excesses of the night before. The boys loved Brooksie, but they had a healthy respect for Dawson, too, and rightly so.

We lost the Test series, but it would be wrong to blame the fun we had for that. Injuries were a significant factor, especially the pulled hamstring that cost Gareth Edwards his place in the third and fourth Test matches. Besides, you should have fun on a Lions tour; it is one of the great experiences of a young rugby player's life. As I have conceded, there were times when the fun went too far, but at least this was a happy touring squad. If you ask me whether I would prefer to be with them or with the poker-faced lot who toured Australia in 2001, never did anything except train and study videos of opponents and still lost the Test series, it wouldn't take me very long to decide. And remember, the 1968 Lions did especially well in the provincial matches, losing only one out of sixteen, although, of course, we knew full well that Lions tours are judged on the outcome of the Test series, not provincial games.

What of the players? Well, Tom Kiernan was a good captain and a very deep thinker about the game. He got the best out of people, which is always a great trait in a successful leader. Maybe, though, sometimes he was too honest. Bob Hiller was back-up No. 15 to Tom and you couldn't have had a better man around on a Lions tour. Bob was the bane of Ireland for several seasons, as he always seemed to kick a vital goal that turned our matches with the England sides of his era. He was a fine player, as well as a tremendous guy, and it was most unfortunate that his tours with the British Lions in 1968 and 1971 coincided with two key figures in his position on each trip.

In 1968, Kiernan was captain, which meant that Bob had virtually no chance of making the Test side, injury excepted. By the time 1971 had come along, a Welshman who had become rather well known had again squeezed out Hiller from the Lions Test full-back position. His name was J.P.R. Williams. By then, J.P.R. was probably the best full-back in the world, but Hiller was one of the reasons why the 1968 and 1971 Lions lost only one of thirty-six provincial games they played during the course of those two tours. That was some record. As I said earlier, the tide had begun to turn for the Lions in the southern hemisphere, and players with the attitude of Bob Hiller were a key factor in that equation.

Another player to excel on that tour was T.G.R. Davies, a player of supreme skills and punishing pace. There was none better than Gerald, but I was disappointed in another Welshman, Keith Jarrett, who had travelled with such promise. Jarrett never really developed on the tour and after just one more season back home he turned professional. Three other members of the 1968 Lions squad, Welsh wing Maurice Richards, English prop Mike Coulman and Irish No. 8 Ken Goodall, were also to go to rugby league, but you just accepted those things. There wasn't anything much you could do about it, even though we in Ireland knew how grievously we would miss Ken. But other players would always emerge and the attitude was, 'So long. Cheerio.'

Of the other three-quarters, Sandy Hinshelwood was all right, Barry Bresnihan was a good one hundred per cent player and Richards of Cardiff played fairly well. Maurice was quite a religious guy and you would hardly have expected to find him rolling drunk in the aisles by midnight or hurling chairs and beds out of windows. Now Richards' Cardiff teammate, the Lions prop forward John 'Tess' O'Shea, was judge in the players' court throughout the tour.

Normally, players were dragged before the court in light-hearted vein for things like drinking too much or some other misdemeanor. But they couldn't pin anything on Richards and so a charge was laid, citing him for 'doing nothing out of place on this tour'. There was no defence to that, because Richards was too nice a guy, so Judge O'Shea said, 'OK, I find the defendant guilty because he has uttered no defence.' You see, the Lions courts were rich in legal framework, with the defendant afforded his full democratic rights.

Anyway, the sentence was then handed down – Richards had to take a glass and smash it against a wall in the courtroom. But then the most astonishing thing happened. He threw the glass against the wall, and it bounced back on to the carpet and never broke.

Jock Turner, the Scottish centre, was another great stalwart on that tour; a man who stood back from nothing. As for the half-backs, Gareth Edwards was, well, Gareth; a masterful player in the making who would flourish in New Zealand with the 1971 Lions and again three years later with the 1974 Lions, back in South Africa. His Cardiff half-back partner Barry John was another genius in the making but, sadly, Barry broke his collarbone in the first Test and never played another Test on the tour. Indeed, injuries bedevilled the tour.

But the reason the Lions lost the Test series 3–0, with one match drawn, was because of us forwards. We were inferior to the hard-grafting South African packs that dominated possession and played a tough, physical game. We were not good enough. I was probably not the line-out forward that some of the guys I played against were and I lacked a bit of the pace that others had, but certainly not attitude. I don't think anyone could ever accuse me of lacking that as a player. I always wanted to be the best. I don't like losers at that level.

Much hope had been invested in the Lions' Scottish lock-forward Peter Stagg, who was regarded as something of a freak in some circles because he stood six feet nine inches tall. Of course, that height is about the minimum requirement to play international rugby these days, but in those times people peered in bemused fashion at this beanpole of a man. Peter was a nice man, too, but he lacked the steely inner core required to handle the sort of treatment the Springboks dished out to him. The Lions chose to have four-man line-outs in the first Test, a decision I argued long and loud against because I knew that the South Africans would target Stagg and that he wasn't up to handling it. But we went ahead with it and the inevitable happened. Peter was too spindly and the Boks just took him out.

Of the other forwards, Syd Millar was very solid, as you would expect. John Pullin, the England hooker, was a great player, while the two Taylors in the back row, John of Wales and Bob of England, played very hard rugby. Jim Telfer, too, was hard, but he didn't have the pace you need in South Africa at the base of the scrum. But it dismayed me that the Lions scored only one try in those four Tests and it was scored by a forward. Myself. Apart from that, all we could do was to kick penalty goals – eleven by Tom Kiernan, spread over the four Tests. That statistic alone was sufficient to damn us in my eyes, but our problem was we had no ball or if we did get some it was delivered going backwards under pressure. Such possession is more a liability than a resource.

We trained well enough and there was always some fun around the corner, with Brooks in charge. However, you can have the happiest tourists in the world off the field and the best team in the world on the training ground, but none of that necessarily counts when you get out on the field on match-day, especially when it comes to Test matches. There is nowhere to hide in those pressure-cooker games and we were found badly wanting in them.

Our players started questioning themselves when things started going wrong, which is why the mind is so important in rugby football. I honestly believe that, despite the fact that we did all the work in preparation, when we were confronted with the best of the southern hemisphere, we crumbled. We had this feeling of being inferior. Physically, we could prepare, but mentally we were not strong enough. Mankind discovers the power of his mental faculties in adversity. Ours were insufficient to handle the task before us. Today, it is different for we believe in ourselves. England proved that in the 2003 World Cup; we didn't. Not deep down. We were not convinced we could win.

The South African game was based on the scrummage and that wasn't wrong. I wish it still was today, in teams all around the world. I always believed that you could dictate an entire game from your scrummage, with your half-backs and back row, but much of that has changed in modern rugby. I was glad to see England underlined that fact in winning the World Cup.

So, we lost the series, yet in a sense the 1968 Lions had laid the base for what was to come in 1971 and 1974. Dawson led the way in showing what could be achieved, not only with the 1968 Lions, but also as coach of Ireland at that time.

Of course, you couldn't even dip a proverbial toe into the water of greater organisation in the game without upsetting one group of people. Among the establishment, there was much grumbling along the lines of who did these coaches think they were, wanting to change things and take the players away for proper pre-match preparation, to cut down on the number of cocktail parties the players attended on a Lions tour, and so on? I looked at this old brigade and shook my head in dismay. They simply could not see the reality, which was that if we were ever going to be anything other than just whipping boys for the southern hemisphere countries, then these changes had to take place. But these people, the so-called and often self-appointed 'guardians' of the game, had taken it upon themselves to keep the administration of the sport at the top level almost a closed shop. Reality was not allowed to intrude.

I was sufficiently fed up with it all that I had virtually made up my mind not to tour again with the Lions when I returned from the 1968 trip. On the flight home I was sitting next to the Welsh prop-forward on the plane, pondering all that had gone before. John O'Shea, Tess as he had become known, leaned across and asked, 'Would you do it all again?' I said that I doubted it. I'd had three Lions tours and we'd won nothing, not a single Test. At the time, I couldn't imagine wanting to go through that painful experience a fourth time, but of course once I got back on the rugby field I didn't stay depressed for too long.

In 1970 there occurred a most extraordinary event in the annals of Irish rugby history. Irish rugby has had more than its share of characters down the years; it has perhaps been the single defining quality in an Irish rugby team. But few characters have been greater than Tony O'Reilly, a rugby player of remarkable talent for the British Lions on tours of South Africa in 1955 and New Zealand in 1959. It is said that O'Reilly played his best rugby for the Lions, rather than Ireland, and general opinion holds that to be true. By 1963, at the grand old age of twenty-six, O'Reilly had just about finished international rugby and had already embarked upon the career structure that would see him become Ireland's most successful international businessman. His final game in the green jersey had apparently been against Wales in 1963 and a suitable send off it was, for Ireland won in Cardiff 14–6, the first time they had won on Welsh soil since 1949.

Tony later worked his socks off in business, being head-hunted by the American food conglomerate H.J. Heinz Ltd. and becoming a key figure in their organisation. Thus, by 1970, he was working in London and filling out physically, as befits a man taking regular lunches and dinners with important business associates. Yet suddenly, whilst in this state, O'Reilly received a call to play another international match for Ireland, against England at Twickenham in 1970. The whole episode was absolutely hilarious.

Getting injured during what passed for training in those days took a bit of doing, believe me, but Bill Brown, chosen on the left wing for Ireland in that game, managed it as we gently warmed up. That night, therefore, a message was delivered to a rather over-weight businessman in a suit and tie, entertaining his guests in a London night club. It read, 'Brown injured, cannot play. Report HAC ground in City of London, 10 o'clock Friday morning, to play England on Saturday.'

It is a wonder that O'Reilly did not fall down dead from the shock. He hadn't played international rugby for seven years and the game had moved on a fair bit in that time. When we saw him strip off for training the next morning, let's just say he no longer looked the athlete he once was. He looked nowhere near fit. We'd had to wait for O'Reilly to arrive at the training ground, but eventually this chauffeur-driven Mercedes came slowly through the gates. O'Reilly stepped out to a great cheer from the waiting Irish team, after which a volley of healthy verbal insults was fired in his direction. Tony took them with impunity as he has always done, a mischievous grin spread large across his cheeks. He went to the enormous boot of his enormous car and dug out his playing kit, before strolling into the changing rooms to get ready.

You warmed up by running around the field three or four times. I absolutely hated it because I was not built to do it. On most training runs, the backs would be at the front and the forwards at the back, with me always last. I always ran at the back because you could cut corners off the field and make the torture a bit shorter. Invariably, it was a lonely journey at the back, because there was nobody as ill-suited to this activity as me. But on this particular day, lo and behold, I looked beside me and there, puffing and panting, was our brave left wing. O'Reilly's cheeks were wobbling around like a blancmange jelly, the sweat running down his face like droplets of water on the outside of a window. Eventually he turned to me and gasped out the words, 'I'm a bit worried about tomorrow.'

That, I suppose, might go down as one of the great human utterances of the twentieth century. Forget about some bloke landing on the moon and going on about 'One small step for man . . .' So I said to O'Reilly, 'What are you worried about, you've been through all this before,' but he said, 'The England wing, Keith Fielding, is very fast, probably the quickest player in the world.' It was clearly imperative that some confidence was instilled in our new wing for the morrow, so, being as helpful as I could, I promptly offered the following advice: 'Well, Tony, I wouldn't worry about that too much if I were you, because by the time he runs around you, he's going to be bloody tired. And if he comes near you, I suggest you just shake your jowls at him, because you're sure to frighten the daylights out of him.'

So match day came and we got on to the field and there was great excitement in the crowd, particularly among the London paddies from Kilburn. But it was a very wet day and there was a huge patch of muck in the shadow of one of the old stands. Ian Shackleton, the England outside-half, kicked the ball and it came down and stopped dead in this pile of muck. It never even bounced, just came down, went plop and stopped right in front of O'Reilly. The great man looked briefly around, presumably to see if his chauffeur was on hand to pick up the damn thing, and when he realised he was the only man there, he went down on the ball just ahead of the English pack who were thundering towards it. O'Reilly disappeared, ball and all, in this pile of muck.

Anyway, eventually the whistle went and a scrum was called. As the teams broke up, there was this momentary lull, with everyone looking and waiting to see what state O'Reilly would emerge in. Then suddenly, with him still on the ground, this guy shouted out, 'And yer can kick his fuckin' chauffeur, too.' Even O'Reilly burst out laughing at that. Alas, Ireland lost a drab match played on a drab February afternoon, 9–3, and I think Tony was probably the first to conclude afterwards that his lengthy and distinguished career was at last at an end.

Tony has always been able to make people laugh, which is an endearing trait. He had been asked to write an article in the programme for that game and he was also to be the guest speaker at the dinner after the match, long before he was chosen to play in it as a replacement. Not many players get to do all that in one game.

O'Reilly was one of those guys who saw rugby chiefly as relaxation. I remember once playing against his club, Old Belvedere in Dublin, and it was one of those days when Tony obviously didn't want to know. The ball seemed to evade him because he just didn't want it. He obviously had other things on his mind and when it came to half-time, he just disappeared. He came back on just before we kicked off for the second half and it transpired he'd gone off to make a phone call. He was probably fixing up a business appointment for that night over dinner, but that was Tony, he just saw rugby in another light from the rest of us.

Once that 1970 Five Nations season was over, an Irish international squad headed off for a short tour of Argentina. It was a trip I'll never forget. When I look back at it, I think some people must have thought it was an Irish joke, when we got home and told them about it, because the fact was that we wandered straight into the middle of a revolution in which they assassinated the president.

We flew into Buenos Aires, the capital, on what we thought would be a cracking little trip with some interesting sight-seeing, and all we got was views from our hotel windows of street fighting and bullets whizzing past the windows. It was like something out of a movie. There were police vehicles tearing down the streets, water cannon used on protesters and the place was in uproar, with the sound of explosions going off on a fairly regular basis. You couldn't say we were under house arrest, but we couldn't leave the hotel for three days. Eventually, they appointed a new president, things quietened down a bit and we managed to go and play a bit of rugby. It seemed hilarious, but of course it was no laughing matter for the thousands of people who just disappeared and were never heard of again.

When we finally left the hotel and travelled through the country, we saw what a beautiful place it was, in a geographical sense. We went from Buenos Aires to Rosario, right across the pampas. It was a lovely land, but behind the beautiful scenery lay an ugly reality. I'd been to South Africa and seen what I thought was fairly grim poverty, but the shacks, filth and squalor we saw on the outskirts of Buenos Aires were something else entirely. It shocked me, and I wasn't alone. Nor did it take much to work out why there was a revolution going on. These people had nothing to lose by fighting for change.

On the rugby field, they weren't averse to a bit of fighting, either, but this was cowardly stuff. We got down in the first scrum of the match in Rosario and when Ronnie Lamont went in to bind onto the side of the scrum, his opposite number stood up and just kicked him in the face. I don't know what was the most arresting sight – the blood pouring down Ronnie's face or his look of shock and amazement. Syd Millar, who was playing tight-head prop that day, stood up to hit this guy and there was a bit of a scuffle. But the guy obviously realised that taking on Syd in a prolonged battle would not be terribly clever, so he started to run. Syd chased after him to finish the job he'd started and these two were joined by some of us and the referee, most of us shouting, 'Come back, come back.' It was like a scene out of the *Keystone Cops*.

Eventually, the referee caught up with them and they were brought back to what we might call the scene of the crime. The perpetrator was duly admonished but that was the extent of his punishment. Later in the game, however, that same player had to be carried off the field after an unfortunate collision between his face and an Irish fist – although I simply can't remember who that fist belonged to. I suppose he happened to be in the wrong place at the wrong time. I only went to Argentina once as a player, but that was enough. I didn't want to go back and go through all that again. The trouble was that the Argentine males seemed to regard rugby football as an extension of their macho lives and they had to impose themselves and prove what splendid young fighting bucks they were. Believe me, you can do without all that sort of nonsense on a tour. And I don't mean just the revolution.

When we left Buenos Aires to fly home, we boarded a Varig Airlines plane. It wasn't full, for the very good reason that it was going to stop in Rio de Janeiro. It was going to be a long flight from

Rio to London, so some of the boys took sleeping pills. I didn't, because I never touch the things. Anyway, we waited on the tarmac at Rio and, presently, more passengers began to board. In fact, so many were coming on board that I began to think we had seats on Noah's ark and everyone left on the land was joining us. Quite soon, they were standing in the aisle with all the seats taken. Of course, the plane couldn't take off with people standing up, so everyone was ordered off. Guys in our group who were getting really drowsy were roused from their slumber and we all slouched down wearily in a corner of the departures lounge, the Irish party surrounded by army officers with machine guns. This didn't look terribly promising.

Things got progressively worse from then on. All our passports were collected up and taken from us; meanwhile, the other passengers were put back on the plane. It then took off for London. A wonderful sight, that was; our plane rushing down the runway and lifting off into the blue yonder with us sitting around at machine-gun point, back in the terminal building. We asked them to call the Irish ambassador, but they wouldn't do that. Then it emerged that we were going to be put under house arrest, because they claimed that we were drugged. Honestly, I've been called some things in my time but a 'druggie'? Never. I don't think even my fiercest New Zealand rugby opponent would have accused me of that.

After more delays, we were taken to a separate building within the airport and detained there without our passports. For *three* days. An armed guard was put on the door to make sure no one could leave. After some time, the ambassador did arrive, but he wasn't able to throw much more light on a mysterious affair. All the authorities would say was that they suspected drug abuse was widespread. Now Irish rugby was not always in the pink of health, but to resort to massive drug abuse within the team? This was absurd.

On the third day, we'd just about had enough of the nonsense. Perhaps they realised that because suddenly the doors were opened and we were told we were allowed to go. They escorted us back to the terminal building, where we clambered on board another aeroplane with the glee of drowning men discovering a life raft in the middle of the ocean. To this day, none of us really knows the truth, but I suspect that the plane was overbooked and the easiest thing to do was to chuck us off.

One member of our party came home looking particularly dishevelled. In fact, he got off the plane in London without any shoes on. Peter McMullan was the rugby correspondent for the *Belfast Telegraph* and had been with us throughout, covering the tour. You can imagine what the heat was like in Rio; we reckoned Peter had had the same shoes on for days on end, and they were smelling a bit, to say the least. So while Peter was asleep one morning, I quietly opened the window of our temporary jail and threw them out over a wall. You do these stupid things when you're on rugby tours. When he woke up and came to, he thought someone had stolen them and went around looking for them. He had to come home in his socks. They were mad days.

CHAPTER 8

Bloody Friday

By the time that the 1968 British Lions had left for their tour of South Africa, I had moved to a branch of the bank in Coleraine. While we were away, the manager died, so that when I got back certain changes had taken place and I was sent to the new University of Ulster, located between Coleraine and Port Stewart. We had what we called sub-branches outside the main centres, and these operated by means of an official from the main branch going out to premises somewhere in the small village or community, being available for people to do their banking business for a few hours on a given day. Then the official would return to the main branch, perhaps at 2 p.m.

One of these sub-branches was in a place called Castlerock, where there is a super little golf club. The sub-branch was actually in the foyer of the local hotel and the official virtually took over the reception area for two or three hours. He changed money, took in lodgements, provided change for shopkeepers for the week and issued cheque books. In other words, he carried out a normal banking service.

When I got back from that Lions tour, the bank asked me if I would go up to the new university site and run the banking facilities that were going to be needed there. They were still building the place and there were no students, but other people around used the facilities I provided from my mobile home, which was my office. I was paying workmen, looking after the contractors and assisting the university heads in establishing financial practices. At the end of the month I could be carrying in my case anything up to £30,000. Now this was before there were problems in Northern Ireland and you could carry such money with you. You never thought about the risks of robbery. The following year, 1969, the first students arrived and trouble with a capital T hit Belfast. But Belfast was an hour and a half away from Coleraine and we just read about the Troubles in newspapers. There was no sign of anything amiss in Coleraine.

One Thursday afternoon in May at around exam time, however, there was suddenly a great commotion shortly after lunch. It was a beautiful day and the sun was shining, but word was hastily passed that there had been a bomb scare at the university. I assumed that someone had not done enough work for their exams and had phoned the university to say there was a bomb, hoping the examinations would be postponed. You can't put anything beyond these students, you know. When it happened I was in my little office, so I gathered up all the money into my bag and evacuated the university. I walked across to this grassy bank – I seem to have been attracted to banks all my life – and sat down to await developments.

Now at this university, there was a real character called Professor Newbold. I had put my bag of money underneath my head, sat back in the sun and was awaiting developments. I lay there with my eyes shut and it seemed marvellously peaceful and pleasant, with the sun beating down. Meanwhile, the university was filled with police and army personnel searching for the alleged bomb. As I lay there, I suddenly heard a voice above me say, 'Will you cash a cheque?' I looked up and it was Professor Newbold. We kept the transaction to an even amount, because I didn't have any coins for change, and no sooner had I completed that transaction then I looked up and saw a long line of people queuing on the grassy bank, waiting for the banking service I was providing. I worked my way through them, just as the police and army worked their way through the university in their fruitless search. Security? I never even thought about it, but how naive I was. Subsequent events were to change my way of thinking dramatically.

There had always been strong ties between the banking official and the local community. Of course, local people knew me through rugby football, but I had been around for a few years by this stage and they knew who I was anyway. In fact, banking was one of the closest relationships you could have. I liked my clients and I would go and visit most of them; they didn't come to see me. By going out to see them I was able to build up a picture of their circumstances and needs, so that when I was at the bank poring over papers and finances I had a clear idea of what they were trying to achieve. I also felt that it was important that not only was the bank supporting them, but I was as well, as their bank manager. I saw it as a very close relationship between the client, his accountant and myself as the banker. If you wanted people to have a sound business, you had to do that level of work.

If people came into the bank to see me and said, 'Look, I have got a problem,' I would think, thank God, because he knows he has a problem. I would invariably be able to help. But when you rang someone or had them in to see you to tell them they had a problem, they would sometimes reply, 'What problem? I have no problem.' That was when the difficulties arose, because it was obvious in some cases that people had no idea that their business was in trouble. The fact is that the first place where a problem emerges in business is at the bank. It might be turnover, profit, anything, but the bank is usually the first place where a business problem is identified.

I was always an outdoor type of guy, so I enjoyed getting out into the local community, visiting farmers in their farmyards and that sort of thing. I'd ring them up and say something like, 'Charlie, I'd like to pop over to see how you're doing. Have the kettle on and be ready in about an hour.' Talking is a national occupation in Ireland and no one ever minds having a chat – sharing the craic, as we say – so maybe half the conversation wouldn't be about finance. However, I'd listen to the person's views, his ambitions and targets, and all the while I'd be gleaning information concerning the investment my bank had made in this particular man. Was the bank's money safe? Was he a sensible, hard-working man who would accept the challenge before him and make a success of his business? I would like to think I was one of the first managers to shape the job in that particular way, because my fellow managers were horrified when I told them how I had clumped through a muddy farmyard in Wellington boots, or crossed a field ankle-deep in dirt and grime. They claimed their clients wouldn't want them to go and see them in their own locations, but I strongly disagreed.

After Coleraine and life among the university officers and students, I was transferred to what they call the lending department in Belfast. I was there for about three years and it was tremendous training from a banking point of view. In the sense of learning about life, I suppose you could say I was introduced to a world that at times resembled fairly closely my idea of hell on earth. For this was Belfast city centre in the 1970s and the terrorists regarded anything within the city as fair game for their murderous activities. From the comparative peace and quiet of Coleraine, I was catapulted into a world of explosions, threats, blood, loss of life and murder. I can tell you, those years were the most terrible indictment of the evil human beings can inflict upon a society, including innocent bystanders.

I worked at Royal Avenue, in the centre of Belfast, and our department handled applications for loans from all over the province. I was an assistant to a controller of lending. My job was to look at the applications first, put my remarks on the sheets and then pass them to the controller. By this time I was thirty and had had a reasonable amount of experience in the banking business, but not, alas, in the world of living amidst a terrorist campaign.

There weren't many days when we were not outside the offices due to a bomb scare. On some days, we might be told not to go home because there would be a bomb planted somewhere nearby. In Royal Avenue, close to the offices where I worked, there was an old broken-down hotel, the Grand Central, which was used as an army billet. My offices were directly opposite this building and I suppose if I'd been more streetwise I might have anticipated what could happen.

One day I went out for lunch to get my usual sandwich and a small bottle of orange juice. I walked up Royal Avenue, saw this van parked and thought to myself, 'That's a funny place for a van to be sitting.' Of course, there was no one in it. I walked back to my office, which was very close to where the van had been left, but no sooner had I arrived then sirens started to pierce the air. I looked out of my window and there were police and soldiers running everywhere, clearing the streets. It quickly dawned on me I shouldn't be where I was for very much longer.

By this time, I was the only one left in the office, so I quickly ran down the fire escape at the back of the building. There was an old wino with a bottle in his brown paper bag sitting with his back against the railings near the bottom. Suddenly two soldiers appeared from nowhere, picked him up as they ran and dragged him around the corner and out of the way. This guy didn't understand what was happening and tried to fight the two burly young soldiers. It was a moment of hilarity in a deadly serious situation.

I was running too – literally, for my life. I knew that if the police and army were trying to clear the streets, they must have been alerted about a bomb in the van. And terrorists did not leave bombs in vans in that location to cause a bit of traffic congestion. The bank had a big administrative office nearby, in Waring Street, and I decided to make for that. In such circumstances your mind becomes crowded with a thousand possibilities and you find it hard to think coherently. So to start with, I ran in the wrong direction – towards the actual car bomb. I quickly realised my mistake, with the aid of shouted warnings from the army, and changed direction. Of course,

I was used to running around a rugby field and this presented no problem to me, but I never ran around a rugby ground with my heart pounding because an enormous bomb might explode at any second and blow me to oblivion.

That day I didn't reach our other office. When I was about ten yards short of the door, this huge bomb went off. The explosion was massive. I am sure that older readers who lived through the Second World War and experienced such things would understand my recollections of that event. The ground shook as though an earthquake was happening, the air was filled with the aftermath of the shock and flying objects, and the windows in the building seemed, peculiarly, to go out and then back in again. I was thrown against a brick wall and then onto the ground. For a moment, I lay there as the earth trembled. Until you experience such things you really cannot understand the sensation. It is scary, truly frightening.

Eventually, after an hour or so, I picked my way back to the office through a sea of rubble and broken masonry, carpets of glass, broken down buildings, debris, alarm bells ringing constantly, which created a pounding in your head, and other mess. You knew, deep down, that death had occurred this day all around you. Your mind was disconcerted, your senses scrambled by such an experience, but when I got outside my offices, I confronted an awful sight. The Grand Central Hotel, which had probably stood on that site for around a hundred years, had completely disappeared. It was just a heap of rubble. You knew, from that one glimpse, the awesome power of explosives and the frightening capacity of the men of violence to kill and maim as they pleased. No accountability, no conscience, no feelings, nothing at all from killers who might as well have been emotionally dead in terms of the pain and anguish they had dealt out to their victims without the slightest compunction.

Inside our office there was paper strewn everywhere. My desk had gone, as though workmen had come in and carried it away completely. We had two doors quite close by and one of these doors, which had been blown clean off its hinges, was embedded in another. It was haunting. It had knifed straight through the second door like you might put a knife through butter and leave it standing there. It was simply unbelievable. When I went down to Royal Avenue some while later, I found sheets of paper on which I had written notes earlier in the day. They were just blowing around in the light wind, amidst an eerie, evil calm that had descended upon the city in the aftermath of this carnage. There were so many, it was a complete waste of time trying to collect them all. The event was a reminder to me, a very brutal reminder, that in the overall scheme of life rugby football came very low down the order in terms of importance.

But if I felt that this was a day I never wished to see again, there was worse to come. There always is from people who have no regard for the sanctity of human life, who believe they can 'persuade' others to their cause by blowing up their friends and families. If only they had brains with which to think, they would realise the futility of their actions, and indeed how such violence imposes a fierce will and determination upon the aggrieved to fight back, never to surrender or concede an inch. By perpetrating such outrages these people move even further away from the chances of their ambitions and targets ever being met.

Bloody Friday in Belfast, 21 July, 1972 was a day when death touched almost everyone in the city. Nine people were killed, 130 seriously injured, but all who were there knew they had been within an ace of passing into the next world. On a single day, the terrorists of the IRA planted and exploded twenty-two bombs around the city within the space of seventy-five minutes. Those who thought they had escaped one explosion fled directly into the path of another, to be blown to pieces or horribly maimed. I was working in my rebuilt office at Royal Avenue and we could hear the explosions going off at regular intervals. We wondered what on earth the world had come to.

By three in the afternoon things had become so bad that head office sent out a directive that all staff should try to make their way home – as carefully as possible, they added. I got outside my office and saw scenes of chaos and destruction I never want to see again in my life. I had not the slightest idea of the safest way to go. You just didn't know whether you would walk around a corner and there would be a huge explosion. Fear stalked the streets, like an assailant.

I had to get to Ballyclare, which was where I was staying, but I had no car. I'd gone to work by bus, but of course there were no buses running by this stage. Even if there had been, there was no way anyone would have headed towards the central Belfast bus station. So I decided to run a mile or two towards a patch of ground at the bottom of the M2 motorway, where I knew some people left their cars before heading into the city centre. I reasoned that I might hitch a lift out of this hell into the safer ground of the country.

But no sooner had I gone down the stairs of our building and got outside, than I heard another huge boom close by and the air was again filled with flying objects. This particular bomb was at Smithfield, somewhere behind my office building. I started to run, but almost immediately saw the extraordinary sight of an exhaust pipe flying through the air towards me. If it had hit me, I would have been flattened and probably killed. Shrapnel, remember, was a huge killer of soldiers in the trenches in the First and Second World Wars. The exhaust pipe flew past me and smashed into a window just where I had been standing seconds earlier. It unleashed a shower of broken glass that would have cut down a human being anywhere in its path. My great fortune was that I was sufficiently far away to dive to the ground and escape the murderous shards of glass as they flew over my head. After that, I ran. I ran so hard and so fast that the sweat was pouring down my neck inside my business suit. I didn't care; I knew that if I was to survive, I had to get out of this hell hole.

When I got to the waste ground I wandered around in a daze. I thought to myself, 'How on earth am I going to escape this madness and find some sort of sanity?' Just then, I heard a shout behind me. 'Willie John, Willie John . . . over here. Quick.' It was a good friend of mine who lived in Ballyclare, waving to me to go to his car. He'd done the same as me, run out of the city centre to his car. Like everyone else, he now just wanted to get out of this terrible place on this awful day. We jumped into his car, drove out onto the road across some rough ground and roared away up that motorway as though the bats out of hell were after us. Huge New Zealanders aiming to kick me to shreds at the bottom of a ruck? Angry Welshmen trying to throw punches into my face on a rugby field? Neither even began to compare with this level of fear.

I had never been so glad to get away from Belfast in my whole life but, sadly, these experiences were almost becoming commonplace for those of us who worked in Belfast, although Bloody Friday had plumbed depths hitherto unknown even to most terrorists. The worst thing was, these outrages were almost coming to be accepted; certainly, no one was doing anything much to stop them. There were politicians talking about things like 'an acceptable level of violence', whatever that might mean. This was the sort of sub-standard leadership we in Northern Ireland were getting.

Yet even in the darkest hours, we still somehow found room for humour. Perhaps that was what kept us sane; I don't know. Frankly, when I look back, I honestly wonder how we did live through it all. Of course, some didn't; they were blown to pieces or maimed for life. Their lives changed forever on such dark days, but perhaps even in the direst adversity, you need to find humour in a situation. Maybe it helps you retain your sanity. One such moment came on a night when I went out for dinner with my wife Penny and some friends, who had a relation home from Canada. We went to a place called La Mont House, which had been rebuilt after being blown up. It was on the other side of Belfast from where we lived.

At that time, of course, and indeed until quite recently, there were roadblocks by the side of the road, manned by local UDR police officers and also British Army soldiers. These roadblocks could pop up at any time, day or night. The police or army officers would stop you and ask where you had been, where you were going and generally try to see whether you were suspicious or not. For those of us who lived in Northern Ireland through those years, they were a regular part of our lives. We'd had a good night at this restaurant and when we came out we were in quite good spirits. There were six of us, and we were all quite big. I knew we couldn't all get into this Volvo, so I volunteered to clamber into the boot for the ride home.

We were coming into Belfast city centre over the Queen's Bridge and I could hear them talking in the car. The next thing I heard my friend say was, 'Oh hell, there's a road check.' You could hear this conversation going on in which the usual questions were being asked, and it was all very civilised, but then the policeman or army officer said to Jim, 'Can I have a look in the boot, please?' I knew then that trouble was coming. I heard Jim say, 'I don't think that's a very good idea,' but, of course, the police and army boys immediately thought something was wrong. Moments later, the boot was flung open and my eyes focused upon a couple of soldiers holding guns aimed right at me. They thought they'd found either a terrorist or a corpse. They shone in a light, and I half sat up in my cramped compartment and greeted them with a cheery, 'Good evening officers, how are you?' They looked back at me, smiled and said, 'Good evening. I hope you are well.'

I found living through those times very frustrating, because it was only a tiny minority of people who were doing the bad things. The greatest weapon in life is fear and one person can create that fear in an entire community. Frustration? Yes, because it was so unnecessary and people were losing their lives, but for what? They talked about targets, but what targets? Most of those who suffered were innocent people. How could they be targets? It is only cowards who hit innocent people. I don't mind people who stand up and fight, but this had nothing to do with that.

On Bloody Friday I saw bodies being picked up, just blown to pieces. Or should I say, parts of bodies. There would be an arm or a leg or part of a chest lying along the pavement or in the road. When you see such things you wonder at the evil in some people. At that time my sister Sadie was working in the Royal Victoria Hospital and she was in the middle of this carnage as it unfolded. She told me sometime later that she worked for two whole days, forty-eight hours, without a break. Body bags were unzipped in front of her and pieces of bodies were brought in; there was blood everywhere and injured people were being carried or limping into the hospital.

It was horrendous, but Sadie coped, because she had been trained to do so. It was when she went home that the worst of it started, from her point of view. She was suddenly and very violently ill and sat at home in tears, wondering at all she had seen. She had been strong when she had needed to be, but when the actual emergency was over, it suddenly hit her that these were living people who had been blown to bits.

I confess I don't understand how the minds of people who perpetrate such outrages operate. When I left school and went out into the big world, I soon saw that the world didn't owe me anything, but that if I was prepared to help myself and give, there were lots of people who would help me. However, I couldn't understand how those who were giving so much to society, such as businessmen who were creating employment and stability, could be blown to bits by people who were not contributing an iota to society. That this tiny minority could be so destructive and affect the lives of so many others was terribly frustrating.

Life for a bank manager in Northern Ireland was far from easy. One day a manager found himself in the back of a taxi carrying some money, a ransom to take into the border area. He'd been forced to do so by terrorists back in the city who were holding his staff hostage. There were several managers who were kidnapped during those years and held for ransom. I am appalled to say that it was part of life here. In this particular case, though, it was a controlled situation, because the police knew about it and were watching, so when the pick-up was made, the culprits were caught.

As a bank manager, you were very vulnerable. You had to take different routes to work, vary your travelling times and operate under firm security guidelines. It was all part of your daily life. You adapted to it because you had to, but for those of us who had families they were especially worrying times, because we were always mindful of their needs and safety.

There were plenty of bank holds-ups, too, of course. It didn't happen at my bank, but I was just lucky. When I left the lending department in Belfast, I moved to Ballymena, as deputy manager of the Broadway branch, and while I was there an edict was made that we had to erect bandit screens. This bullet-proof glass was regarded as one way that hold-ups might be averted, but I found that I couldn't hear customers properly through those wretched screens. I therefore rang head office and told them I wanted the screens taken down. I said I could take the screens down in twenty minutes myself with a screwdriver, but I wanted the appropriate department to remove them. They told me we would be too vulnerable without them but, as I pointed out, if someone walked in with a machine gun the screens wouldn't save anyone.

You might have thought rules and regulations would have emerged triumphant from this little contretemps between one individual bank manager in a small Northern Ireland provincial town and an edict issued from on high at headquarters, but you would be wrong. I got the screens taken down within three days, and this had the most extraordinary effect. No, we didn't have masked gunmen visiting us on the hour, every hour. What we did have were profits that quadrupled very quickly, and do you know why? It was because the word had got out that we wanted to talk to our customers and would not let anything prevent that. I heard people talking about it in the streets of the town. Someone said that they were fed up dealing with anonymous bank people locked away behind screens and someone else replied, 'Oh, you want to go down to the Northern Bank. They're much better there and they've got rid of all that nonsense.' Once we had set the precedent, other banks began to realise what was going on and in the course of time they took their screens down, too, but by then we had taken an awful lot of new business, presumably from them.

I liked working in Ballymena. These were my kind of people: frank, honest and upright citizens. Life was not easy for them, but they were people of character and fortitude. As mostly Northern Ireland Protestants, they were directly in the firing line of the terrorists who were trying to kill and maim people simply to make their political point. Now I respect people who stand up against cowards and bullies and who fight back, in whatever way, and these people in Ballymena did that every day of their lives. Simply by walking into the centre of town, by doing their shopping and visiting the bank or wherever else they went, they were sending a message to the terrorists – you will do not deter us; you won't force us to cower in fear in our houses.

I respected those people deeply for their attitude as, I am certain, did all right-minded and decent people throughout the entire island of Ireland, north and south of the border. As someone once said, 'All people are not evil. Do not condemn all for the sake of the few.' Which is true. There may be a few rotten apples in every basket, but you do not condemn the entire basket load because of the few bad ones. The same went for society at that time.

So in my working life, I faced many difficulties. Even when I went off to play rugby there were threats made against me, so that when I played for Ireland I was subjected to close scrutiny. Armed detectives would patrol outside my hotel bedroom door in Dublin and the same would happen when Ireland played in Scotland, England or Wales. When I questioned this with the security people, they told me that they were concerned about certain unspecified threats that had been telephoned to the police. Of course, the people who send such threats are just cowards, but there were inevitably some people who didn't want to see me play for Ireland and were especially opposed to the sight of an Ulsterman leading Ireland.

You will always get some fanatics, a few hotheads, but I believed that most reasonable people were happy enough to see me lead Ireland. All I wanted to be judged on was my form on the field, not my politics off it. A sportsman or woman should never be judged on the latter. The trouble was, you never knew whether these threats were genuine or not. I remember being in Scotland one year and we were told that a couple of us were under threat, and I was certainly one of them, but you were always left wondering whether it was real or unreal.

Threats made against sportsmen are always unsavoury. They put the individual in a very difficult position. In 2003, the England cricket team received much criticism for refusing to play in Zimbabwe during the World Cup, but I was not one of those doing the criticising. In fact, I had a lot of sympathy for them. They were going into an unstable society so it was difficult for them and I could understand their reluctance to go. From what I understand, their security could not be guaranteed one hundred per cent. That was a situation where the administration should have stepped in and taken a decision much sooner than it did.

Yet, shining through it all, and as a bank manager I saw this time and again, was the sheer will of the people to stand up, get up on their feet again and go forward once more. They were not going to be cowed and beaten by murderous thugs, and were not prepared to allow their lives and beliefs to be changed by a pack of cowards who planted bombs and then ran away for their own safety, leaving others to face the terrible consequences. Had such cowards only bothered to read their history books, they would have known from the Second World War that bombing people generally installs a fiercer determination among those who survive. It happened in many British provincial towns, like Belfast, in 1940 and 1941 and especially in London during the Blitz. Willpower and spirit surged despite the atrocities then. Much the same happened now. We as a people in Northern Ireland were determined never to bow to such despicable acts. Such qualities are buried deep within the fibre of the good people of Northern Ireland, and indeed Britain, in my view.

In Belfast there was this pleasant little arcade in the city centre, but one day someone put a bomb in it and all the small shops were blown up. So they rebuilt their shops, in time, but not long after the work was completed, another bomb was planted and the replacements were destroyed. I remember going through that arcade one morning after they had rebuilt it a second time, and there was a little man beside his shop. He was doing the sign writing for it, painting it and putting his name on top in stylish letters. I went back to my office and remember saying to my colleagues how wonderful it was to see the will of the people; that very afternoon, another bomb went off and blew it to bits again. I thought to myself, 'How do people keep standing up and saying they will build it again and again, and build it stronger and better?' But they did.

I could not say I lost any really close friends or family during the Troubles, as so many people did, but certainly several people whom I knew were killed. The guy who stands out in my mind was John Haldane, who ran a family business involved in timber importing. When he launched it, I went along and helped him create some publicity. I had played with him in the Ulster team of the 1960s, when he was a No 8 forward. He was a tough player, six feet four inches tall, and a big man in more senses than one, with not an ounce of bitterness or hatred in his body. He came from Newry, the border town.

A couple of weeks after he had held the event to mark the opening of an extension to his business, some guy walked into his office one morning and blew his head off. But why? Who authorised this? Who sent the killer out to do it and for what purpose? Would it transform the entire political situation in Northern Ireland? Would it assist the cause of the Catholics and persuade the Protestants to make major concessions? Of course, the answers were no. John had done nothing against anyone. He didn't want to be part of that process and he employed Catholics and Protestants alike as an example of his tolerance and fair-mindedness, yet he lost his life. But for what?

His death is the one that I cannot get over completely. I'd been with him only a few days before he died and he'd been cheerful, optimistic and looking ahead to a better, brighter future for himself, his company and Northern Ireland. Within days all that hope was gone, wrecked by a mindless thug with a gun. You have to say, any society that tolerates that sort of thing – and no one has ever been convicted of John's murder – has become sick. It is all to do with this thing called fear. It is the easiest thing in the world to create fear and if you don't deal with it, it grows like a cancer and then people are too scared to do anything. Still today, there is a bit of that. Now, it is difficult to get evidence for anything. People know that an individual has done something or they are in it up to their necks, but they are not prepared to give evidence. Worse still, there is not a political will to deal with it. Sometimes it seems as if violence and robbery are now virtually decriminalised.

Generally speaking, I rarely stray into politics, but I want to give David Trimble some credit for what he has done. I am amazed he has been able to bring the Northern Ireland people so far, but he has tried to take a positive view as to the way forward. Go back five or six years and there is no way he could have done what he has done, but at this stage all I can say is that the results of the elections held in November 2003 were very much predictable. It seems to me there is every reason to believe it all could and probably should have been signed, sealed and delivered three years ago, as was anticipated by the people of Northern Ireland, but now people are not prepared to accept this position any longer. The present position is stalemate, so let's hope some progress can be made in the near rather than the distant future.

Even through the darkest times, sport helped to heal wounds. This is where I have a great belief in sport per se, because without it, where would we be? It brings people together. Sport teaches everyone who participates a discipline. Whether it is soccer, hockey, tennis, athletics . . . anything, it induces qualities whereby someone must win and someone lose, but at the end of the day, the loser says, 'You were better than me today and good luck to you, but maybe I'll beat you next time.' There is an in-built tolerance in that. Sport, I believe, has been a great example for all those years of what can be done. I don't mean just rugby, but all sports. For wherever two sportspeople of different religious beliefs have come together and played a sport together, there has been a fostering of relationships amidst healthy competition. There has been a forum, if you like, for tolerance and understanding. That has to be welcomed.

Rugby football certainly stood up and was counted in those times. There were very few games that had to be cancelled. Those that were certainly were never cancelled because of fear or anything like that. The only times games were called off were perhaps when trains could not get through from Dublin or somewhere in the Republic. One day we were due to play Galwegians in Belfast. Now their journey was long indeed. They would have caught the train from Galway to Dublin, changed stations there and caught the Belfast train at Connolly station. It was a particularly bad time in Northern Ireland, with all sorts of problems, especially in Belfast and on the border, and on the Wednesday night before the game the telephone rang at the Ballymena clubhouse. A man called Chris Crowley, the president of the Galwegians club, was on the line, and some of us thought we knew what message was about to be delivered.

'Sorry boys, but we can't make Saturday; there's just too much trouble over where you are,' was what some expected to hear, but on the contrary, Crowley had phoned to confirm that they would be with us and, because of the problems, they would be travelling in a fleet of cars all the way from the west coast of Ireland. They had arranged this because they weren't prepared to risk delays by train. They came a day early, too, in five or six cars, and we made such a fuss of them. The game was played and that Saturday evening in the bar afterwards was one of the happiest the old place had ever known. We knew at times like that we did not stand alone in Belfast. Our many friends from the South, good people like us, were reaching out and saying to us, 'Keep going, keep your heads up and your resolve strong. You will emerge and beat this minority. Furthermore, we will come to play you to show where our loyalties lie.'

But then, rugby ties between the North and the Republic were never in question anyway. Even during our school days, the ties were close, for there were always inter-school, inter-club matches. I am convinced that education is the key. You must have kids playing together, sharing the same sporting field so that you can have understanding. That is why rugby football has come together throughout Ireland, because we have been able to have some grasp of other people's views, show tolerance towards them and respect one another and each other's different opinions. We can do those things thanks to rugby football.

In my opinion the Churches have been very divisive in the north. I am sorry if I offend some people in saying this, but in my view almost every war and every problem is created somewhere along the line partly by religion. What the division of education inside Northern Ireland has meant is that people of opposing communities have grown up denied the right to an understanding of others and their views. How Church people can advocate and implement such a policy I do not know.

All you can say is that maybe my view is not one in the wilderness, because the power of the Churches has waned enormously in more recent times. The influence of the Catholic Church especially has suffered greatly, having lost so much credibility because of instances of child abuse by certain priests. Equally, however, I feel the Protestant Church has also lost its way. I am no great church-goer, although I do attend church occasionally; sadly, however, my children never go, and I wonder how many other parents in Northern Ireland would have to admit exactly the same thing. Very many, I suspect. I believe this is because young people have become disillusioned with the role of the two Churches on either side of the Northern Ireland divide. So many opportunities to play meaningful roles in helping to create a better future for our young people have been lost by Church leaders. I believe that young people feel the Churches have failed them and, in a sense, they have voted with their feet by refusing to go to church.

I may be no Bible basher, but I was brought up to understand and respect religion by my mother. She was a very devout woman, a true Christian, and she taught us right from wrong in a most forthright way. We had to attend church each and every Sunday and we all did so until we were well into our teens. I am no atheist; I do believe there is something in the teachings of the Churches. They try to set standards that people should be trying to achieve in their everyday lives. That is good and right. But it was confusing that they both condemned evil acts, and then provided Christian funerals where paramilitary trappings were involved. Surely you cannot have it both ways. You cannot proclaim that you live by the Bible, the holy book, and yet not condemn, utterly and without reserve, evil acts, no matter who has perpetrated them. There has been too much evasion of responsibility among both Churches.

The problem is that, while it is right and proper to have respect for the churches themselves and the meaning of God's work, we would do well to remember that it is only frail and mortal human beings who are in charge of the churches. As we have seen on countless occasions, those people whatever they may be dressed up in, in terms of church robes, are no different to you and me – they have their strengths but they have their weaknesses. In some cases, they have been proven not very decent at all. But this is where it all falls down and perhaps explains the decline in attendances at churches, not to mention the indifference of so many young people to the Christian message. I regret this but I believe both churches, especially in Northern Ireland, are to blame for it. As for other areas and different countries, I cannot comment upon those because I do not live there.

If the churches are ever to arrest this decline, then they must start to show themselves willing to change. You have to appeal to people and that means young people, not just the older population. Churches must remember that indoctrination is no longer a tenable path because people think for themselves nowadays. We have moved on, for better or worse, from the days when youngsters were told something and that was it, or the local priest decreed what action should be taken in a certain situation, and his word went un-challenged. There was no debate, no room for people's views to be aired or discussed. Frankly, I believe it is better that we have left behind those times. For the fact is, as we have seen, under that system we ran into serious difficulties. It was the path to failure because human beings trod it. Today, by contrast, youngsters do question their parents, and people do challenge what the priest or vicar says. Or they ignore him altogether and just get on with their everyday lives. It is the church alone that has to bear the respon-sibility for that situation.

I have a friend who calls on me from time to time. He lost his wife about two years ago and I asked him how he was getting on. He said he was managing, but he enjoyed company. On that front, he said, he'd had a visit from the clergyman the other day. 'Ah,' he said, 'he's a waste of time, that boy.' I asked him what he meant. Simply this, he explained. 'He came to see me, but he didn't stay long. He'd said he wanted to pray for me and for my soul and I told him he was wasting his time. I told him, you boys have been running around and preaching for 2,000 years, but you're getting nowhere. All this missionary work you're doing, you're only making it worse. You need more money every year, but you're not getting anywhere with it. About 100 years ago, half a dozen boys would go into a field and beat the hell out of each other with sticks. Whoever was proven the strongest man, the rest would do what he said, because he was the boss. Nowadays they fly up to 60,000 feet, bomb to bits hundreds of thousands of people right around the world and you guys are still running around preaching. We had a situation in Iraq where two of the most famous Christian nations in the world sent planes up that high and killed all those innocent people. Now you tell me, how is that Christianity? The whole thing is a lot of nonsense.' I said to him, 'But Bertie, what was his reply?' 'Oh, he just got up and left. He didn't have a reply.'

I've seen just about every side of human beings in my lifetime. Enormous courage, dedication, kindness and fortitude on the one hand, allied with unity, understanding, coming together, working as a team, and embracing one another mentally and physically. Then on the other side of the fence, I've seen despicable cowards who haven't got the courage to go out and confront people face to face, preferring to blow up people, killing or maiming them, ruining their lives. I believe you can only live your life as you see it and as you think is best. Those things have been happening for as long as man has lived on this earth and they will keep on happening. All you can do is, in your own way, show by example that it is better than that. Show that human beings can be kind and tolerant and understanding of others and their viewpoint. Because if the world adopted this process, then ninety per cent of the wars and fights would never arise in the first place. This is why I believe that the young people are so important.

I'll give you a simple example of what I mean. In our rugby club at Ballymena, we were always taught as young men to paint the walls, the dressing rooms and public areas, to help out and assist the club. We were always told to make our club better, even in the smallest way. So we became used to helping out. We lads would go and help the club when a major event was on, doing whatever was required to make it all go smoothly. Then in the summers, we would sometimes go up to the club and get involved in some of the painting or other activities that went on when the season had finished. This, I felt, followed faithfully that creed: do all you can, do your best. Then hand it on to the next generation. But I prefer to focus on all the countless numbers of young people all over Northern Ireland who are doing any number of jobs and tasks to help other members of the community. I take my hat off to them. They go and assist their families, some help out at old people's homes, they raise money for charitable causes by doing things like charity walks or runs, or sponsored events. In each case, they are contributing to society, helping out, doing selfless work and assisting other people. Those are the youngsters who we should remember, rather than the ones who have no desire to help others in life, but instead prefer to cause trouble and waste their lives. You will always get people like the latter group in any society, but we must all remember that they are only a small element. We should simply celebrate all those who are striving to get ahead, to help make their lives and the lives of others better. Don't make it worse. I wonder, will we as a generation be handing on a better world, a better place to live when we pass that torch to those coming up? In some respects, yes, but in many ways, the sad answer is, no. I think a lot about that – what generation would not feel ashamed to say it handed on a worse world to its children than the one it inherited?

We have a lot of great youth today, no doubt about it, but we only ever really hear about the bad ones, those who want to destroy, to pull things down, to be negative. It is my firm belief that we must reach out to those young people, to put our point over to them. Let's make society better and hand it on to the next generation in better shape than we found it. We may not reach out to everyone, for there will always be good and bad, but I believe there are large numbers that we can influence for the better.

So what of the general situation today in Northern Ireland? All you can say is that the majority of people are angry about what has happened. How can you have trust when a politician puts up on a blackboard a list of promises and never keeps to them? We had an agreement here based on those promises and British prime minister Tony Blair convinced people that they should sign up for it, but once they had voted for the agreement, those things did not happen. Those promises were forgotten. Now you have 400 murderers of both denominations released onto the streets who never served much of their sentences. Today, those guys are walking around the streets sticking a pair of fingers up and saying to certain people, 'I shot your mother or father.' I just ask, how can you have a society based on that sort of nonsense?

CHAPTER 9

The Coach Who Saw Rugby as Opera

A s I told you, after the 1968 tour I was sick of forever losing in a Lions shirt. But when 1971 came along I was still around and, more importantly, I had seen attitudes changing throughout British rugby. When I heard that Carwyn James, the Llanelli coach, was to coach the party, my hopes were raised still further. Here was a man, I had been told, who knew and understood the game and had a proper dialogue with his players in terms of how it should be played. Best of all, he was not interested in going all the way to New Zealand just to have a bit of fun on the basis that losing the Test series was inevitable. I too had had enough of that nonsense.

Any rugby team needs key performers who set the standards that others can follow. If you're a leader or a senior player you must establish the benchmarks so that others can understand what you want and where you are coming from, and that you are not prepared to tolerate anything that is below those levels of performance. There might be only three or four key performers in a given side, but those individuals must be of such quality that others look up to them. When you see one of those key performers in action, other players follow them, because they are inspired by their words before the match and also, crucially, by their actions and behaviour on the field.

When key people do something spectacular, everyone is lifted. I was extremely heartened that there were many genuine world-class players who would be available for this Lions tour – players like Gareth Edwards, Barry John, John Dawes (who was the captain), J.P.R. Williams, Mervyn and Gerald Davies of Wales, Mike Gibson, Ray McLoughlin and Fergus Slattery of Ireland, plus other out-standing rugby men such as Delme Thomas, Derek Quinnell, John Taylor, John Pullin, Gordon Brown and Sandy Carmichael. Initially, Ray McLoughlin led the Lions forwards, until he had to return home through injury. After that, I took over.

Bob Hiller, the English full-back whose cheery style and total commitment I had admired in 1968, was also there again, although once more destined to be back-up No. 15, this time behind the formidable J.P.R. Williams. Another Welshman who was powerful and full of purpose was John Bevan from the Cardiff College of Education. Then there was David Duckham, who would flourish on the tour as a left wing, ironically once he had taken Bevan's place in the Test side for the last three Test matches. I did not see any quitters in that lot, people who would be put off their game by a flurry of punches. Rather, I felt I knew the mettle of such men; I suspected they would just dig deeper and become even more bloody determined to win, especially if, when the chips were down, the New Zealanders resorted to their usual tricks.

Wales were the power side of that time. They had won the Five Nations Championship in 1969, shared it with France in 1970 and then won it again outright in 1971. With the nucleus of their side – nine Welshmen were chosen for the first Test of that Lions tour in Dunedin – there was a hard core of determined, skilful players. It is a point worthy of mention that the London Welsh club, which had been sweeping all-comers aside with a brand of wonderful attacking rugby played at real pace, had contributed seven players by the time the tour finished, one of them as a replacement. However, not every player selected proved a raging success, a point to which I will come.

This time, when we went to Dunedin for the first Test, as we had five years earlier, things were very different. There was no feeling in my mind that we were like kids beside the men of the All Blacks. By the time the first Test arrived, we had played ten provincial matches and won the lot. Chief among these, in terms of results, was the 47–9 thrashing we inflicted on what all the locals thought was a very strong Wellington side, at Athletic Park. Again, I remembered what had gone before. In 1966, the Lions had gone to Wellington and been hammered 20–6, one of three provincial matches we lost before we even got to the first Test. No wonder we duly lost the Test match.

This time it was completely different. Barry John, who sadly was to retire far too soon from the international game – in fact within twelve months of returning from the Lions tour at the ridiculously early age of twenty-six – masterminded the operation of the team behind the scrum with some brilliant performances. Mind you, Barry was the first to admit that with a powerful pack of forwards to deliver the ball and then Gareth Edwards inside him at scrum-half and a centre pairing of John Dawes and Mike Gibson, he was surrounded by superb players. In fact, there was quality just about everywhere you looked in that side and some very fine rugby players were completely unable to break into the Test team.

By then, at thirty-one, I was a senior player, and the selectors said to me, 'You'll be available, of course.' I looked them in the eye and told them what was in my mind. I said I'd come home in 1968 pretty clear that had been my last visit with the Lions, although I admitted I'd seen a new attitude emerging among some key players in the Five Nations. Of course, when we'd had the chance to spend some time together after internationals, some of us players had got together and discussed our thoughts on a variety of topics, the 1971 Lions tour included.

I told the selectors I was only interested in going if we were going to win this time. Their response was encouraging. 'This time we're going to pick the players who can do the job,' they said – and they were as good as their word. Quite early on in the tour I began to feel confident that this would prove to be the breakthrough in terms of finally seeing a Lions team able to compete with the best of the southern hemisphere. Finally, the Lions selection process had been conducted in a proper way and the players who were chosen had a single purpose and a determination to succeed. The good guys who were not quite good enough on the field were left at home.

The selectors also made one crucial, big decision that was to be at the heart of what the Lions achieved in New Zealand that year. Choosing a coach who was not in charge of a national side was far from the norm. Those picking British Isles teams in the past had hardly been what you would call innovative or daring. They followed the conventional route, did the accepted thing and adhered to the creed of precedent. But not on this occasion.

Carwyn James was selected as coach, even though he had not coached the Welsh national side. Carwyn had been coaching Llanelli, most successfully, too, as their famous 1973 win over the touring New Zealand All Blacks at Stradey Park would testify, and his philosophy was that the Lions' play should flow, chiefly in the form of the outstanding backs we had. I appreciated and enjoyed that sort of rugby and the fact was that we had to play like that because we really weren't good enough in the forwards. I doubt whether we ever got more than 40 per cent of the ball and without our backs we would never have won the Test series.

No one can ever diminish the role played by Carwyn James. He was a unique man, but very difficult to get to know. Indeed, in some ways, he was a complicated man, but when it came to rugby football his view was simple. He wanted his players to play, to enjoy the experience, to take responsibility, to have the capacity and backing to make decisions themselves. We loved that as players. He had this vision and one day he said to me in the middle of a conversation, 'I see rugby football as a piece of opera, a piece of music. It is something that can flow like music and opera and can be beautiful to watch.' He loved the notion of a flowing game and a classical three-quarter movement, with a wing scoring in the corner.

But he was no mere romanticist, for he had a special ability when it came to leadership. He would sit his players down and ask them, 'Which way do you think we should play this game? How do you see it? What do you want to achieve?' Various guys would talk and Carwyn would ask questions that would prompt the specific answers that he wanted to hear. At the end of it all he had us saying what he had wanted to tell us all along, but we felt we had contributed, had been brought into the decision-making process and that brought us together. I always regarded it as a shrewd tactical approach on his behalf.

Off the field, he was often alone. He and the manager, Doug Smith, a tough, durable Scot, would share some fun with us for a while – Carwyn the quiet one, sitting in the corner, Doug the noisy one – but then the two of them would go off and have their dinner together. Doug seemed to know when to withdraw and keep that management screen which was very important. What a far-sighted decision it was to put Carwyn in charge, though, because, without putting too fine a point on it, he transformed not only that tour, but also the way British Lions tours were approached. Carwyn James has to be the greatest Lions coach I ever worked with.

Very few people had even won a Test in New Zealand and we really weren't given very much of a chance. When we stopped off en route in Australia and promptly lost our first match, 11–15 to Queensland, the critics had a field day. 'This lot won't live with the

All Blacks' was one of the kinder headlines. At times like this, I tend to find a quiet corner, light up my pipe and have a quiet puff and a good think about life. It does you no end of good to think deeply about decisions you have made, about how you could have done better in a given situation and how you might best approach the immediate future. Thus, when I thought about it, I wasn't especially worried that we had lost our first tour game. That happens. I still had enormous faith in the management and the players around me. Indeed, for the first time on a Lions tour, I felt I was in the company of men who would not take a backward step once we got into the cauldron of rugby in New Zealand.

But if Carwyn James was the best Lions coach I knew, then Doug Smith was the best manager, too. Smith had been a Lion himself, touring as a centre with Karl Mullen's team to New Zealand in 1950. He was a big man in every sense and came from the London Scottish club. It was the combination of the two that worked so well, for they had a tremendous rapport. We all pulled together, but Carwyn never lost his focus on what he was trying to achieve. However, no one should go away with the idea that it was all plain sailing on that tour, all a bit of a stroll in the New Zealand winter sunshine. It wasn't. We had a few down days and there were quite a lot of other guys who didn't come up to expectations, which was worrying for Carwyn. It meant his selection opportunities especially for the Tests were severely reduced.

One of the key things in rugby union is to have players going on to a field bouncing because they are as fit mentally as physically. If you don't have that, you have serious problems within your ranks. We saw that with the 2001 Lions in Australia at the time of the second Test. They had won the first Test and, when we sat in the crowd at Melbourne awaiting the start of the second Test, I watched closely as the Lions ran out. People around me were saying we were going to give the Aussies another stuffing, but I saw no sign of that bounce when the Lions emerged. Before the match started, I said quietly to someone, 'I am worried about today. I don't think we will win, because I don't like the body language I see among the Lions.' They weren't bouncing; they looked tired and not ready for another Test match. So it proved.

Of course, you always get rabble-rousers in any company. And there will always be a few nights when things go a bit awry, but that's life. Life is not like a plateau – it has too many peaks and troughs for that. Take an Irishman called Sean Lynch, of St Mary's College and Ireland. He was thrown in at the deep end on that tour when both Lions first-choice props were punched out of the tour in the Canterbury game before the first Test. Lynch coped tremendously with the actual rugby, but he couldn't really cope with the concept of touring. He was homesick and distracted at times. I remember on his better days, trying to talk to him, but Sean would hide himself away. Then sometimes he'd go berserk. Once or twice, I recall Fergus Slattery and myself putting him to bed at 8 p.m.

Lynch was just one of those guys. He was as far away from home as he possibly could be and he didn't want to be, so he'd try to stir things up, for instance by throwing things around and shouting and carrying on. He was totally irresponsible at moments like that, yet he still gave one hundred per cent on the field, and we needed him – with Sandy Carmichael and Ray McLoughlin having to fly home because they were so seriously injured in the Canterbury match, Lynch became a key member of our Test pack. However, it was a good thing the New Zealanders never knew how unpredictable one of our key Test pack forwards could be in his darker moments.

Others, too, stood out for their exemplary behaviour off the field and magnificent form on it. Edwards and John were supreme at half-back, a partnership which was beyond the range of anyone the New Zealanders could select against them. John utterly destroyed the New Zealand full-back, Fergie McCormick, in the first Test, dragging him this way and that across the field with his cleverly directed kicks. He teased McCormick like a cat playing with a mouse, so much so that McCormick never again played international rugby for his country. But mentioning Gareth there brings me to a character called Ray 'Chico' Hopkins of Maesteg and Wales. People forget that Gareth only played the first quarter of an hour of the first Test because he pulled a hamstring. Chico took his place and was absolutely superb. Chico was a great scrum half and had all the cheek of the day, just like Gareth. This was the biggest test of his life and he came through it superbly.

I was leading the forwards that day and we were giving Chico rubbish possession at the line-outs. He was nattering away at me, complaining at the sort of ball he was getting, from every phase: line-outs, rucks, mauls and so on. In the end, I could take no more of it. 'If you don't shut your mouth and get this ball out to Barry John, I am going to stand back and let [Colin] Meads come through the line-out and hit you. Then you'll really have something to complain about,' I told him. Never heard another peep from Chico after that, but he was a superb, gritty performer.

Believe me, you needed hard, gritty people who could raise the morale in such circumstances. When we went to Dunedin for the first Test of that tour, the conditions were dreadful, on and off the field. It had been pouring with rain, sleet and snow. They had played two or three curtain-raisers (the preliminary matches they used to allow on the Test grounds in the southern hemisphere before the start of the main international) and the surface had turned to liquid mud. Our dressing room had just two old wooden benches, full of splinters, in the middle of the floor, the paint was peeling on the walls and condensation was dripping from the seven-foot high ceiling. Psychologically, it was the worst place in the world to be, and didn't the New Zealanders know it? Doubtless, it was all part of their pre-match preparation.

Just ten minutes or so before kick-off time, I asked John Dawes, the captain, if he minded if I took the forwards out of the dressing room for a meeting. He agreed and I got them together in a quiet corner and told them what they could expect. I said it would be hard and tough. We could expect them to run at us until we were physically sick, but we were going to knock the buggers down until someone cracked, and it had better not be us. Well, Barry John kicked off, Ian Kirkpatrick caught the ball and they started running at us in waves. We hardly touched the ball for the first ten or fifteen minutes and I had aches and pains all over my body. I was not alone. When the whistle blew at the conclusion of a ruck, there was Sean Lynch, our prop forward, on his hands and knees, covered in mud. He looked up at me and said, 'Jaysus, you warned us about this, but will somebody count the bastards, because I've tackled thirty-seven of them already.'

In midfield, Dawes and Gibson played superbly; it was probably the height of Mike's entire career. Always a wonderfully gifted player, he flourished in this supreme company, showing his great timing and vision in all he did, as well as offering a rock-solid defence. Few players in that Test team fell below the very highest of standards.

We set up the entire tour by winning that first Test in Dunedin 9–3. It was the first victory for the British Lions in a Test match since they had beaten New Zealand in Auckland in 1959. Then we lost 22–12 in the second Test at Christchurch, but bounced back to win the third Test in Wellington, 13–3. The crucial last Test ended in a 14–14 draw, after J.P.R. Williams dropped a sensational goal from far out. Barry John contributed 31 of the 48 points we scored in the four Test matches.

We used only eighteen of the thirty players on the tour for the Test series, which was some going in such a harsh rugby country. The only two changes were Duckham for Bevan after the first Test, on the left wing, Gordon Brown for Delme Thomas in the final two Tests, and Derek Quinnell for Peter Dixon at blindside flanker, in the third Test. That was all.

What a change it all was from 1962. Then, we had been sent out to the southern hemisphere by men who had selected the Lions squad as the cream of British and Irish sporting society. The trouble was, they were sending us out to be slaughtered. But things changed, chiefly because this time, nine years later, we had the players. I came home not just a happy man, but a relieved one. At last, I felt, I had looked the cream of the southern hemisphere rugby men hard in the eye and not blinked first. We had nailed the myth that the Lions could never take on the All Blacks in their own backyard and triumph. We had shown that with the right planning, proper selection of the best players, whatever their character, and a strong coach and manager, we were just as good as, if not better than, the New Zealanders. Because not only did we win the Test series 2–1, but also we won every single one of the twenty provincial matches we played, up and down the two islands of New Zealand. Only the very best touring teams come away with a record like that and I was not alone in holding my head high as we boarded our plane at Auckland airport for the long flight home. There had been a job to do and we had done it. Superbly well, I thought.

I had some good off-the-field memories, too, because we had some fun times there, like the night I ended up with the *Sunday Times* rugby writer Vivian Jenkins in a stranger's home somewhere in New Zealand. We met a man at a function and he invited us back to his home for drinks. He left and Viv and I followed on, but when we got to the street we couldn't remember the number of the house. It was a long street, too, but we finally saw a house with a lot of lights on and thought that must be where the party was. So we went up to the front door and it was ajar. In we went, but we couldn't find anyone. Still, we thought it would be OK.

Viv was hungry and said he wanted some food, so I looked in the fridge and found bacon and eggs and set about cooking a meal. As the smell of bacon wafted around the house, a lady suddenly

Above: Leading out the Lions in South Africa; Gareth Edwards is right behind me.

Below: In action for the 1974 British Lions in the 4th Test of our record-breaking tour of South Africa. The great Springbok flanker, Jan Ellis, is just behind me, facing camera, on the left of the picture. Fellow lock Chris Ralston is behind my left shoulder.

Above: **Action from the 1968 Five Nations Championship match in Dublin. Here, I seem to be getting the better of that great Welsh line-out jumper, Delme Thomas. Ken Goodall is to my right. Ireland won, 9–6.**

British Lions tour party to South Africa 1974:

Top row: J.J. Williams, D. Milligan, S. McKinney, M. Burton, R. Bergiers, L. Ralstion, A. Ripley, T. Grace, R. Uttley, F. Cotton, T. David, A. Old, G. Evans, A. Irvine.

Second row: J.P.R. Williams, M. Davies, I. McLauchlan, G. Edwards, A. Thomas (Manager), W.J. McBride (Capt.), S. Millar (Coach), K. Kennedy, G. Brown, S. Carmichael.

Third row: T. Neary, I. McGeechan, L. Rees, W. Steele, F. Slattery, P. Bennett, J. Moloney, R. Windsor.

Left: Training with the Lions.

Below: It's a thoughtful job, this coaching lark! Watching Ireland train prior to the 1984 Five Nations Championship season.

Giving my all for the Lions in South Africa in 1974.

appeared in her dressing gown at the bottom of the stairs. She looked as though she'd seen a ghost. 'Who the hell are you?' she said. 'Oh we're friends of your husband. We met him at a reception and he invited us over for drinks,' I said. 'Hope you don't mind us getting something to eat, we're starving.' 'But my husband has been with me all evening and he's just taken the babysitter home,' she said. And then in came her husband. When he heard the story and saw me in my Lions blazer he roared his head off. We stayed and had bacon, eggs and a lot more besides, plus drinks. What a night.

Qualities such as strength of character, determination and a willingness to stand up for what you believe in were at the core of what the British Lions achieved in New Zealand in 1971. Unfortunately, six months later, we in Ireland had seen a complete reversal of such qualities by so-called men of rugby football.

The Five Nations Championship of 1972 had started wonderfully well for my country. We had gone to Paris and beaten a very handy French team 14–9, and followed this up with another win away from home, 16–12 at Twickenham. This was the day when Kevin Flynn and Tom Grace scored famous tries, as we powered past England's new-look team. Ah, memories. Where would we be without them?

What excited most of us in the Irish squad that night in London after the game with England was that we were only two matches away from a Grand Slam. And both matches, against Scotland and Wales, were due to be played in Dublin. Now Ireland had not won the coveted Grand Slam since 1948 and excitement in Ireland, both north and south of the border, steadily intensified once we had won at Twickenham.

Sometimes it would be hard for an outsider stumbling into the party on a Saturday night after an international match to know who had won and who had been beaten. If you won you celebrated and if you lost you drowned your sorrows – which amounted to the same thing, because you all ended up pretty happy at the end of the evening. Now wasn't that a nice way to end a day of international rugby? One thing was for sure – the following morning you all felt in the same condition, so everything was certain to have levelled out by then.

So, that night we had a good few drinks to celebrate what we had done and what we might be able to achieve in the remainder of the season. But alas, our hopes of a possible triumph were to be dashed in the cruellest of ways. There would be no Grand Slam for us that year, not even a share of the championship. In fact, the championship was not won by anyone because Scotland and Wales both refused to travel to Dublin to play us.

There was no disputing the fact that the Troubles were causing plenty of headlines in Ireland at that time. In fact, when I was playing rugby football for Ireland and the British Lions, I had quite a high profile in public relations terms and there was a list that appeared somewhere, although I never saw it, with my name on it. I was told by the police it was a terrorist organisation's death threat list. Now what that meant, I have no idea – I cannot even begin to get inside the minds of such people, nor would I ever want to – but the security people were sufficiently concerned to come to my house and put in lights and panic buttons and that sort of thing. I just told Penny that the bank was doing it for all its managers to keep them safe. I never let on about any death list. I personally was never threatened, but then you never are, because that's not the way it works. It operates on fear, but I believed that I had to get on with my life, not bow to terrorists but keep my head up and hope my time had not yet come.

So rugby football had lived through an awful lot in Ireland over the years, yet the game had always carried on, whatever the background and however difficult it may have been. North, south, east and west, we kept playing together and coming together to play for

Ireland. In the green jersey of Ireland, the northern Protestants stood shoulder to shoulder with the southern Catholics. Nor did anyone in the squad give a thought to a man's background. He was a colleague, a teammate, and it made no difference whatsoever where he lived and what religion he followed.

Rugby had proved itself bigger than any man of violence, for it had conspicuously refused to allow itself to be intimidated by anyone, whatever their views. It was something of which all of us involved in rugby football in Ireland felt intensely proud. Imagine our feelings, then, when we were let down – and I mean those words – by the administrations. It was not the players from Wales and Scotland who were to blame but their governing bodies who claimed that the violence in the north might have repercussions in the south. But by whom against whom? Those gentlemen who took the decision to abandon their matches with us that year failed Ireland, failed their own countries and failed the game of rugby football. In my view, they should have been ashamed of their actions.

And why did they refuse to show up? I believe they were just scared, that was the bottom line of it, but what we could never understand, nor did they ever offer a valid reason to explain, was who was going to do anything to them? What were they going to do to players from the other Celtic countries for coming to Dublin to play a game of rugby? I thought then, and I continue to hold this view to this day, that rugby football must be bigger than anything that is political. Otherwise we might as well give up everything.

A lot of people in Ireland, myself included, felt badly let down by so dreadful a decision. To me, it was the sickening sight of people being cowed by terrorists, men of violence who were not even worthy of discussion in the circles of decent men. No thought was given by them to the fact that rugby football, throughout its history, had always stood up for what it believed in. They brushed that aside without a thought in those committee rooms in Cardiff and Edinburgh. So many decent, law-abiding people who had eagerly anticipated the two matches were left out on a limb by decisions I can only describe as craven.

For a bank manager from Northern Ireland who had seen death and destruction, heard the boom of explosions in the city where I was working and read so closely of the loss of life, this decision smacked of cowardice. Nothing more or less. It was a good thing the people of Northern Ireland were not prepared to capitulate in such a weak manner at the first sign of trouble. But above all, it sickened me because we in Ireland had kept rugby football strong through the dark days. That others could not recognise that and stand alongside us by fulfilling their fixtures saddened me immensely. Our friends had let us down.

Their attitude contrasts with that of my own family and countless others who endured those terrible times in Northern Ireland. How would life be here today had we just caved in like the Welsh Rugby Union and Scottish Rugby Union?

My wife and children have always been a great support to me. I'm glad to say I have always managed to keep them out of the spotlight and free from any trouble. But it couldn't have been easy for Penny at times. My son Paul always did his own thing anyway. which was something I fully supported. He was his own man, his own person. My daughter Amanda was great, too, and has done her own thing, made her own path in life.

I always tried to be my normal self and carry on. Really, you felt, you had to battle on, try to continue your lives in as normal a way as possible, however hard that may have been at times. If you had sat down and thought about it all, the terrible violence, bloodshed and the killing of innocent men, women and children, you would have gone mad. You could have despaired over it, but that wasn't me. I suppose, too, that had I sought a business opportunity elsewhere, such as the South of France, through one of the great clubs down there, I might have been offered the opportunity to flee Northern Ireland for safer (and warmer) climes. After all, the English lock-forward Nigel Horton left his job in the police force in the Midlands and went to Toulouse in the 1970s to run a cafe/bar and play for the local club Stade Toulousain. Indeed, I imagine some people would have encouraged me to do something like that, perhaps reasoning that it wasn't worth it, staying in Northern Ireland with all the trouble going on.

But do you know what? Had I done that, had I ended up running a cafe or working in an office somewhere such as Toulouse or Biarritz, I would never have been able to live with myself. I would have felt I'd run away, that the men of evil had won a small triumph, over me at least. I'd have felt I had deserted my many friends still living in Northern Ireland, and anyone who knows me understands I am just not like that. I feel that if you run away from something, you give in to the things you don't believe in. I was never prepared to do that.

I'll tell you another truth, something I've never really spoken about publicly. I never wanted to go because I admired and respected what rugby football did in those times in Northern Ireland. It was good, a wholesome example and a pillar of society. There were always people around who would say, 'Can we help; can we do something for you?' Now I'm not saying you only found that wonderful spirit through rugby; manifestly, that would not be true. But I came across it time and again through my involvement in the game and it warmed me, comforted me, made me feel good about people. Whenever it happened, I knew that all people were not bad, that it was just a tiny minority who were trying to make the lives of the vast majority miserable.

I include people in the Republic as many of those who offered help. They too were like us in the north; thoroughly decent folk who abhorred what these evil thugs were doing. I knew that we had to stand together, stand up and be counted. Running away was no solution whatsoever. So I believe rugby football contributed a very great deal. You can't say it exactly cured situations – nothing can ease the pain of seeing husbands, wives or children bombed or shot – but I do honestly believe it eased suffering in some circumstances.

The disappointment of what had happened in 1972, in terms of a missed opportunity on the field, faded relatively quickly. I have to say the crushing sense that we had been so badly let down by people we had thought to be our friends took an awful lot longer to pass. I think the best way to describe the feelings of all Irish people over the entire business was reflected in what happened the next season, when England were due to come to Lansdowne Road for the Five Nations fixture. Whether they would come or not had been endlessly debated in the media.

In the end, England travelled. When they ran out at Lansdowne Road for the start of the international that February afternoon, I for one had never heard a roar like it, on any rugby ground anywhere in the world. I was winning my 42nd cap that day and I'd played the game all over the place, but the warmth of the welcome and the noise was unique in my experience. It was the occasion when any English supporter walking down Lower Baggott Street in Dublin's City Centre had a job getting a pint of the dark stuff himself in any pub. Friends ushered the English fans into the pubs and lined up pint after pint for them, which was another example of the wonderful brotherhood that has always existed in this game.

But there was a reason why England turned up that day that, to my knowledge, has never been revealed publicly. About ten days before the game there was great speculation about whether the match would actually be played. Around that time, David Duckham, the English three-quarter whom I had got to know very well on the 1971 Lions tour, rang me at home. David had got married three months earlier. He said that his wife Jean was not at all happy about him going to Dublin and he feared he would have to cry off. I said to him, 'For God's sake, David, you are the one guy

England keep picking. If you cry off, the others will too and the game will be off.'

Of course, wives were invisible as far as the committee men of the national rugby unions were concerned. Certainly, they were never invited to go to international weekends or anything like that, but I suggested to David that he bring Jean over with him, and that the wives of the Irish team, including Penny, of course, would look after her and make sure she had a great time. As for playing the game, I told him I would be out on the field with him; we all would be. I saw no danger at all in that situation.

David said he'd call me back in half an hour, after he'd had a chance to chat it through with Jean. He did so, but came back to me in just ten minutes. 'OK,' he said, 'Jean agrees. It's on.' So they both came over, the match was played and Jean had a superb weekend. There was a lot of looking down noses by the RFU committee men, who seemed to disapprove of a player bringing along his wife for the weekend, but they didn't know the real story. I certainly have no doubt whatsoever that if David Duckham had not done what he did, the match would not have gone ahead. What David and Jean did at that time for the future of rugby football was incalculable. Suffice to say that that cemented still further the strong friendship between him and myself. Today, I regard David as like another brother to me. We talk a lot, see each other often and even go on holidays together.

We beat England that day, 18–9, and at the after-match dinner, John Pullin, the England hooker and captain, brought the house down by standing up for his speech and saying simply, 'Well, we may not be much good, but at least we turn up.' The entire company, every man in the place, stood up and roared his approval at that remark. I can tell you, strong men had tears in their eyes over it. I was just one of those who felt thoroughly moved by the whole experience. But that was what rugby football could do.

It could also still do a lot on the field. On 27 January 1973 I played in a match that is still being talked about, and watched endlessly on video, thirty-one years later. Quite extraordinary, that, but then the Barbarians versus the 7th All Blacks at Cardiff that day was a game that justified entering what you might call rugby union's Hall of Fame.

Those All Blacks had included some of the players whom the 1971 British Lions had beaten on their tour Down Under two years earlier. Yet New Zealand teams never stay in the doldrums for very long. Captained by Ian Kirkpatrick and managed by Ernie Todd, those All Blacks came to Britain, Ireland and France for a 30-match tour and had beaten Wales, Scotland and England by the time they went to Dublin to meet Ireland. Our spirited 10–10 draw with them that day denied them what was known then as the 'Grand Slam' of the British Isles.

One week later, Ray McLoughlin, Mike Gibson, Fergus Slattery and I lined up against them again, this time in the Barbarians' jerseys, before a sell-out crowd at Cardiff. It was the traditional end of tour match, which was always arranged against a major touring team.

Of course, being the Barbarians, we were not allowed to have any coaching – well, not officially, anyway. But we managed to sneak Carwyn James, the man who had masterminded the Lions success against the All Blacks in 1971, into our hotel on the Friday night and we sat down for a chat with him.

Carwyn reminded us of one crucial factor. He said, 'Now remember, the All Blacks don't like the ball being run back at them. They have never had to cope with that and they cannot do so. Therefore that is what you should concentrate on doing in this game.' We did that all right; we cut them to pieces.

Well, I suppose you cannot launch counter-attacks from much deeper than Phil Bennett managed in the first few minutes. A kick downfield by Bryan Williams rolled towards our goal-line and

Bennett scampered back to pick it up. I assumed, like everyone else in the team, that he would bang it into touch and we would have a line-out. But Phil was a little genius who would light up South Africa on the next Lions tour in 1974. He side-stepped two or three opponents with some dancing footwork, setting in motion the movement that Gareth Edwards finished with a thrilling dive into the corner at the other end of the field.

That set the tone for the whole match, and what a remarkable game it was to become. Yet on that Friday morning it had all the makings of a complete disaster because both Gerald and Mervyn Davies, two of the finest players in the world at that time, cried off through injury. Two Welshmen replaced the two Welshmen: Derek Quinnell at No. 8 and John Bevan on the wing, for Gerald.

It was a match that had everything. The skills, the passing, the running and the kicking were superb. I have been happy ever since to say that I was on the field that day. It was a privilege to participate in such a wonderful match.

When Gareth scored, I think I was still in our half, puffing along but cheering with the crowd. The whole match was played at a hundred miles an hour and the good thing was that we got quite a bit of ball to give our backs. That was what Carwyn said – just get the ball and feed your backs. They can do the damage.

It was traditional for the Barbarians to select an uncapped player in their teams. The responsibility in this case fell to Roger Wilkinson of Cambridge University. He was to go on and win only six full England caps in his entire career, but participating in this match earned him a place in rugby folklore. He did all right in this game, too. He would not have been the most powerful scrummager in world rugby history, but he won some line-out ball and played his part. I packed down alongside him that day but never saw him again until we held our thirtieth anniversary reunion of that game. It was a strange feeling meeting up with him again after all that time.

I would like to think that amazing day and the outcome of the match, and also the 1971 Lions tour, helped to break down what had until then been almost a fear of, and certainly too deep a respect for, New Zealand's rugby teams. Until then, their reputation alone had given them a crucial advantage over most teams from our part of the world. By winning in New Zealand with the Lions in 1971 and then beating them in such style for the Barbarians two years later, I think we showed that New Zealand rugby teams were, after all, only human, and therefore perfectly beatable. Today, of course, that aura has gone and teams beat New Zealand quite regularly.

But what of the Barbarians today? Well, I'm afraid you have to say that nothing better illustrates the decline of the game than the virtual demise of the Barbarians, a wonderful concept that high-lighted all the best qualities the game had to offer. You only have to see the state the Barbarians are in today to understand where the game has descended. Players refuse to represent their country at a World Cup because they are too committed to a club that is paying them. Materialistic desires have meant that they would rather turn their backs on their country than give up a pay packet for a month. I keep going back to the clubs because that is where the game is born in terms of young players. It's like a pyramid: if you don't have the base, you don't have the pinnacle, and I don't believe the base is any longer near right.

I lament the decline in influence of the Barbarians because they represented so much of what was good about the sport. They espoused values such as friendship, courtesy, and comradeship on the field and fun off it. Nothing too much wrong with all that, in my eyes, but there you are. Times have moved on and sadly left them behind.

CHAPTER 10

The Roar of the Lions

Around this time, another momentous event lay on my own personal horizon, although I knew about it some time before the general public was made aware of it. In 1974 the British Lions were due to return to South Africa, and quite early on it was quietly suggested to me that if I were available for the tour, I would in all probability be nominated as captain. I would be thirty-four years of age during the tour, a comparatively old man, I felt, to be tearing around southern Africa in the company of a lot of young rugby bucks. However, by the end of that 1974 Five Nations season I had won 49 caps for Ireland and was their captain, so I suppose I qualified on that count, because at least I'd had some experience of leading men.

There were two ways of looking at the possible Lions job. It would be twelve long years since I had first arrived in southern Africa with a British Lions touring party, and what a painful experience that had been. By the end of that first tour, I was bruised, had been kicked and was as sore as hell, but it made me a man. That is what that tour did, not only for me, but also for a lot of other people. I survived and it was to prove to be a great learning curve.

Then I'd been back in 1968 and, although we'd lost again, I could see the new shoots of a better approach, a fresh attitude at last appearing. That belief had been proven in the toughest proving ground of all, New Zealand, in 1971 with the Lions. But now there lay before me the chance to go back to South Africa and show that British and Irish rugby really had changed, that it had learned the hard way and that we were no longer the pushovers that we had been all those years earlier.

However, I knew too that being away for so long would place another great burden on Penny. The children were young and she had a great deal on her hands. Nor was it as though I were leaving her in a beautifully relaxed, peaceful corner of a quiet, tranquil country. This was Northern Ireland and bombs were still going off all over the place at regular intervals. But my respect for Penny has always been immense and it deepened still further when she said to me, 'You go if you want to and if you feel you can do the job. We will be fine here.'

A little later, when the touring party was announced and the media had the chance to interview players and, sometimes, their wives, a reporter asked Penny about me going on another long tour. I'll always remember her reply. 'You can't live with a man if he hasn't achieved what he really wants to in life,' she said. I thought about those words then and I've thought about them quite a lot since. To me, they just demonstrate my wife's great maturity, vision and willingness to carry on and be practical. Not a lot of women, I suggest, would have looked at it from that point of view. I am still grateful to her, to this day.

The backdrop to the tour was proving far from easy at home, though, for South Africa was not a popular place to visit. The debate over apartheid was raging. One school of thought was that connections should be kept open through tours, so that the South Africans could be gently persuaded to the viewpoint of the outside world as to the horrors and impracticalities of the apartheid system.

The contrary view was that all ties should be cut, thereby isolating South Africa from the outside world. I strongly favoured the first option, but a lot of people were against the tour. Even Harold Wilson, the then British prime minister, said publicly that we should not go. When the four home unions' tours committee reiterated their determination to see the tour through, Wilson instructed all the embassies in South Africa to sever any ties with the touring party. Now I'm a member of the British Empire and that was not a very pleasant message to my ears. In fact, it deeply annoyed me, but I never discussed it at the time – as you will no doubt be aware by now, I am one of those people who, if I believe in something, will always see it through.

Once the touring squad had been announced, there was a lot of pressure on the individual players. They were being telephoned by outsiders and urged not to go. I didn't want the tour to fall down but I knew that if it was going to, it would do so before we left. All I felt was that rugby football would never have existed if we had allowed it to become embroiled in politics.

At that stage I had played the game for close on twenty years and I felt that I had to help preserve it. I was very clear in my own mind that my going to South Africa would neither encourage nor destroy apartheid, but I felt it might just help relations because, for the first time, we were due to play a coloured team and also a black team. So I hoped that it might even begin the process of breaking down the notion that a white man could not play against a black man on the same sporting field in South Africa. At least the 1974 Lions were going to demonstrate to all South Africa that such a law was nonsensical.

In the event, it was to prove an amazing experience. We had to have special permits to get into their areas, but to play a match in front of 50–60,000 black faces was something entirely new. They were hugely enthusiastic, too, and gave us a great reception. The game against the coloureds was another memorable occasion and we had the chance to mix and chat with their players afterwards over dinner, which we all thoroughly enjoyed. We saw that as something of a breakthrough, which was important.

There was so much more debate and far more widespread protests against touring in 1974 than in 1962 and 1968. This was because the anti-apartheid movement had really been built up by, among others, people like Peter Hain, who is currently the leader of the House of Commons. The anti-apartheid message had spread around the world and the protesters had become much better organised, but I was appalled at such tactics as showering a rugby pitch with shards of glass and tacks. Protests had become a popular thing and all sorts of people who had never been to South Africa, and had no idea of the situation out there, clambered upon the bandwagon. Certainly, it took on a much higher profile than either of the two previous Lions tours I had been on. Then, two years later, would come the Soweto riots.

At the height of the protests about the tour, the Lions squad that had been chosen came together in London. Anti-apartheid demonstrators were chanting slogans and holding up banners outside our hotel, the press was full of the issue and every politician who ever craved a headline was crawling out of the woodwork to give his two-pennies-worth, as they do. Alan Thomas of Wales had been chosen as manager with Syd Millar of Ballymena and Ireland as coach. I liked that idea from the start; Syd was a no-nonsense type of man who knew rugby football down to his cotton socks. There would be no barmy, deluded selection ideas on this tour with him around, I knew that for sure. Nor would there be any misunderstanding as to how we should take on the South Africans. Syd was one of the toughest front row-forwards I had ever known in my life and it was pretty clear that all his plans would begin where he knew best – the front row. Rightly so, too.

When the chosen squad met up, both men gave their views on the tour to the assembled players and then it was my turn to speak.

I stood up and said, 'I realise all the pressures you are under. For my part, I have no problem listening to these people [the protesters] and their views, but why aren't they respecting my views as well? It's not all one way.' I could see twenty-nine faces scrutinising me and listening to my words as I went on, 'I know there are pressures on you and there must be doubts in your minds, but if you have any doubts, I would ask you to turn around and look behind you.'

There, at the end of the room, two huge doors were then pulled symbolically open. Once that had been done, I spoke again. 'Gentlemen, if you have *any* doubts about going on this tour, I want you to be big enough to stand up now and leave this room. Because if you do have doubts then you are no use to me and you're no use to this team. There will be no stain on your character, no accusations if you do so, but you must be honest and committed.' Not a soul moved. And I believe that was the moment when the 1974 British Lions united and we became a special team. When we went off to South Africa the next day, there was a special bond already among us, quite unlike any I had ever known before on a Lions tour.

For several weeks before that, there was all the preparation and thinking that had to be done. For me as captain, there was the challenge of those amateur days in bringing together men from as diverse backgrounds as teaching, coal mining, the legal world, steel-work, carpentry and all manner of other professions. Forging a common spirit and keeping everyone happy while they were living in each other's pockets for the next three and a half months would inevitably be a major task. Qualities such as tolerance and under-standing would be of primary importance and all this I outlined to the squad.

So we sat down and prepared for what was to be a momentous tour, my last as a Lions player. This was my fifth tour as a Lion and I was very aware of having enjoyed such longevity as one of British and Irish rugby's most privileged elite. All that I had seen in 1962 on my first tour had left a deep impression on me. So when we went back in 1974, under my captaincy, I made sure that the players in my charge would also gain great benefits from the trip, off the field as well as on it. Standing up and speaking in public was something few of them had ever really done or were used to, but I was determined that this would change. I wanted them all to imbibe thoroughly in the culture and friendship of the tour, to be approachable and to meet as many people as possible. This tour would not be about us Lions huddling in our private rooms and only rarely venturing out to meet the public of South Africa.

When we reached South Africa I told the guys I wanted them to go and talk to various schools, although admittedly and sadly, these were mainly whites only. However, we did attend one school for coloured youngsters, somewhere near Pietermaritzburg. We created what you might call an adoption scheme, whereby thirty schools in the country each adopted a particular Lion for the duration of the tour. Wherever we were, two of the Lions would go out and talk to a couple of schools in that area. Now some of the guys, like Andy Ripley of England, could handle this with complete aplomb. Ripley worked in the City of London, enjoyed the company of complete strangers wherever he was and was totally at ease chatting to them. Then there were players like Bobby Windsor who was at the direct opposite end of that particular spectrum.

Not much fazed the Duke, as Bobby Windsor was known, on the field. He could handle everything that the most gnarled, grizzled front rows representing France, South Africa or New Zealand could throw at him. But the notion of going to a school on his own and standing up in front of a few hundred kids and speaking to them reduced Bobby to a trembling wreck. His first response was perhaps inevitable. 'Sorry, I'm not going. Can't do it,' he gasped in panic. 'Bobby,' I told him, 'you have to go. There is a commitment and, anyway, it will be good for you.' I promised to go with him to the first event. There were 700 children at morning assembly. I asked

Bobby to stand up when I introduced him and tell them who he was, where he came from, what his home town was like, how long he'd played for Wales and what it meant to him to be a Lion in South Africa.

Bobby shook like a frightened rabbit to start with, but when he finally got talking, the infectious humour we all knew from sharing rugby times with him began to emerge. The kids loved it. He was marvellous and it was so good for him and his confidence to prove to himself he could do it. He achieved something that day he'd thought he would never be able to do. Furthermore, I'd say that, without exception, every man in that 1974 Lions squad could stand up in any company by the end of the tour, give his view on things and talk with people he had never met. I regarded that flourishing of young men as one of the greatest achievements of the 1974 Lions.

You see, I had an ulterior motive in all this. After each match that the Lions played on tour, the tradition was for the captain to stand up and make a small speech at the after-match function, thanking the host union for staging the game, the opposition captain for a good hard match and the referee for handling it. You'd say a few pleasantries, tell a joke or two and everyone would be happy, but I wanted to change the tradition a bit on this tour. I wanted the players to make the speech just as much as me. Why should they be slouching in a corner at the back of the room, cracking jokes among themselves about their captain while he had to concentrate on his speech?

I therefore called on a different Lion each time to speak at the after-match games. I didn't even tell them who it would be until we reached the venue. Nor was it confined to after-match functions. We might train at a local school in the town where we were staying and lunch would be laid on for us afterwards. Someone would have to stand up and thank our hosts for their kindness and the boys took it in turns. For it was always important to say thank you. The 1974 Lions never forgot that lesson.

When we sat down and had a team meeting, I never led it with my views. I'd ask a player sitting somewhere near the back of the room to stand up and give us his thoughts as to how we should approach a certain situation. Nor was this confined only to the Test side. I would want the input of everyone on the tour, whether he was in the Test team, on the bench as a reserve or in the stand as a squad member not involved on Test match day. I had picked up this tactic from Carwyn James in 1971 and, like him, I found that very often the players came to the same viewpoint as the one I'd originally held. But it was far better to have others giving their opinion than for me to lay down the law and say this or that is what we will be doing. No questions, just do it. I didn't believe in that dogmatic approach at all. By this method, we ensured that the players believed in what they were doing, because everyone had bought into the scheme.

One of the aspects we had to discuss with the players was the issue of referees. I knew from painful experience what it meant to have a Test match refereed by a man who lived just up the road. He was bound to be influenced, because any human being would have been. The game was asking the impossible to put men in that position. You always knew which way the 50–50 decisions would be given. So before we played our first game, I called all the Lions together and spoke to them about this subject. I said that every day we went on a field to play, we had to be better than the 50,000 or 60,000 people around us. We had to be better than the conditions. We needed to be better than a non-neutral referee. And we had to be better than the fifteen guys opposite us, every day for the next three and a half months.

They proved themselves a remarkable Lions squad because they bought into all this and achieved it. In three and a half months, no one was disciplined. On every day in every training session, they worked like hell. They all got on well together, another vital factor. Of course, there were occasionally tense times, because we are all different. There are some people everyone finds it tough to get along with, but they all stuck with it, learned the value of tolerance and also the importance of doing the essential things every day. Most important of all, in three and a half months we never once talked about losing. I never heard that word used throughout the tour. We were winners.

Yet we didn't only work hard; we also played hard off the field. The fun we had off the field was important, because as I've said, life is about peaks and troughs. You need some down time to relax, before you get serious again and build up towards another peak. On that tour, we picked our peaks; various games, not just the Test matches. Tough matches like Western Province and Northern Transvaal were highlighted. There was an implicit understanding that we had to be at our very best for those peaks. The rest, we felt sure we would win.

I believe there is a great secret in life. It is realising when to work, and when to play. Those 1974 Lions had it and that was most important. I didn't have to tell them when it was time to go to work, nor did they need much invitation when it was time for a piss-up. But I knew I could rely on them when I needed them to be at their best. Not so many Lions captains have been able to say that without reservation down the years.

These players had something else that has completely disappeared from the game today, too: loyalty. It is a word you never hear now. You don't hear it in business, in the workplace or on the sports field. You certainly don't hear it in rugby football and I find that sad. I played twenty-three years for my club and would never have moved to another. I'd have given up the game before moving. The 1974 Lions showed such loyalty throughout that tour and, again, it was one of the key ingredients in our success. But there was another factor, too.

Now I suppose that many rugby followers will recall with amusement what came to be known as the '99' call on that tour, and I want to address it fully here so that people know exactly how it arose. I had toured either South Africa or New Zealand four times with the Lions by the time we set off for the 1974 trip and, on every tour, I had seen certain key players targeted by someone in a provincial game, often quite close to a Test match. It had happened far too often to be coincidental.

A Lions tour is hard enough without having your best players lined up by some thug in the opposition out to make a name for himself by putting a top Lion out of the forthcoming Test. In my book, that was cheating, and too many players in South Africa and New Zealand had got away with it for years. I was determined they were not going to this time, with me as Lions captain, and so it proved.

When you tour with the Lions, you live on the edge. There are aggressive games against aggressive opponents, for everyone wants to defeat the touring team. That is understandable and exactly how it should be. What was not acceptable were the illegal acts, the taking out of opponents or the kicking of defenceless men, supposedly to soften up both them and their colleagues. That approach sickened me and I steeled myself to deal with it once and for all.

We started the tour with a bang, beating Western Transvaal, 59–13. OK, they were far from the most formidable of opponents we would face, but it was a useful opening. Better still, we followed up with wins over South West Africa, 23–16, and Boland, 33–6. Things were going well, we were winning and the sun was shining, but we were a bit like the American Second World War commander, General Patton, heading across Europe in 1944. 'The weather is foul, all movement is difficult and the German Army has not launched a winter offensive for a thousand years,' he said. 'Which is exactly why I believe they are going to do so.' The next morning, Hitler's Panzers stormed into the Ardennes, catching many Allied soldiers unawares as the famous Battle of the Bulge unfolded. It was the same with us in South Africa. I just sensed something was about to happen. I feared it would occur in our next match against Eastern Province.

You see, by now I knew the way of thinking that went on in certain quarters in South Africa. The feeling among the locals in both South Africa and New Zealand was that if you couldn't beat these guys by playing rugby, then you would intimidate them. Now it worried me if that were to happen, and not just from the physical side of things. If one of my players was going to spend five or ten minutes trying to gain revenge for a punch or kick he'd taken from a player in the other side, he was pretty useless to us. That meant we were effectively reduced to fourteen men for that time, and playing the game at this level a man short is never easy. I knew that we needed everyone to be playing and concentrating totally on the game. I didn't want anyone in my team losing concentration because he was trying to catch up with some nutter and hit him.

You usually encounter the thug element in a provincial game. It's less likely in a Test, but as these Lions were winning and starting to look a very useful outfit, then it was safe to assume that some psychopaths lurking in a provincial side somewhere would decide that they'd target us and see just how tough we really were. This time, though, the louts who made their plans accordingly had bitten off more than they could chew.

The fact was, I had made some plans, too. I was not playing in the game against Eastern Province, and normally didn't get involved in the pre-match preparation for a game I would not be involved in. I would let the captain for the day do all the preparatory work, because he was the one taking the team on to the field, but this time I went to the team meeting the night before and outlined my fears.

I told them I had worries about the game and that there were a couple of guys in the local team who could be a bit of trouble. I was very mindful of the fact that we could not afford to lose a couple of key players with only three more games before the crucial first Test.

173

I told the players I was not prepared to take any intimidation and we should not accept any such rubbish. I said to them, 'Tomorrow, if anything happens, we are all in it together – and I mean all. You belt the guy that is nearest to you as hard as you can. Whether he has been the one guilty of the illegal act has nothing to do with it. If that doesn't stop it, you haven't hit him hard enough. Then, once you've done that, it's all over and we are back playing rugby.'

My attitude was, hurt one of us and you hurt us all, so we'll finish it, we'll stop it. There and then. We never started any trouble in any match on that tour. We were too good for that and just wanted to concentrate on playing good rugby. But if others wanted to do that then they would learn a very painful lesson and that message would go out right across South Africa. That message would be, mess with these Lions and you end up in a mess yourselves. I hoped there would be no need for this policy to be put into action, but in case the need arose, I thought up a signal to alert everyone. The one I came up with was '999', the traditional alert for all emergency services back in Britain, but the feeling among us was that 999 was too long and too much of a mouthful, so we cut it down to '99'.

Let me say at this point that I deny emphatically, as some have suggested, that we planned all this before we ever got on the plane in London. That isn't true. What was true was that on the 1971 Lions tour, under Carwyn James, we had discussed the need to 'get our retaliation in first'. But this was different. After all, we weren't modern-day warriors heading out to the Crusades. We were going on a rugby tour, for heaven's sake, and in an ideal world we would have been protected from such loutish acts by the referee in each game. To think that would happen, though, was to whistle in the dark. So once the tour got going, I could sense something was building. We picked up a few things, too, from the Afrikaans correspondents covering the tour. They suggested something like this was coming. My suspicions were not unfounded.

Gareth Edwards was always likely to be one of the key players on the tour. Why would he not have been? He was the number one scrum half in the world, a player of fabulous quality and class. Any team in the world, the South Africans and All Blacks included, would have given their right arm to have Edwards in their team. I was never in the slightest doubt as to Gareth's immense value to us, so it came as little surprise when Gareth turned out to be the target of the Eastern Province thugs.

At one point in the game Gareth passed the ball and, long after that, was hit with a rabbit punch on the back of the head. I was sitting in the stand, but I'll never forget it to this day. Down went Gareth and, within seconds, down went half the Eastern Province team. Almost before I could blink, there were five or six of the local team laid out on the pitch. It looked like some terrifying tornado had just swept across the ground, flattening almost everyone in its path.

It was very obvious that the entire local team was working at a considerable disadvantage. They had no idea what was about to happen. Players who were standing around suddenly found themselves on the ground, their jaws aching or bleeding. Others were hit so hard that they didn't feel anything for some time. One of our players was Stewart McKinney, from the Dungannon club in Northern Ireland, and he hit this guy next to him so hard that he went down like a pack of cards. He just crumpled from the base and slowly collapsed. He never knew what hit him and the fact that he personally had not done anything wrong was irrelevant. Any of the Eastern Province players unwise enough to try and fight back found themselves confronting four or five Lions, with inevitable results. It looked like carnage and it was – which was exactly the desired effect.

Of course, the publicity was blown out of all proportion once the media learned what had been going on. Yet ironically that helped us achieve our ambition, because the whole of South Africa quickly got the message that one traditional option open to them down the years to help beat a touring Lions team had suddenly been closed off.

The first time it happened to me personally, or at least whilst I was on the field, was in the match against Northern Transvaal, shortly before the vital third Test. No coincidence that, by the way; the South Africans knew that Test would be the point of no return for them, because by that time we were 2–0 up in the series. So the nonsense started again. One of our players was hit illegally and I shouted out '99'. But by then we were so proficient at it that three of their guys were already lying on the ground, knocked nearly senseless, by the time the rest realised what was happening. When they saw their pals lying motionless, few of them appeared to have an appetite to join their mates in never-never land.

Let me tell you straight, I took no pride in helping flatten opponents off the ball when they had done nothing wrong. I did not delight in the carnage that unfolded before me at East London. I wish it had never been necessary to use such tactics, but I wanted the locals to be perfectly clear about it. We were there to play rugby and win fairly and squarely, but if they wanted to start something, then we'd make damn sure we finished it on our terms. Nothing was going to be allowed to distract us from our goal of winning the Test series in South Africa.

I'd been on the receiving end of enough physical intimidation during my previous tours there in 1962 and 1968 to know that the South Africans would understand this message, whereas a thousand others expressed verbally or just in print would go right over their heads. In short, they would ignore them, but they did understand physical violence when it was used against them, because that was the way they operated. They used it when they thought it would give them an advantage. I decided that two could play at that game and that was why we adopted it, *if* we were attacked first. But only if . . .

In 1962, we would never have got away with such a tactic, because the attitude among the British and Irish administrators then would have been, 'Chaps, this just isn't rugger.' The trouble is, that sort of attitude doesn't count when you go to South Africa or New Zealand. They laugh at such an approach and I knew that. We got a lot of criticism for that tactic, but my response is quite simple – look at the record books. I'm not interested in criticism; sticks and stones may break my bones, but words will never hurt me. The guys who were doing the criticising were not the ones who were lying on the ground being stamped on and kicked in the face, or being punched from behind off the ball. So criticism doesn't matter to me. What did matter was winning that Test series by playing high-quality rugby in a fair but physical way. Once the message had got home, we were able to do that and returned home unbeaten on our tour, having won the series 3–0. I can tell you now, if we had not sorted out that nonsense, I am not at all sure we would have been able to do that.

Furthermore, what we did on that tour helped clear a lot of attitudes in South Africa, so much so that when Bill Beaumont took the Lions back there in 1980, they didn't have to contend with that sort of nonsense. By then, the locals had got the message. They picked up a lot of injuries and they didn't win the Test series, but that had nothing to do with foul play.

We were blessed with riches in terms of players on that 1974 tour. Gareth Edwards and Phil Bennett at scrum half and fly half was the finest half-back pairing in the world at that time. They were the critical cog in our wheel, but like all half-backs, their job was made easier by the fact that we had a pack of forwards able to give them the ball going forward. Not even the best half-backs in the world can look very effective if they are receiving the ball going backwards. It exposes them to all kinds of pressures and restrictions.

There were some marvellous forwards, players who, like me, were out there to win this time and refused to be distracted from that focus. Windsor, Uttley, Slattery, Ripley, Ralston, Neary, McLaughlan, McKinney, Kennedy, Davies, David, Cotton, Carmichael, Burton and Brown. Each man deserved a medal for the effort he put into the common cause, because even those who didn't figure in the Test side played their part by doing so well in the provincial games. The fact that we kept winning all those midweek matches helped build up a momentum that we never lost throughout the entire tour. I felt, at last, that I had true men around me, human beings who would cheerfully go into the trenches with me and fight the enemy to the last. It was a feeling I had never had before as a British Lion. As captain, I cannot tell you how proud I was of them. Even now, the small matter of thirty years later, I admire them. When I meet Andy Ripley today, he still calls me 'my leader'. That came from the very special feeling we had engendered for the duration of that tour.

Of the backs, Mike Gibson flew out late because he was doing final law exams, but we were so settled, so established as a unit, that not even the great Gibson could force his way into the Test team. When I saw that happen, I knew that we really had something special happening around us. Tony Neary of England was another world-class player who couldn't get into the Test side. So in my view, maybe only three or four of the whole thirty-man squad did not come up to the standard required for Test match rugby. If we'd needed to, we could have played virtually the whole of the back-up group and still been confident of beating the South Africans. That was a big difference from the 1971 Lions. On that tour, we'd had a magnificent first-choice first XV, but below that you were struggling, because a lot of the rest were not Lions Test material.

Neary was an interesting guy. He was a superb player, akin to Fergus Slattery. He was very disappointed when he didn't get into the Test side. It was a shock to him. I had a long chat with him after the decision had been made, but he mainly sat there in silence, staring forlornly out of the window. He was very upset. The next day, he came back to my room and explained what had been in his mind. He apologised for acting that way, but told me how sad he was to miss out. He explained that he'd always been a bit of a spoiled boy and confessed he'd never had disappointments like that before and he found it hard to cope. He was one of those people who had walked through most stages of his life without ever getting the knocks.

I told Tony the tour wasn't over for him and meant it. It was up to him to prove the selectors wrong but, unfortunately for him, Slattery proved the selectors right by playing so superbly in the Test match. We won and the side hardly changed for the rest of the series. There was a positive to come out of it from Neary's point of view, though, because he buckled down and was also superb in the provincial games for the remainder of the tour.

In 1974, we were fortunate that injuries did not disrupt us. The only changes we made were Andy Irvine for Billy Steele on the right wing for the last two Tests and Chris Ralston for the injured Gordon Brown, who had a hamstring injury, in the final Test. That was all, which was phenomenal for a hard tour of South Africa.

I said that those guys could party when the chance arose and, by God, I meant it. At the happy hour after our win, 28–9, in the second Test, which put us 2–0 up in the series, I announced that I was resigning as captain. There was a stunned silence. 'Until Monday morning,' I then said, once I really had their attention. Great cheering followed. It meant that I could relax like them and not be constantly on the alert. This was in Pretoria and the party we had that night, or at least the so-called happy hour, lasted for four or five hours. We all had to do a party piece; someone sang a song, someone else told a story. Later, much later in the night, in the small hours in fact, I remember waking up, lying in my under-pants on the mattress in my bedroom, with the room going one way and me trying to focus and bring it back the other way. We've all been in that situation. I was aware of banging on my bedroom door, so I turned on the light and looked at my watch. It told me it was 3 a.m.

I opened the door to be confronted by Roger Uttley and Mervyn Davies. Both were pissed. They told me there was a bit of trouble and I was needed downstairs. I picked up my pipe – I never go anywhere without that, especially in times of crisis – and walked down this corridor, somewhat unsteadily, just in my underpants. The first sight I saw was Bobby Windsor with a fire hose in his hands and I sobered up very quickly.

I got to the mezzanine floor, which overlooked the lobby, and there were the rest of the Lions, out of their tree, with pieces of tables, bits of chairs and other furniture strewn about. Most of them were sitting or lying on the floor. It was another of those scenes of carnage we were beginning to get used to. It was very cold in Pretoria at night and there was a fire going in the hotel reception area, on to which they were throwing cardboard boxes and pieces of wood. In the midst of all this, there was one extremely irate hotel manager. He was having a lot of trouble. He was involved in a tirade and it didn't take me very long to work out that he didn't like us at all.

At the end of the tirade, he said, 'That's it. I've had enough of you lot. I'm going to get the police.' I heard this and thought to myself, we've just won two Test matches, we're unbeaten on the tour and this guy is about to destroy all that. I could see the next day's headlines: 'Lions team thrown out of hotel' or 'Drunken Lions darken rugby's name'. It was a disaster about to happen. Anyway, the Lions were looking at me standing there in my underpants, smoking my pipe, so I thought I should intervene. I said to the hotel manager, 'Hold on a minute. I'm the captain of this team. What's the problem?' But the guy obviously considered he had been asked a stupid question by someone trying to take the mickey out of him. He completely lost it. He said, 'I've been through all this. I'm taking no more of it and I'm calling the police.'

Now I'd seen the riot police in operation in South Africa and didn't like the mental images my mind was conjuring up. I could see hordes of them rushing through the door and didn't think they'd be handing out sweets and asking these drunken idiots for autographs. So I said to the manager with what I suppose was an unprepared bout of Irish wit, 'Excuse me, but if you are going to get the police, do you'll think there'll be many of them?' There was a brief silence because the guys downstairs couldn't believe what I had just said. Nor could I believe what I'd just said and clearly the manager couldn't believe it either. The Lions then burst into cheering, as though a great fist fight with hordes of South African riot squad policemen would be the ideal way to round off the night's entertainment, but for some strange reason it changed the whole atmosphere.

The manager walked across the lobby, looked up at me and said, 'That was bloody good, you know.' I replied, 'Look, they're pissed, I'm pissed and you're bloody angry. I will see they all go to bed now and you and I and the management will sort this out in the morning.' The Lions duly departed for bed and it was sorted out satisfactorily in the morning without a word appearing in the papers. Alan Thomas signed a cheque for a few hundred rand to cover the damage and it was all resolved.

I mentioned East London a while earlier. It was never my favourite place on Lions tours of South Africa. It was quite boring, because there wasn't much to do, but it did provide the comic highlight of the 1974 Lions tour. We had been permitted by the management to phone home, making up to three calls a week to a maximum duration of five minutes. If we kept it to that, it was agreed the South African Rugby Board would pick up the bill. Now Alan Thomas, our manager, was a very forgetful sort of man, who would lose things all over the place, all the time. He would mislay his bag, his coat, his room key . . . anything. In fact, he lost his room key frequently. He would wander into the dining room for a meal with his room key in his hand, put it down and wander over to somebody for a chat. Then he'd forget where he'd put the key.

Not very much missed Bobby Windsor on the whole tour and he quickly spotted this little foible. Now, when we checked out of a hotel, the players would be ready on the bus and the last thing the manager would do was to pay the bill at reception. Perhaps Alan Thomas had never had the opportunity to lead men, but one of his weaknesses was that he tended to treat some of them like school-boys, which was absurd. This particular day, a red-faced Thomas boarded the bus. He had a deep frown on his face and it was obvious everything was far from well. He called for the players' attention and said, 'Right, you call yourselves British Lions, the cream of rugby men from the four home unions. You know what the rules are, but it appears that someone has been going to my room without my knowledge or approval and using my telephone. I have a phone bill for 1,500 Rand and I want that player to come here right now and we will sort it out.'

No one on the entire bus moved a muscle in response. You could have heard the proverbial pin drop. After a moment or two, Thomas became even more irate and said, 'Right. I did not want to do this. I didn't think it would go this far and I have to say I am very disappointed, but unfortunately, the guy who did this is a country-man of my own.' Well that immediately cleared twenty-one of the thirty players on the tour, news that was clearly a considerable relief to many. So the rest of us then started shouting, 'Come on you bastard, whoever it was. Be a man. Own up.'

But incredibly, still no one moved. Alan Thomas was by now at the end of his tether. He said, 'I cannot believe this, so I am now going to expose the culprit myself. The number that has been phoned is Pontypool 31748.' Barely had the words left his lips then Bobby Windsor jumped up, looked all around with a feigned expression of anger and shouted, 'Which one of you bastards has been phoning my wife?' The whole bus exploded with laughter. I don't think any of us had laughed so much for years, but that was Bobby Windsor for you. Bobby has an answer for everything, but he was a classic example of how rugby football and, I believe, that tour in particular, helped people. Some guys like Bobby never had many chances in their early years, but rugby came along, showed them what qualities such as teamwork, spirit and cohesion really meant in life and also opened their eyes to the world in general. They returned from those tours better men.

It would not be fair for anyone to look back at the record books and just assume we got lucky on that tour. Lucky we had world-class performers like Edwards and Bennett, J.P.R. Williams, Cotton, Slattery and Mervyn Davies; lucky we largely steered clear of injuries; and lucky the Springboks could find no answer to it. Lucky? Forget it. It was nothing to do with luck. Our preparation, as in all things that succeed no matter who is involved, was absolutely meticulous. For example, if I were leading the team in a match, I would be in charge from the night before right through to the morning of the game and the match itself. The coach had nothing to do with the team from the Friday evening onwards. I knew we had to get our mental preparation right for the Test matches, so on Friday afternoons Syd Millar and I would take the team out of the city where we were staying, into the countryside or up into the hills to some quiet little spot. There we would sit down and have tea in peace. Then we'd just talk about the game and how we saw it evolving.

It was essential for every man to know his job, what his place was, and his role, and what he was trying to achieve. After all that, it was a matter of getting the mindset right to go on to the field. Things like communication were important, too, though. During a rugby match you can't use carrier pigeons to communicate or a tick-tack man to give you signals. So you need to work out prearranged methods of communication, even amidst the intensity of a Test match. All that took time to sort out and discuss. I told the players it was important they had an input out on the field, because I didn't want us getting into a rut of style or pattern if one of them could see the problem and knew how to change it.

It was also very clear to me throughout the tour that, despite whatever else I had done during my career, I had to earn the respect of my fellow professionals all over again. I was playing with some of the greatest players in the world, as I have said, and you don't buy respect from anyone. It is earned. Furthermore, I would never have asked them to do something I wouldn't have done myself. They knew that. They also knew that I would die for them; that was something that was within the whole team. I was just another member of the team; I wasn't anything special.

I think that at the end of that series, that single unit was probably the defining quality in determining the outcome. We had a lot of talent, but skill and class is never enough in a team game. You need a team ethos of one for all, all for one. We maintained that team ethos at all times. When we drove by bus to Loftus Versfeld, the Pretoria ground, for the vital second Test, we sang 'Flower of Scotland', which we'd adopted as our song, right through to the end. The bus had reached the entrance to the stadium and they were waiting for us to get off, but not a man moved until this vivid demonstration of the team ethos and common spirit had been fulfilled.

My job was to encourage, cajole, threaten, urge, blackmail or whatever word was appropriate for a particular player. No two players were identical. For example, you would just give a pat on the back to a person like Phil Bennett, as you walked around the dressing room, speaking to each man in turn. Others you almost had to threaten: 'Unless you bloody well give it everything today, we're never going to get out of here in one piece,' sort of thing. Gordon Brown of Scotland was one of those you had to get going. He was a lazy bastard and I used to say to him, 'When you come back into this dressing room, I hope you can look me in the eye, because that's what you are going to have to do.' He did and he could.

As a leader, you begin to know how guys look at you and therefore how they are going to react, so by the time we came to go out for that Test match, I knew we were going to win. I was certain of it, because, you see, each man knew his role implicitly. For example, so much of our play revolved around Bennett, a wonderful little man. He was the only outside half we had for the Tests, so we had to devise a situation whereby he didn't have to tackle. I didn't want him getting crushed by some brute of a Springbok forward who would put his boots into Phil as he went straight over the top of him. So we sat down with Fergus Slattery, our open side flank forward, and said, 'Look, the one guy they're going to go for today is Phil. He's the smallest guy and they know how crucial he is to us.' I told him it was imperative that Phil must not be involved in any tackling. This meant the South African outside half had to be looking all the time for Slattery whenever they got the ball, rather than trying to crash into Phil. So that was what happened.

Then I told Bobby Windsor that if their scrum half was not looking for him after every line-out, he was failing in his duty that day. As for the defining moment, I'd say it came in that Test when Phil went back to collect a kick ahead not far from his own line. Things weren't going particularly well for us at that stage, for the South Africans were getting stuck in, we were making a few mistakes and the referee was giving us virtually nothing. But then Phil started this superb run out of defence. He jinked his way past a couple of guys and suddenly threw a pass out and J.J. Williams went streaming past the cover to score in the corner. That turned the whole game, perhaps the entire series. There were players in that team who could run all over the place, like Phil Bennett, J.J. Williams and Andy Irvine. In the end, we forwards started running after them, mostly out of curiosity.

That was a momentous day and it had started in strange fashion. In the hotel, before we even left for the ground, I had a sixth sense that strange things might be about to happen. I felt that some bastard might try to jam the lift when we were travelling down in it and therefore, when I left my room to join up with the others downstairs, I walked down all the stairs. I wouldn't get into the lift. Another reason for doing that was that I didn't want to associate with local people in the lift, because already at that stage I was closing my mind to outside influences. We were about to play probably the most important game of our entire lives and I did not want anything or anyone to interrupt my focus on that and what I, as captain, had to do. I suppose my fear that the lift might be sabotaged was absurd, when I look back at it, but it shows those of you who have not been involved in international rugby at such a high level how deeply you have to prepare and perhaps sometimes how paranoid you become.

There is one final thing to say about that tour. Some people said afterwards that South African rugby was at a low ebb, but there are always negative people. The fact remains that when the Springboks went to France a few months after we had played them, they won the Test series 2–0. Then, two years later, they beat the New Zealanders 3–1 in a Test series in South Africa. So I think we can safely discount suggestions that we were up against a side playing at the level of Old Rubberduckians. Remember something else, too. South Africa had never been beaten at home before in a Test series. That was some scalp for us to seize.

Sure, the South Africans made mistakes playing against us, one of them being that they changed their team far too often, but that wasn't our problem. What it probably demonstrated was the amount of pressure we were exerting on them, but they put out their best side each time, as they saw it, and it just wasn't good enough. However, never underestimate the intense pride that beats in every South African's heart when he wears the green jersey of the Republic.

It was a measure of the man that the Springboks' captain, Hannes Marais, took the defeat so well. In some ways I felt sorry for him, for he went down as captain of the first ever Springbok side to lose a Test series on home soil to the Lions. I have always had a very high regard for Hannes. He is a very nice guy and I like him immensely. Again, it was a mark of the man that he agreed to fly to London years later to join us at our twenty-fifth anniversary celebrations of the tour. He came over and spoke at the reunion and that was not an easy thing to do.

That Lions tour of 1974 and what we achieved has to be my single greatest achievement in rugby football. I was captain and we finished the tour unbeaten. No other Lions touring party in history, before or since, has ever matched that achievement. We are in the record books and will stay there because, for a start, there will never be another Lions tour of twenty-two matches. Sadly, those great days when the Lions took the game to all corners of the great southern hemisphere rugby playing nations are over. But there is more to it than just figures in a book. To know that we came through that campaign against all the odds, when the government, several sporting bodies, the media and apparently many other people were against us, took some doing. It demonstrated a singularity of purpose of which I felt proud. We overcame all that, took all the criticism, but stuck together. Thirty years later, that squad is still a close-knit unit, because there is that bond which will never be broken. It was a much stronger bond than that of any other Lions touring party with which I was involved. It was a tough tour, mentally and physically, but we came through it all and earned the title, 'The most successful Lions in history'. That description makes me a proud man today when I reflect on those times.

I was fortunate. I survived to experience those winning tours of 1971 and 1974 and, I can tell you, I was proud of what the Lions had developed into by the time I returned home from my last Lions tour as a player, in late summer 1974. The guys I felt sorry for were those who did not see the great tours that followed the long years of failure with the Lions. All those guys knew was the pain of defeat throughout the Lions tours of the 1960s. To go back to New Zealand and South Africa and beat the bastards in their own backyard was sweet, very sweet indeed. I will cherish that memory until the day I die, but it would have been sweeter still had the good guys from those early years still been around to share it all.

I am thinking of people I really respected both as rugby players and as men, such as Alun Pask and Haydn Morgan of Wales, plus Bill Mulcahy and Noel Murphy of Ireland. They were unlucky. They didn't experience that winning and the deep inner satisfaction of being able to turn around at the end of the tour and say, 'We were better than them.' Poor selection had frustrated players like that as much as myself. I suspected that the attitude in committee rooms was, 'He's not the right sort of chap, not a good enough ambassador to represent us.' Well, people like Pask, Morgan, Mulcahy, Murphy and myself knew, for the most part, that good ambassadors were no good on rugby fields.

What we achieved in South Africa, together with the 1971 Lions' triumph in New Zealand, proved extremely difficult to live with for subsequent Lions touring parties. In 1977, the Lions returned to New Zealand and were beaten; in 1980, they lost the Test series 3–1 to the South Africans. Following a legacy of success is always difficult and it's a fact that both subsequent Lions parties found it impossible to match the deeds of their two predecessors. I can tell you that following 1971 was difficult, although we did it, but we still had some key personnel remaining from 1971, the hard core, if you like. And we still had that winning feeling, but when you look at 1977 and the tour of New Zealand, you have to say a number of mistakes were made in selection.

I think they went back to New Zealand dreaming of 1971 and that was a big mistake. It was a different era but, probably crucially, they didn't have Gareth Edwards, who had turned down the chance to make one final Lions tour. I believe that cost the Lions the chance of winning the Test series. I believe, too, it was a mistake for John Dawes to go back to New Zealand as coach, so soon after being the winning captain there six years earlier. Trying to match the success of the 1971 Lions was always going to be a fearsome task, and I don't think Dawes should have been asked to coach there on the first occasion the Lions went back. Things don't often happen for you twice like that. What is it they say, lightning doesn't strike twice in the same place? Yes, in 1977, they still had Phil Bennett, although he was weighed down by the worries of the captaincy. Phil has said subsequently that he made a mistake by accepting the captaincy, and I must say I was most surprised when I heard he had been chosen to lead the Lions. New Zealand was exceedingly wet and Phil was not as effective there as he was on the hard grounds of southern Africa. Another player who was missed terribly was J.P.R. Williams. Mike Gibson was there, but he failed to make a single Test match and that was another loss to the Lions.

There was, on that tour, the extraordinary sight of the All Blacks putting only three men into their scrummage, because they conceded the Lions' vast superiority at the set pieces. Still, it did the Lions little good, because, although they won copious amounts of ball, their backs generally frittered it away. Meanwhile, it kept on raining, day in and day out. It turned out to be the wettest winter in New Zealand for over forty years, and playing on a series of mud-heaps understandably sapped the Lions' morale. Some might say that with such forward ascendancy, the Lions should have won easily in 1977, but then rugby football is like life – a funny game with all kinds of twists and turns that come upon you unexpectedly. That's probably one of the reasons why it is such a great game.

I remember thinking when I looked at some of the personalities involved in the 1977 tour that it would take very strong leadership to bring all that together so as to create maximum impact. Half the squad were Welshmen and you knew that sometimes the Welsh got very homesick on long tours. More than one Welshman suffered from precisely that on the tour and it didn't help morale one jot. As on all tours, a lot comes down to the manager and the example he sets. Another Scot had been chosen, George Burrell, but from everything I have heard I think he found the going tough as a manager. Even so, the Lions were desperately unlucky to lose the Test series 3–1, because they slipped to only a 10–9 defeat in the last Test at Auckland. But for that the series would have been shared.

In 1980 in South Africa, the Lions were again unlucky, losing the first three Tests by a margin of four points, five points and two points, before winning the final Test. These results proved to me that the great journey I had embarked upon with the British Lions all those years ago, back in 1962, had been thoroughly worthwhile. What had happened had justified my initial optimism that we could one day compete on level terms with the best the southern hemisphere had to offer. That wasn't the case throughout the 1960s on my first three tours. But thereafter British rugby showed very clearly that it had learned the lessons of those painful defeats and, given a fair wind could not only contest a Test series properly in the southern hemisphere, but also have an equal chance of returning home victorious.

CHAPTER 11

The Man Who Pinched Forty-five Frankfurters

After returning home from that 1974 Lions tour I played one final season in the northern hemisphere. In truth, I felt I'd climbed the mountain and had no burning desire to keep scanning the horizon for greater peaks to conquer. Besides, in 1975 I was thirty-five years of age which, while not quite in the walking stick and carpet slippers bracket of society, was getting on a bit for a second row forward in international rugby.

I didn't want to hang around too much longer at international level for a variety of reasons. I wanted to spend time with my long-suffering wife Penny and the children. I also knew that it was time for me to concentrate totally on my career in banking. My employers had been magnificent to me, allowing me time off not just for those long tours, but to go away on weekends and play international matches. Someone always had to fill in for me when I was away and, after a period of time, I became very aware that such generosity could not continue forever. I did want to carry on playing club rugby, but that would be different.

The public, too, were always – and have continued to be – very generous to me, and by the time I retired I was pretty well known throughout Ireland, north and south. I like to think I am one of those fortunate people who can go anywhere and chat to anyone. I hope I have no enemies, because I'm not strong enough to fight them any more if I do. Because I was around for so long, I have a recognisable face. When I played, you may remember, I always wore a headband to protect my ears, which were in a mess. I also used to get a lot of cuts around my eyes, and I was one of the first to wear a headband of Elastoplast or strapping to avoid the cuts. Obviously any photographs that were taken of me showed me in this band. Anyway, I say this not because I am now trying to find employment on a fashion catwalk, but because I am reminded of something that happened to me quite recently, while I was out in Belfast.

I was in St George's market, the fish market in the city, and I saw two old dears having a chat as they did their shopping. I could see them looking at me, and I assumed they were trying to put a name to the face. As I passed them a few minutes later, I heard one say, 'I know, it's Willie John McBride.' They were both in their seventies, perhaps even their eighties, so I smiled as I went by and said, 'Good morning, girls.' They were very excited at being called girls. Anyway, one of them called after me and said, 'Willie John, I'm glad to see your head's better.' I think she hadn't been sure who it was originally, because I wasn't wearing my headband to go shopping. I knew immediately what she was talking about.

So, once the 1975 Five Nations Championship was over, I retired with 63 Irish caps to my name. I was more than satisfied with that tally, having represented Ireland from 1962 to 1975, thirteen years of fun and excitement. It had been a wonderful experience but, like all good things, it had to come to an end. I had to grow up sometime and I felt then was as good a time as any.

My final season in the Five Nations Championship was, in one sense, much like all the others had been. We won two and lost two of our four matches. If I'd had ten pounds for every season that had happened in my career, I'd have had a fistful of notes. As before, we flattered to deceive. We toppled England, 12–9, at Lansdowne Road, on my fiftieth appearance in the championship, and beat France handsomely, 25–6, also in Dublin, six weeks later. But in between we disappointed, going down 20–13 to Scotland in Edinburgh and finishing the season on a really low note, being wiped out 32–4 by Wales in Cardiff. Mind you, the Welsh were in their pomp, with a few guys who could play a bit – J.P.R. Williams, Gareth Edwards, Gerald Davies, Phil Bennett, J.J. Williams, the Pontypool front row and Mervyn Davies. Match that, as they say. The fact was, we couldn't, and lost by five tries to one. I wasn't the only one who finished my career that day; Ray McLoughlin and Ken Kennedy, fellow travellers for Ireland and the Lions down the years, also retired after the game.

So an era came to an end. Well, I thought to myself at some point during that evening in Cardiff, all is not lost. There's always the cat to kick. Or at least there would have been if we'd had one. But it had been a special season in another sense. In 1975 Ireland celebrated its centenary year and the New Zealanders sent a team over to play some matches. They beat us 15–6 at Lansdowne Road, and I was able to see that several of the weaknesses that we had exposed on our successful Lions tour of 1971 had been addressed and solved. That's the thing about the New Zealanders; they study the game and learn from any failings. One thing you can always bet on – they will get it right, and quickly. That is why I respect them so much as a rugby people.

To lead fourteen other guys in a green shirt out on to an international rugby field is one of life's great feelings. I had taken over from Tom Kiernan as captain of Ireland in March 1973. My first match in charge had not been a success, at least in terms of the scoreboard, as Ireland lost, 16–12, to Wales in Cardiff. Mind you, we did beat France, 6–4, in Dublin five weeks later to end that year's

1973 Five Nations Championship. However, even though I was thirty-three at the time and knew I was unlikely to be in the job for very long, I felt extremely honoured, because it's very special – to head out knowing that, whatever their personal idiosyncrasies, those fourteen are with you and won't let you down.

Ireland, of course, have probably had more players with personal idiosyncrasies, more characters, than any other country in their time, and I found that playing alongside two of them in particular was wonderful. Willie Duggan and Moss Keane must have been laughing and cracking jokes from the day they were born. They've certainly never stopped since and I count myself fortunate to have shared the company of such great men.

Willie hated all the training associated with rugby football. In fact, he loathed it so much that it is a wonder he ever got to play the game at international level. Of course, he was good enough, but Willie's idea of hell would be hard work for hours on end on a training ground, yet when he got on the field, he would die for you. Not only that, but he was one of the finest No. 8 forwards of his era. He was one of those hard men whom you never saw get injured on the field. One day, he arrived late for a training session and I was talking to the team. I said we would start with a ten-minute warm-up, at which point Willie lit up a cigarette in the dressing room. He did have the good grace to stub it out on the floor after a few puffs, but promptly said of the training, 'Jaysus, I think I'll give that a miss today.' I looked hard at him, because I obviously didn't want this to become a general attitude, and then he came out with this wonder-ful line. 'Warm up?' he said, 'I'll be all right there, because I've had the heater on in the car on the way up. I'm warm enough.'

Moss Keane's face would not have moved a muscle at that remark. He'd have fully understood the logic in Willie's argument. I think the first time I saw Moss Keane was when he came up to Dublin to university, from Kerry, and started playing for Lansdowne. He was a great man of Munster. Moss was big and he got a final Irish trial. This was in the days when we had probables versus possibles as a trial – or rather the hopeless against the no-hopers, as one wag put it. Anyway, I was captain of the probables and Moss was included. Unlike the former captain of Ireland who lined up his men in the dressing room before a final trial and sent them onto the field with the stirring words, 'Good luck to yer all and every man for himself,' I emphasised the need for a collective effort. Well, Moss knocked a few men down, won line-out ball, which he was bound to do really given his size, and overall played a good game.

Usually, the team for that forthcoming 1974 international match, which was to be against France in Paris two weeks later, would have been published on the following Monday, but for some reason they announced it on the Saturday evening after the trial match. Well, Moss was chosen so, of course, we had a celebration at his first cap. Now this was not a particularly good idea, because if you have a celebration in Ireland, the following morning you some-times don't know where the ground is.

I can remember going down to the Lansdowne club around midnight and after a night of beers we started on a few more. Now Moss Keane can drink in this life; in fact, I've never seen anybody who can drink like him. By the small hours, most of us couldn't even stand up never mind go to the toilet, but Moss got up, went to the toilet and when he returned, said, 'Right lads, I'm away home.' There was a general chorus of disapproval, with guys shouting, 'Ah no, Moss, you're on another pint here now,' but Moss said, 'No, I'm finished now. I'm going home to prepare to play for Ireland against France.' More loud cheers . . .

But Moss wasn't just heading back across the city. He was driving off towards Kildare. By car. We heard later that he was apparently doing quite well, actually managing to stay on the road although weaving around a bit, when he was spotted by a Garda patrol car somewhere out in the suburbs. They followed him for a while and then pulled him in to the side of the road. Now Moss was well known in and around Dublin and everyone loved him. The patrol officer looked in the car, saw Mossie and said, 'Ah, now Mr Keane. We've been following you a while and have reason to believe you've been taking alcohol.' Moss looked around and said, 'Officer, you know, it's been a good day.' And he explained the whole story.

He'd been playing for the probables in Ireland's final trial and had heard soon after the game that he'd been selected for his first cap. 'So you've had a little celebration?' suggested the officer. 'Just a couple of pints, perhaps?' But Mossie, who is as honest as the day is long, looked almost insulted by this suggestion and replied, 'Ah, no, officer, not just the couple. I've had nineteen pints of Guinness.' The officer looked at him, shook his head and said simply, 'Mr Keane, I wish you hadn't told me that.' So he produced the breathalyser and said, 'Mr Keane, I'm going to have to ask you to blow into this bag.' And do you know what big Mossie said? He looked at the officer and said, 'Officer, do you not feckin' believe me?' I can tell you now, all these years later, there had to be a lot of sweet-talking done to get Moss off that one. In the end, I don't think he ever blew into the bag; some sort of a deal was done. But that was Moss.

So we went off to Paris to play at the Parc des Princes on 19 January 1974. It was a disappointing outcome for us. It was 6-6 with two minutes left to play and France kicked a penalty to win 9-6. But I remember the night after much better than the match itself. Now, I don't know if Moss had ever been to Paris before, but I can tell you, he struggles a bit with English. As for French, he wouldn't know a single word of it. Not that I am a great speaker of the language, either, but I felt that, as captain of the team, I ought to keep an eye on the new caps, Vince Becker and Keane. Both incidentally, were from the Lansdowne club.

Becker, who only won two caps in his career, both during that 1974 season, went off somewhere else with friends and I was left with Moss. Now all he ever drank back home was Guinness, but you couldn't really get the black stuff at many places in Paris, so he was drinking everything else. I thought, well, he's a big man and you never know what might happen, so I'll keep an eye out for him. Well, we must have covered most of Paris that evening and Moss had a big night. Sometime after midnight he said he'd got a big hunger, which seemed strange because we'd been to the official banquet at the Grand Hotel and they don't exactly stint you there on portions. But Moss wanted to eat and I thought that was good, because I'd prefer him to be hungry rather than thirsty.

We found a street with a lot of little cafes and shops – I think it was in Montmartre – and I parked Moss up against this wall, because by now he was weaving around a bit, what with all the funny drink he'd had and wasn't used to. I said I'd go and get some chips or something and he was to wait there, outside the shop. Well, my French wasn't good and it seemed to take a long time to make the guy understand I wanted a really big bag of chips. Anyway, Moss kept putting his head around the corner, staggering into the shop and asking what was happening. In the end, he couldn't contain himself any longer. He came into the place and saw that the guy was also selling frankfurters. Moss waited until the guy turned his back and then grabbed one of the frankfurters and headed out of the shop.

The trouble was, Moss didn't realise that the guy was still cooking the frankfurters and forty-five of the wretched things were still attached to the one Moss had grabbed and was eating. A trail of frankfurters ran across the floor of the cafe, like a moving army of ants. I'm standing there with my mouth open (not because I'm hungry, just through astonishment) and the guy then turns around and sees this stream of his frankfurters disappearing around the corner out of his shop. He went berserk, absolutely berserk, as only the French can. Arms waving, shouting, appealing to whichever god he worshipped: the whole thing. There was a terrible commotion.

Soon, we heard the dreaded sound of the police sirens. The gendarmes were on their way.

Moss and I stood with our backs to the wall – incredibly, he was still trying to eat as much as he could – and there were people and frankfurters all over the place. I said to Moss, 'Keep your back to the wall, Mossie. We can fight what's in front of us, but we can't fight anyone behind us.' But I don't think it came to warfare. The gendarmes, recognising two big Irish rugby players still dressed in dinner jackets and black ties, realised who we were and what had happened. It was smoothed over somehow and we went back to our hotel, never to hear any more about it.

Moss Keane's language is terrible. Always has been. We were playing in Scotland at one stage, I think in a Barbarians game or something like that. It was definitely some sort of a centenary game because there were players selected from all the four home unions. Moss and I were playing, and so was Andy Ripley. I remember in the bus, it must have been in the Borders area, we were travelling after playing the day before. Now Moss is no fool; he went to university and got a degree and all that. He might not act that way, but Moss Keane is a very bright lad. As is Andy Ripley. This meeting of Mensa minds came together as the beautiful countryside of the Scottish border region flashed past the window.

Suddenly, Ripley came up with this intriguing line of questioning for Moss. 'Moss,' he said, 'you see that hillside over there? How many fir trees do you reckon there are on it?' Moss looked over, thought a bit and then said, 'Ah, don't be bloody stupid. How the hell should I know?' So Ripley said, 'Now Moss, it's like this. In your mind, divide it into sections, count roughly how many are in a section and then multiply it. I'm not wanting an exact figure but an approximation, an estimate.' Moss says, 'Ah yes, very good, very good.' And he has another look and presently he says to Ripley, 'Yer know, there could be 5,000 trees up there.' Ripley says, 'That's near enough, Moss.'

So we drive on a bit and these two blinding geniuses, sitting together in front of me, come into conversation again. Moss says, 'Ripley, do yer see that hillside there? Do you see all those sheep? Tell me how many sheep are on that hillside.' Ripley looks at this field, thinks for a moment and then he says, 'There could be 2,500 sheep on that hillside.' Moss says, 'That's not bad, that's near enough, but tell me this. If one sheep runs over to the other side of the hill, how many would be left?' Ripley says, 'Oh come on Moss, don't be silly. It's obvious. There would be 2,499.' There is a pause for a moment. Then Moss says, 'Yes, I thought you'd say that, but there's one thing, Ripley. You know feck all about sheep. If one sheep went over there, they'd all feckin' go.'

I'll tell you about another great character who used to play for Ireland, although he made his debut after my time in the team. His name was Ginger (G.A.J.) McLoughlin of Shannon. He won his first cap in 1979 and in 1982, by which time I was involved in selection, and he was chosen to play against England at Twickenham. We had not travelled with a great deal of hope, even though we had beaten Wales in Dublin two weeks earlier, but by half-time it was clear that we had a chance if we could just improve a little in the second half. Perhaps, we thought, one individual moment of genius might turn the whole game. We had little idea that that one moment would come from a certain Shannon prop forward.

Someone shoved the ball into Ginger's hands about twenty yards from the English line, probably because there was no one else to give it to. No matter, Ginger somehow resisted the urge of all forwards to collapse gratefully onto the ground, from where it could be recycled for the backs. He kept going, kept pumping his plump thighs and suddenly the English line came into view. It was what they call in Hollywood a 'slo-mo action'. More and more players clustered around him, but Ginger refused to give up his hold on the ball. He was being pulled and twisted this way and that, but was still making steady progress towards the line. Anyway, Ginger kept going and eventually crashed over the line with half a dozen Irishmen and a few Englishmen hanging on. The referee Alan Hosie of Scotland gave the try and, soon after, Ireland had won a famous victory, 16–15.

I never saw Ginger all evening at the Hilton Hotel in London, where the RFU held its after-match banquets, but at about 2 a.m. there was Ginger standing around in the foyer amidst a group of friends. He was explaining to them how Ireland had won. I patted him on the back and said well done. I told him he'd be living on it for a good while when he got back to Limerick and remember him looking at me, with his eyes a bit bloodshot, and saying, 'Yer know, Willie John, it wasn't easy.' To which I replied, 'Oh no, it's never easy beating England, especially at Twickenham. In fact it's never easy winning any international game.' Ginger was still looking at me, but a pained expression spread across his face. He said, 'I'm not talking about that, I'm talking about scoring the try. Yer know, it's not easy driving those Englishmen back over their line when you've got to pull the whole feckin' Irish pack with you at the same time.' That was classic Ginger. I can tell you, it was an education to travel with guys like that.

France and Wales dominated the championship during my playing time. From 1962 to 1975 they won it every season apart from once, when we won it, in 1974. England beating Wales at the end of that season gave us the championship, but it was a bit of a peculiar feeling because we weren't even playing that day, having completed our programme two weeks earlier. But the French and the Welsh justifiably ruled the roost, for both countries were much better than the rest of us.

In the 1960s and 1970s, France had some superb players. They won the Grand Slam for the first time in 1968 with the little Camberabero brothers at half-back, directing operations like a couple of Napoleonic generals. In my era, the French were always well organised and they had some wonderful rugby people who seemed to make each occasion special. The Boniface brothers were fabulous players for their club Mont-de-Marsan and their country, until Guy was tragically killed in a car crash. Then there were players like Christian Darrouy, Jean Gachassin, Jo Maso and Monsieur Le Drop, Pierre Albaladejo, a wonderful kicker of the ball. The production line never seemed to stall; others in the same mould included Pierre Villepreux, Jean Trillo, Jean-Pierre Lux and Andre Campaes. All of them were great entertainers, runners with serious pace and silky skills.

Unlike some in the British Isles, I did not find France particularly dirty. Certainly, they never stood for any nonsense, but I never had a serious problem with them. There were always a few fists and fingers around, but that was international rugby. I wouldn't count that. But at that time, France were anxious to let their ball players gain possession and show their skills. When they did that, you knew you were in trouble.

They were a lot more innovative in their approach to the game than the rest of us. They would try things from short penalties that none of us had ever seen before, still less attempted. When you played them, above all else you had to try and prevent them from starting to run and getting on a roll. We used to sit at home in Ireland before a match with the French, reminding ourselves we had to watch the blind side against them. We had to shackle their scrum half, sit tight on their fly half and be careful about the back row, and so on. At one time, they were using the blind side at the breakdown a heck of a lot because, of course, it is the most vulnerable place for a defending side. We had a rigid system whereby almost the first player to the breakdown went straight to the blind side, so that at least there was someone there to stop the French exploiting quick ball and attacking down that short side.

But the fact was, every single year you had to cope with something new when you met the French. I admired their innovation, their willingness to look afresh at aspects of the game and come up with some intriguing new ploy that they would try. Very often it worked, too. Other countries that could, and indeed should, have been showing similar invention, like England, were staid. If England's traditionally big pack of forwards didn't win the game off their own bat, then that was invariably the end of England in a particular match. But the French had such wonderful skills to accompany their rugby brains, and their coaching and preparation put them well ahead of most others at that time, the Welsh excepted.

I always enjoyed playing against France. I had many a tussle with those wonderful ball-handling, tough, talented and durable forwards Walter Spanghero and Benoit Dauga, not to forget Elie Cester. Dauga was a lamp-post of a man who could also run and handle like a modern day forward, yet this was thirty-three years ago. I was brought up on a farm, but Spanghero's hands were like great buckets and twice the size of mine. Later on came more superb backs, such as the charismatic Serge Blanco and Philippe Sella, plus outstanding forwards such as Jean-Claude Skrela, Jean-Pierre Rives and Jean-Pierre Bastiat. Until rugby changed with the coming of professionalism in 1995, if a French back line ignited, then there was nothing you could do but admire it. The skill level of those guys was extraordinary. They could take opponents out of the game with just a single flick of their hands.

I doubt whether there is a more spectacular sight in the game even today than a French team in full flow. There is a certain movement and elegance to their running that is marvellous to see. For sure, it has changed a bit now, because they only really select giants behind the scrum and, as a result, you don't see as much of the dexterity, delightful touches and sharp skills that their players used to typify. Power is now the key. But their rugby reminded me of what Carwyn James said about rugby football being opera. It hit the high notes, all right, when the French were on song.

After the French came the Welsh and their period of domination, which was to last through to the end of the 1970s. Wales, in fact, were the team I liked playing against least of all and I found them the most difficult during my international years. We had one or two unpleasant incidents with them, like the Brian Price affair, when he chinned Noel Murphy. Some silly things that went on in our games with them went unpunished and perhaps that left a sour taste.

I liked to think I was a hard but fair player, but I got a bit tired of the stupid antics that occurred in games against the Welsh. I mean things like jersey-grabbing when you went to get the ball or holding players down on the ground off the ball. None of which is to deny that those Welsh teams produced some wonderful rugby, played by fantastic players, many of whom became great friends of mine. Wales were the most successful of all the teams in the Five Nations around that time, although I did feel that they always had one or two players who let them down.

I don't believe it was a freak, that era which Wales enjoyed. I prefer to believe it was the direct consequence of having such a strong club rugby structure. They may have been fortunate that, for instance, the minute Barry John retired, in came Phil Bennett, another world beater. But Wales had fine players throughout their team and an awful lot more in reserve. Their club rugby was tough and competitive, and prepared the players for the step up to international level. That is the biggest difference today and partly explains why Welsh international rugby has declined so far. The great structure that underpinned it for all those years is no longer there, so the players have not come through as they used to.

But then, Wales still had steelworks and coal mines from which hard men emerged to play rugby football. Sadly, all that has now gone. Rugby was a passion for the Welsh, as much a part of their lives as going to chapel and singing, something they also did memorably. They sang those great hymns, such as 'Guide Me Oh Thou Great Jehovah', with the same deep-seated fervour as they took on to the rugby field. It was wonderful to experience it at first hand. Their brilliance and superiority were akin to that of the Australian cricket team today.

It must have been wonderful to play in that side. Many have been the times since, that I have sat down with some of my Welsh friends and talked about how and why that position of such strength was somehow frittered away. Now this may sound an off-the-wall idea, but I honestly believe it was Maggie Thatcher who destroyed Welsh rugby. Why? Quite simply, because she closed the coal mines and introduced widespread privatisation which, of course, undermined the steelworks in Wales. When both industries were thriving, Welsh rugby teams had a tough core of men from whom to select their sides. When Wales was forced to become much more of a white collar industry country, there was never the same strength in Welsh national teams.

But we shouldn't forget another reason for the decline of the game in that great country. Rugby football ran into problems in the schools. The great grammar schools that had produced so many fine players began to die out and teachers no longer wanted to spend their Saturday mornings or midweek evenings out on the training ground, teaching youngsters the vital elements of the game.

When teachers stopped doing all that vital work, pupils began to drift away from the sport, finding other things to do. In turn and in time, this affected the clubs, for their supply line of talent was damaged. As if all that lot were not enough, in the mid-1990s professionalism arrived and it is an open secret that Wales has never coped with the professional side of the game, chiefly because they just haven't got the money in the country. Yet crazy things still happened in Wales under professionalism and people lost their heads. The Welsh Rugby Union is today grappling with enormous financial problems, partly as a result of all that, but also due to the debts incurred building the Millennium Stadium.

Whatever the reason, the fact is the valleys have been decimated. I find them sad places to visit today. I saw them when they were buzzing, full of people, busily employed and vigorously pursuing their two great traditional passions: rugby and choir. Today, to my mind, they are like haunted places, lonely and sad.

Do I see Wales ever regaining their once eminent position of strength in the world game? No. There is certainly no sign of it. Some of the things that have happened there have been farcical. People better qualified to know than I tell me that Wales threw away a glorious chance of rebuilding their whole structure when officials from the WRU arrogantly turned down an offer from the English clubs to set up an Anglo-Welsh League. That could have been the salvation of Wales as a rugby nation, a return to classic fixtures such as Cardiff v Gloucester, Swansea v Bath, Harlequins v Llanelli and Newport v Wasps. But the WRU refused to budge, demanding too many entrants on their part. The English couldn't see it working with as many as eight or nine Welsh clubs and the idea fell on stony ground. Welsh hopes collapsed with it.

One of the most absurd things that has ever happened in Wales was the playing of players who turned out not to be eligible for Wales after all. One of them, who had claimed Welsh ancestry, played twenty-five or so times in the Welsh jersey until someone found out that his grandmother came from Lancashire after all. I mean, how demeaning is that for a Welsh cap holder? It would be like an Irish team including an Australian whose mother came from Birmingham. I just ask, why were those players allowed to play? Surely there was a system to check their claims and surely someone was in charge of that system? And why was it allowed to go on for so long? Did they want to bury the truth when they found it? Or is 'burying the truth' the way our game is run now? If so, how is any game going to become healthy?

One man who had a key role in Wales's success was Ray Williams, one of the first exponents of the art of coaching. Wales turned to coaching some time before the rest of us. In Ireland, by contrast, coaching was still frowned upon. As the old joke went, the only coach we ever knew was the one that ferried us to the stadium. It certainly took a long time for the IRFU to be persuaded that this was becoming an essential element of a national team's preparation. People like Ronnie Dawson and Ray McLoughlin played vital roles in that process, but neither ever got enough credit for the part they played in helping to drag Irish rugby, kicking and screaming, into the twentieth century.

Scotland, too, had some gifted players in my time. Andy Irvine was a sublime player, but you simply didn't know what to expect from him. When you watched a tape of him in action, you thought there was no way he should have got away with what he did. But then he'd go out and do the same in the next game, so you knew it was no fluke, just pure skill.

Andy was just one of those players whom I think would have preferred to beat ten opponents and score, rather than half the number. In his world, that wouldn't have been anywhere near as exciting. We played him on the wing in 1974 with the Lions, but he didn't enjoy the same freedom there as at full-back, where the Scots played him. He was a high risk all right, and he certainly made some crucial mistakes, but he also won plenty of games for his country and whenever he played he entertained thousands of supporters who loved his style. You can't do better than that.

Another interesting Scot was Alistair McHarg, whom I always found tough to play against, because he was so lively in broken play. He could play lock or in the back row, but he covered a remarkable amount of ground. I don't know about his scrummaging ability, because I doubt if you can cover the field in that way while giving everything you have in the scrums, but there was a lot of emphasis on scrummaging and maybe that was where Alistair fell down. Perhaps he was too loose a player. I used to stand up sweating and bloodied from a scrum or maul and wonder how the hell McHarg could turn up in some of the positions he would be found in if he was doing all he was supposed to be doing up front. I believe that counted against him when it came to choosing Lions teams of that era, but he suited the Scottish ideal of keeping the ball moving and having a mobile pack.

And England? In my day, we had a chance against them, because they were disorganised and kept on changing their team. They had so many clubs they could pick half a dozen sides, whereas in Ireland, our base was much smaller and we had to keep faith for longer with players. When we played England, you would never know who would line up against you. It was like a sporting game of musical chairs played by their selectors. There was a hard core of perhaps three or four players, like David Duckham, whom they usually selected, but the rest changed constantly and that is why they were not more successful in my view.

It seemed to us on the outside that England didn't know the true worth of their players. Alan Old was a case in point. People used to say the Yorkshire fly-half was only a kicker of the ball, but I saw on the 1974 Lions tour what a superb distributor he was, too. As for back row players, England had all manner of them available. Peter Dixon was a Lions Test player before the England selectors chose him and he was just one example. Roger Uttley was another superb player and a great man, a fine tourist and a guy who could laugh at most things. Not a pretty sight when he faced you at 2 a.m., though.

However, all many of the England players seemed to want to do was to 'get a cap'. Once they'd got one or two, they seemed to lose interest and go off and do something in the City. They didn't seem keen on being part of a team for a few years, perhaps because there was this widespread image of their selectors changing most of the side as soon as they lost a match. That happened quite often, although of course it's all very different today.

While I'm ruminating on the players I played with and against, I'll tell you about the best Irish team I ever played with. It was the side chosen to face Wales in Dublin in 1970. Wales came to Lansdowne Road looking for the Triple Crown and they had an array of stars in their line-up, including Edwards and John at half-back, J.P.R. Williams at full-back, John Dawes in the centre, Stuart Watkins on the wing and forwards of the quality of Delme Thomas, Denzil Williams and Mervyn Davies.

Our team was as follows: Kiernan (captain); Duggan, Bresnihan, Gibson, Brown; McGann, Young; O'Callaghan, Kennedy, Millar, McBride, Molloy, Lamont, Slattery, Goodall. The key to this side and the reason it was the best I ever played in was the back row. Slattery was a fantastic, tearaway, open side flanker who pestered the life out of the opposition half-backs and won copious amounts of loose ball on the ground. Lamont was a wonderful, hard-driving blindside flanker who could take the ball forward and was as solid as a rock. Ken Goodall was arguably the finest ball-handling No 8 forward Ireland have developed in the last half century. His distribution, speed, ability in attack and defensive play made him an outstanding performer in any country. It was nothing short of a complete tragedy when he suddenly decided to turn professional and was lost to the union code. That back row had everything: pace, defence, handling skills and support play. The combination was perfect.

Ken Goodall and I often used to travel to training at Ravenhill; when the rumours about him going to rugby league began going around I told him not to get involved with this because it was only about money. You wouldn't have gone from Ireland to join a rugby league club in England at that time for any other reason than finance, but Ken was quite young, in his early twenties, and he had just got married. In those amateur days your rewards came later, usually when you were nearing the end of your career, and I suppose I was already taking a longer view than Ken was prepared to do at that time.

I certainly never saw Ken as a rugby league player. He was about six feet five inches tall and had a long back, which definitely wasn't the build for league. I never thought he would succeed there and I told him so. I told him he'd be making a big mistake if he went, and that the advantages of remaining in union, with all its contacts in so many fields, could be just as valuable to him in the long term. However, young men are young men and I later learned that on the day I had that long chat with him he had already signed. That greatly disappointed me, but life moves on and these days I see Ken from time to time. We always chat and are friendly, but he doesn't talk about the sporting past very much now, perhaps because he didn't last very long in league. What is saddest of all is that I don't think he made a lot of money out of it either, but I suppose he and his wife felt that as a young couple they wanted as much money as they could get and as quickly as possible. That is only human nature.

I believe that if Ken Goodall had stayed in rugby union, he would have become one of the greats of the sport. There's no disputing that fact. He had already gone on one Lions tour, in 1968, but I think he would have been an absolutely key component in what the Lions achieved in 1971 and 1974. Yes, we would have been selecting from enormous strength in depth with Mervyn Davies around. But remember, Ken could play blindside flanker, too. He would have gained a huge amount of knowledge on those tours and would have become another Mervyn Davies, I think. He had all those great attributes. In fact, he had everything a great back row man needs. On the day he left for rugby league, Irish rugby suffered a grievous blow.

Several years earlier, the league boys had come knocking on my door. I had played a match in Yorkshire for Ulster and it was just one of those days when everything came together. The ball bounced kindly for me at one moment in the game. I picked it up and smashed through a couple of tackles on my way to the line, where I scored a try. Not long after, I got a call from someone saying they represented Salford rugby league club and they wanted to meet me.

They came over to Ireland and we met at the Manor Hotel in Ballymoney. I was working in the bank at the time earning about £20 a month and, in a quiet moment in a fairly dark corner, they opened up the box they were carrying. In it, I was informed, was £5,000 in cash and it was mine if I signed the contract they had in their briefcases. It was very tempting, I must say, but I knew I was never built to play rugby league and I had grave doubts about the whole venture. I said 'No, no, no,' and they left. That was the end of it.

When I look back, I realise more and more how lucky I was to play in rugby union. It was a game that catered for tall and small, fat and slim, characters and quieter ones; all types of humanity. It was a game for everyone. Yes, there were weaknesses, but you covered those and that was the secret of the game. That is what made it such a great sport.

I use the past tense deliberately because I don't think it is a great game anymore. The game then was based on fun at a social level and attack at the higher levels. Both values have been totally compromised in the modern professional game. A defensive game is not an attractive one and a game shorn of the fun element is also a poor shadow of what it was.

I don't, in fact, believe it will ever be possible for rugby football to recapture those great times, because not only is it now professional, but society has changed forever, too. Communities are not as strong and attitudes have altered. You don't have the family values now that you used to have and how many one-parent families are there out there? How many non-working mothers do you have today? Rugby football has changed because society has. At the end of the day, the game can only reflect and mirror society, but rugby certainly hasn't changed for the better and I don't think you'd find anybody who would seriously dispute that assertion.

Players are fitter, faster, stronger and bigger in the modern professional game. Forwards handle like backs, backs tackle like forwards, but so what? It has not led to a better game. It's not a game for the likes of Gerald Davies, Barry John or Phil Bennett today – and how sad is that? How can a sport have isolated players of smaller stature, who had the most brilliant skills and who provided endless entertainment for supporters throughout the world, so completely? Players like that couldn't survive in the modern game, because they would be smashed to pieces.

So now all we have is a game played by huge men, whether they are forwards or three-quarters, all trying to bash into each other and win a bruising physical contest between two teams with fifteen men strung out across the pitch marking each other. Yes, this may be a different game and some marketing men may say they are attracting new supporters and a younger element. They may be, I don't know. But what those people don't tell you is what rugby football has lost through this transformation. No one talks about the absence of these wonderfully talented players who lit up the entire sport.

It is a game, furthermore, with a completely different emphasis. Everything is now about profit. No one speaks of the obscene amounts of money flushing through the system at the top level, or the dire straits the sport is in at the junior level. Nor do people talk of the huge sums of money that are being paid to players, all of which is disappearing out of the sport, through their pockets. I'm sorry, but that isn't the game I knew, loved and played for twenty-three years. In fact, it has little in common with it. How professionalism has changed the game of rugby football is a theme close to my heart and one I shall return to.

CHAPTER 12

We Didn't Even Know About Bananas

I got up one morning and had a hell of a shock. My knees were creaking, the shoulder muscles cracked. 'What on earth is going on?' I asked my wife Penny. 'Er, old age,' she suggested, helpfully. I could see she had a point. I had been retired for five years from the international game, but had continued to play for my club, Ballymena. By now, though, I was forty and had been in the first team for twenty-three seasons. In fact, I had played in four decades for the club; I started in the 1950s and finished in 1980. I was lucky because I'd had no serious injuries, apart from that break while playing against France back in 1962. But when you reach your late thirties and the watershed of forty as a rugby player, recovery is a big problem. By the time I quit I found I was struggling to recover from a match in time for the one the following week. Some days, I could hardly get out of bed. Training was no help. All that was doing was making me even more tired.

There was another thing about it that I didn't like. You had young whippersnappers coming up against you and clearly thinking they could sort out this old man. They seemed to regard the prospect of knocking my head off, because of who I was, as great sport. I thought otherwise. When you get to that age, you don't like being knocked about and jostled around too much because it hurts for another week. But one day in a match we played in Galway, this problem became a serious issue.

One guy had tried to intimidate me straight from the kick-off and I'd warned him a few times about what might happen. I was later told someone in his club had put him up to it. I had hoped the warning would be enough to end it, but it didn't make the slightest difference. He was pulling my jersey when I went to jump for the ball in the line-out, obstructing me and things like that. Worst of all, he refused to get the message. So when it happened once again, I belted him. Now I was never a dirty player and it took a lot to persuade me to act, but once I hit people, they generally knew about it. The trouble was, on this occasion I hit him so hard he had bleeding in his head. I was seriously worried.

I pretty much decided there and then that it was time to retire. The game was beginning to change anyway, and quite dramatically. Some players in national teams were starting to experiment by eating all these funny foods to get them fitter, leaner or mentally more alert or whatever it was. I looked at all this and thought to myself, 'In my day we didn't even know about bananas.' So I finally hung up my boots. Lots more time with the family, Saturday afternoons out in the garden, quiet Saturday evenings at home rather than beside the bar at the club – that sort of thing.

The day I retired at Ballymena, as that creaking, groaning forty-year-old, I felt the game at that level was still pretty much what it had been the first day I walked into it. It was still full of good, honest, physical, healthy competition, clubs were filled with decent people and it provided young men with a wonderful springboard for life. One of the customs of those times at Ballymena was that win, lose or draw, you always sought out your opposite number after a match and took him into the bar to buy him a drink or two.

We had a happy hour after every game at the club. It usually went on well into the evening, during which time we would have fun, sing songs and share a meal with the opposing team. Perhaps the nicest thing was that the opposition would stay with us during the evening, so you had this great feeling that rugby football was doing what it always did best, namely bringing young people together in convivial surroundings and getting them to relate to one another. The same system operated at other clubs when we went away, too.

To me, one of the greatest tragedies of the modern game is that all that has gone. Players play the game and just clear off among themselves. They don't bother to mix with the opposition and I think that's sad, because that's when you create friendships. Those were great years at Ballymena, made special by such traditional practices, and I was enormously encouraged to see they still survived in 1980, when I finished playing, even though professionalism has wiped all that away from the entire top tier of the game.

By the time I quit, they had started to bring in all those fancy line-out calls, which you hear in every game today. You know the sort of thing. 'Geronimo,' some burly hooker shouts out and a certain player knows the line-out ball will be thrown to him. But while I was still playing club rugby, total confusion usually reigned over such calls. That was because by the time we had got out on to the field no one could quite remember whether 'Marilyn Monroe' meant that the ball would be thrown into the middle part of the line-out, or that some tasty blond had just been spotted in the crowd by one of the forwards.

One day Joe Graham, who was one of our little props and who was always a quiet guy, was asked while he was standing at the bar where we were with some of the line-out codes. 'PCR,' he replied. 'PCR?' we asked. 'What the hell does that mean?' 'We've had the pressure outside, we've had the control of the ball and now we're at R, which is relaxation,' he said, clutching his pint of Guinness. There wasn't really a lot you could say to that.

No sooner had I retired, than they asked me if I'd coach Ballymena, so I did that for a while and found I enjoyed it. Then Ulster, my province, asked me to coach them. I seemed to be gathering coaching jobs like a child gathering daisies in a summer field, but that led to some fascinating experiences around Europe. Ulster rugby at that time was at a bit of a low ebb. Like an idiot, I casually mentioned to someone in a clubhouse that I wouldn't mind taking away a young squad of Ulstermen, to try and build something for the future. Just a short tour somewhere. 'Maybe the South of France,' said Penny hopefully, when I told her about it when I got home. Well, it didn't take long for the phone to ring. Ulster were keen on the idea, all right. The venue? Lovely St Tropez, or Monte Carlo perhaps? 'They must play rugby there, surely,' said Penny. The answer? Er, Romania. Funny thing, that – Penny seemed to lose interest straightaway.

We planned to play three games in ten days and took a party of twenty-two players, which had been slimmed down from an original list of sixty. Now remember, this was 1980, when the dictator Ceausescu was still building concrete palaces to his memory all over the country while his people starved. So, following the Boy Scouts' maxim of 'Be prepared' we planned accordingly. Two stone in weight of Mars bars were loaded on to the plane with the rest of our luggage. 'Going trekking up Everest?' someone asked, helpfully, at the airport.

I had a contact at Bushmills whisky and we took three cases of their special nectar. To drink among ourselves, on a rugby tour, I hear you ask, incredulously? No, to bribe the local officials, of course, because that was how the system worked in the Eastern bloc. I figured that a bottle of Bushmills might gain us all kinds of advantages. Why, we might even get an extra lump of cold luncheon meat for supper one night.

I joke not. When we eventually reached Bucharest after travelling from Belfast, they took us to this place. I wouldn't call it a hotel. I went up to the little room I had been allocated and it had a brass bed, which was all right; we were tired, so I slept, but there was no restaurant or anything there. We stayed there for three days and every day they came and collected us, so we piled into this old bus with hard, wooden seats and they took us, clattering and clanking, out to an army camp, where there was supposed to be food. Always keep your soldiers happy by making sure at least they get fed – the first rule of a communist dictator.

We sat down at some long trestle tables in this canteen. On the plates were five pieces of what they called black bread. Then they came and poured some coloured water, which they called tea, into the mugs. Then other pieces of bread arrived, but there was no butter, jam, sugar, milk or anything like that. The bread was hard and some dubious-looking meat was eventually presented, drowned in a nasty-looking grey liquid, which I tried hard to convince myself was gravy as I ate it – because you had to eat it; you just didn't know when you might get anything else to fill your stomach.

The next meal we were given there consisted of gherkins and spam. Of course, the boys got fed up with it fairly quickly. On the second evening, when we trooped into this grim-looking canteen, nothing happened for a while. The boys picked up their knives and forks and banged them on the table, chanting, 'We want food. We want food.' Then some bread arrived, which bore an uncanny resemblance to the previous day's offering. Now, being a bit of a wily old bird, I'd had a suspicion that the day before we'd been given old bread and I'd quietly put a cross on the bottom of one piece with my pen. I said to the boys, 'Hey, that bread was here yesterday,' and they said, 'How do you know?' So I said I'd prove it. I picked it up and almost pulled a muscle, it was so heavy. It was definitely confirmed as yesterday's when I turned one bun over and there was my cross on the bottom. One day they told us we were having soup for lunch, which sounded promising. It was coloured soup, like a consomme, but it wasn't quite as thick as consomme . . . We lived like this for ten days. It was unbelievable.

Rugby in Romania in those days was not played by actual clubs, but chiefly by the army, the universities, the plumbers, the electricians. That was the way it worked. So if there was a match between the plumbers and the electricians and the showers didn't work and the shed had no lighting, well, you were in the best of company to get it all fixed up. We won our first game against Dinamo Bucharest, which was a tough match. Then they took us to the venue for the next game, which turned out to be about three hundred miles away by bus, only twenty miles from the border with the USSR. It was a university city. They were very kind to us and they tried hard, but the meal we had that night looked as though it had been transported from the previous canteen in Bucharest.

The night before the game in this university city, the president of the Ulster branch, the manager, myself and one or two others were invited to a lecturer's room at the university for a meal, but it wasn't much different. Probably more vodka, but no more food. Towards the end of the gherkins and spam course, a man came in, walked up to me and said, 'Mr Willie, it's wonderful to have you here and we really want to look after you. Is there anything you would like?' Trying hard to keep a straight face, I said, 'Well, there is just one thing I really would like and that's a bowl of vanilla ice-cream.' My friend said, 'Mr Willie, I will go immediately.' He was as good as his word. He went immediately through the swing doors in the room. But he never came back. That was twenty-three years ago. I figured he was probably shot, poor chap, when he went into the kitchen and asked for vanilla ice-cream.

Every day there was a problem with food. One day on the bus, I asked if we were going to stop and eat and they said, 'Oh, Mr Willie [no, it wasn't the same guy], we've got half a kitchen in the back of the bus.' When we did stop and they got out the food, we discovered a small misunderstanding in their translation. It was actually half a chicken – between twenty-seven hungry men. Our last match was against an electricians' association. We beat them and were invited to an after-match get-together. There was no food again, of course, nor any beer. The only thing they had to drink was vodka. Personally, I don't like vodka, and if you drink it after eighty minutes of exertion, you are drunk within about thirty seconds. So the situation declined fairly rapidly. I remember the local players standing around, watching bemusedly, as our guys got more and more silly. Daft rugby songs, laughing and giggling – the opposition were scratching their heads and obviously thinking to themselves what strange people we were.

I had a brilliant time coaching Ulster. We turned things around so well that in the early 1980s, we beat Wellington, the touring New Zealand provincial champions, at Ravenhill, and then the following year, by which time I was chairman of the Ulster selectors, toppled the touring Australians. Ulster then went on to win six inter-provincial titles. It was a great era, which produced some super players from Northern Ireland. In 1982, when Ireland won the coveted Triple Crown, we contributed players like Trevor Ringland and David Irwin to the Irish team. Both men were to go on and win places on the 1983 British Lions tour of New Zealand. Keith Crossan from Instonians was another who appeared in the Irish side that season.

Towards the end of 1982, speculation began to mount as to the likely management team for the Lions tour to New Zealand the following year. They were to play eighteen matches, the same as the 1980 Lions in South Africa. But Lions tours can be decided by all sorts of strange things. Earlier I talked about how early Lions tours were bedevilled by poor selection and by the selectors' apparent determination to choose 'the right sort of chaps' to represent British and Irish rugby. That seemed to be the chief criteria, but at least by 1980 we had moved on from that scenario, although weird decisions still occurred. The first came when a senior official from the game had a chat with me and suggested I become one of the candidates to coach the Lions. Now this hit me like a wet fish across the face. I was only coaching Ulster at the time; what about the coaches of the four home unions, which was the traditional hunting ground for Lions selectors to find a coach ? Did that mean they were less than thrilled at the talents of those available?

Since Beaumont's team had returned from South Africa in 1980, there had certainly been some unusual outcomes to the Five Nations Championship. Not in 1981, because France won it and took the Grand Slam by beating every other nation, but in 1982, Ireland won the championship for only the second time in thirty-one years and the following year, 1983, Ireland shared the title with France. The traditional strong nations, like Wales and England, were no more than also-rans in those years.

Anyway, against this background I was called for an interview to the East India Club in London, which was where the home unions habitually resided. Social airs and graces may have been collapsing for years outside the heavy doors of the St James's club in Pall Mall, but inside it was as though Singapore had not yet fallen and the king still reigned. Old gentlemen were gently woken to be told that dinner was now being served or peered suspiciously over their copies of the *Daily Telegraph* and *The Times* when a newcomer dared enter the hallowed surrounds, a tie and jacket were always required to eat in the dining room. There's nothing wrong in my mind with maintaining decent standards in society, but you could say this was like stepping back into the days of Empire.

I had quite a good interview, ostensibly for the role of coach to the Lions, but was somewhat surprised to be telephoned a few days later by a member of the committee and asked if I would consider not being coach after all, but manager. I asked who they had in mind as coach and they told me it was Jim Telfer of Scotland. I knew Jim well enough from playing against him for many years, but also from touring with him as a Lion in 1966 and 1968. I told the committee member I was prepared to go along with that idea and within a few hours he had telephoned back to say I had been appointed manager.

Soon, Jim and I had met and written down the names of a hundred possible candidates for the thirty places available on the 1983 Lions tour. Of course, you always leave room on your list for those players who come through unexpectedly and simply demand inclusion by their excellent form, but we needed a nucleus of people and set out to try and find them. However, some dark clouds were building up in our particular sky.

England finished last in the Championship that season and they had changed their captain from Steve Smith to John Scott halfway through the season. Scotland, who lost three of their four games, changed their captain from Roy Laidlaw to Jim Aitken after the first three games. Wales had a middling sort of season, winning twice, drawing once and losing once. Eddie Butler had remained captain throughout, but hardly struck us as a potential Lions captain. Ireland had the best of it, in terms of the home unions, beating Scotland, France and England, although they lost to Wales. Thus, Ciaran Fitzgerald, the Irish captain, became a strong contender to skipper the Lions, because he'd shown his leadership qualities.

One other man would have been an obvious Lions captain: Peter Wheeler of England. But England had finished bottom of the championship and with Ireland winning it, there seemed little reason to ignore Fitzgerald's claims. Furthermore, when Ireland beat England 25–15 in Dublin, Fitzgerald had taken three strikes against the head from a pack that included Wheeler, so how could we justify taking Wheeler ahead of Fitzgerald? Colin Deans of Scotland was the other candidate and he was playing well, but in terms of the Lions party, England's demise during the season was seriously bad news. Slemen, Dodge, Smith, Wheeler, Blakeway,

Syddall and Scott could all have expected to make the tour, but in the end none of them did, although Smith did join us late on, as a replacement.

Besides this, there was an even more serious difficulty with which we were grappling. For quality, I would say it was the worst Five Nations Championship we had seen in years. Wales and England drew 13–all in Cardiff and thirty old women would have provided a better spectacle. It was awful. Scotland weren't great, either, and Ireland were the best of a bad bunch, so it became an extremely difficult selection. How we longed for some supreme talent of the kind that had hallmarked the 1971 and 1974 Lions parties. Alas, there were precious few like that this time.

The choice of captain was discussed for hours, but we couldn't get past Fitzgerald. I felt I knew his qualities. Primarily, he was best at taking the team on to the field, handling the final build-up and the motivational aspect on the day. Jim Telfer was a very organised guy and there was, and is, no one as genuine in rugby football, so I thought to myself, this will all work.

How wrong I was to be, but the fact was, even when we were at the selection stage, we weren't bubbling, because nothing had come out of the Five Nations Championship that suggested we were about to go to New Zealand and beat the All Blacks. I knew from personal experience that requires a very special group of players. I knew we didn't have that this time, but just hoped we could forge a really special, close-knit group, a unit maybe without stars, but one that would prove the match of the Blacks.

One player I felt we did need on the field in New Zealand was the big English lock forward Maurice Colclough, but he had a knee injury and would have to get fit on the tour. We were told it would take three weeks, so we decided to live with that. If you have quality available everywhere, you don't need to go down that road. The player isn't fit, so he doesn't tour. But we didn't enjoy such a luxury for this Lions tour.

The news got worse and worse. At the medical testing in London when we all joined up, it was found that our other key lock, Donal Lenihan, had a hernia and he was sent home. This wasn't news to Donal; it was something he had played with for almost two years. He had planned to get through the Lions tour and then have it fixed, but he was sent home, much to the shock of everyone, myself included. Mick Molloy, the Irish team doctor and my former playing colleague, rang me and said, 'This is a nonsense,' but the decision had been made and we'd lost probably our top lock, given his outstanding form that season.

What we also found when we got to New Zealand was that there was an anti-Ciaran Fitzgerald thing in the English section of our own media. They had wanted Wheeler there as hooker and captain. They couldn't accept Fitzgerald, especially after Wheeler had been omitted in favour of Deans, but this was our media being anti, so no prizes for guessing what the New Zealand media picked on straightaway. As if that lot wasn't enough to be worrying about, 1983 was also the time of the first rumblings of professionalism. There was the Kerry Packer plan to set up a rugby circus and all sorts of players were alleged to have signed up for it. Several Lions were said to be involved and you could hardly say that helped the tour go smoothly or successfully. Once again, the New Zealand media had a field day.

At one stage, so much material was being written in the papers about rebel tours and players who were supposed to have signed up for however much money that the tour seemed almost incidental. It was an extraordinary situation. I called a press conference and told the guys this had to stop. I said that if any of them had the slightest evidence that a member of the Lions party was definitely involved in any commercial circus, then I wanted to share that information and would take appropriate action. But if not, I said, please let us get on with the tour and concentrate on the rugby in front of us, not some hypothetical occurrence somewhere else in the world.

Of course, no one produced a shred of evidence and that did calm things down for a while, but it had been highly disruptive. Meanwhile, on the field, things were going just as badly. Terry Holmes, sure to be a key man at scrum half, got injured and had to go home. Nigel Melville, his replacement, was injured before he had even completed his first game and also had to be replaced. Steve Smith took his place. Replacements arrived at regular intervals, like buses along an Auckland street. Eddie Butler, Nick Jeavons, Ginger McLoughlin and even Donal Lenihan flew out, as several of our key forwards, like Jeff Squire, went down like flies.

But another aspect of it all troubled me. While Jim Telfer's style of coaching was tremendous in the build-up to a game, he was also doing everything right up to the last minute; in other words, virtually taking the team on to the field. By doing so, he wasn't allowing Fitzgerald as captain to do what he was good at. Suddenly, I found Jim would be leading them through events on the day of the match, taking them to the dressing room and instructing them, right up until kick-off time.

Because of Telfer's domination, Fitzgerald's role became meaningless. All he did was just trot out on the field first. It wasn't working, so I confronted Jim over it. I pointed out he wasn't being fair to Fitzgerald, who was already under huge pressure from the media, but Jim told me that was the way they did it in Scotland and it was the only way he knew how to do it. They had always done it that way and he couldn't change now. Anyone who knows Jim Telfer is aware that one thing you cannot do is change his mind. I made my point, I warned him it could all end in tears, but I knew nothing would change in that respect because of the nature of the man. Sadly, I was right.

I had learned long ago that you give the locals nothing when you tour a country like New Zealand. By that I mean don't offer them a thing with which to come back at you on the rugby field. But our media blundered straight into the trap without even thinking. They wrote endlessly that Fitzgerald could not even throw straight into line-outs and, lo and behold, the local referees began to pick up on this. So then they began to penalise him even when his throws were straight. It became absurd.

At another stage of the tour, there was a fresh problem caused by the New Zealand media. A local rugby writer rang me and said it had been alleged that our back row forward Eddie Butler had herpes. What had really happened was that Eddie's skin had rubbed in the first match he'd played, because it was his first game for sometime. You got this rash sometimes when you started pre-season rugby training and that was all Eddie was suffering from, but the local media wanted to spread a story that he had herpes. The guy wrote in the paper that the All Blacks might refuse to play the next match because of fears about this alleged condition. It was just another of the tricks the locals used to get up to in order to get any sort of advantage over the touring team, but this was the nonsense we were up against all the time. Of course, we had run into this sort of stuff before in New Zealand, but never as bad as this. This was real venom. Frankly, it soured almost the entire tour.

When we got home after losing the Test series 4–0, as well as losing to the Auckland and Canterbury provincial sides, some players, like Ollie Campbell of Ireland, John Rutherford of Scotland and Bob Norster of Wales, said they had learned a lot of valuable lessons. Other players just breathed a sigh of relief it was all over. Some came back bloody annoyed – and they were the guys you wanted in the team.

I wrote a long report after that tour about the mistakes of the itinerary, the value of proper preparation and the lessons that should be learned in all sorts of ways. I said I would be willing to go and talk to the management of the next Lions tour so that there could be some continuity as to the problems we had faced and how they might be anticipated and solved before the next tour got under way. I didn't hold my breath, waiting to hear back from the home unions.

I never did, of course, and I'm sure that today that report is stuck somewhere in a drawer, quietly gathering dust. I'm also willing to bet it was never referred to again. I certainly never heard any more about it.

Of the players, there were a few who came through it all as outstanding men. Ollie Campbell, for example, was superb. It was a shame that he and John Rutherford were vying for the same position in the Test team, but in some ways we sorted that out by putting John at centre in the third Test. Both were good footballers and men with the right attitude, something you couldn't say for so many of the rest. Sadly, too, we lost Terry Holmes so early on. Little Roy Laidlaw was a one hundred per cent player and a superb tourist, but he just didn't have the high quality we needed once Holmes departed.

Dusty Hare was invaluable from a place-kicking point of view, but he had very little attacking instinct, as I'm sure he would confirm. Hugo MacNeill was hit and miss. He could be brilliant or terrible. Robert Ackerman was a hundred per cent committed, but very young and just didn't have the mental balance required to handle a tour like that. I think he was probably homesick for much of the time. Roger Baird, Trevor Ringland and John Carleton gave their utmost, and David Irwin was a one hundred per cent player. Michael Kiernan didn't really show his best and only had about two good games. He could have been a good player, but he lost confidence. Clive Woodward didn't count. He never contested a place for the Test side and really, in many ways, didn't want to know about the tough stuff, yet he had been on the previous Lions tour, in 1980, and should have been one of the key guys on tour. However, he wasn't near the Test team at any stage, because he seemed disinterested and played as though he was. Why? That's Clive.

Of course, Clive has been an extremely successful English manager with the intelligence to know that his success is based on having a strong team around him. As he said when he was approached about coaching the 2005 Lions in New Zealand, he would want to take his back-up team with him, key men like Andy Robinson and Phil Larder, who have done such good work. Clive has successfully convinced the RFU to pour millions of pounds into the senior squad and by winning the World Cup he has proved he was right, but unfortunately none of the other home unions can afford to put that sort of money into their national sides.

Of the Lions forwards in 1983, too many were not up to it – Bainbridge, Boyle, Beattie, Butler, Jeavons, Jones and Milne. Price was steady, Paxton also did quite well, but Winterbottom was all right, nothing special. As for Colclough, sadly he wasn't up to it at all. He didn't want to know about the physical stuff, which is a hell of a disadvantage when you're on a tour of New Zealand. Lenihan came out too late; McLoughlin should probably have been there from the start and we could have got him properly fit. Norster played well and was one of our few strengths. Jim Calder was limited as a player, but none could doubt his one hundred per cent determination. I admired, too, the way Fitzgerald stuck gamely at what became an impossible task. He took all manner of stick, but kept his head up and kept playing. Deans was solid and performed well.

Someone else who gave everything he had was John O'Driscoll. He, too, earned my admiration. I remember against Auckland, he was injured twice. He scattered someone at one stage in the match, the player, the ball, everything. Afterwards, in the dressing room, he asked our doctor to have a look at his side. There was a nodule on it. John had cracked a rib and it was literally protruding. He had played with that for over half an hour. It must have been total agony, but he never complained. It was during that time I saw him scatter that opponent, but John was that sort of a player. If we'd had fifteen like him, we'd have beaten the All Blacks hands down.

Even so, we should have won the first Test in Christchurch. If Ackerman had given the unmarked Ringland the ball instead of trying to score himself, we would have won, but a New Zealand team that was not much better than us scraped home, 16–12. We also lost Holmes and Ike Stephens through injury in that match. When Squire was also invalided out of the tour, we had lost our first-choice men at scrum half, prop, lock (Lenihan) and No. 8. These were blows from which we never recovered, simply because we did not have sufficient quality replacements available.

New Zealand was, as ever, a harsh, unforgiving land on the rugby fields. Nigel Melville was hit a cowardly illegal blow that ended his tour, while Fitzgerald was stamped on and kicked to pieces in another game. This, we were told, was part of the game; he should have got away from the ball. Or so the locals said, but I remember Ciaran's back and it was in an unbelievable state.

After that particular game, I asked the local media to come to my hotel room so that we could study the incident together. They were not a brave bunch of men; only one did. The rest didn't want to know, because they believed that anything on the ground in New Zealand was bloody good meat. They had this thing about rucking the ball and I had no trouble with that. I'd toured there enough times to know the ways of their world. But the video of this particular incident showed our captain a good three yards away from where the ball was. Nevertheless, he was stamped upon and kicked to pieces. I'm sorry, I played the game as hard as the next man, but that had nothing to do with rugby football or any sport. It was out-and-out thuggishness, nothing more, nothing less.

Jim Telfer's total, almost fanatical, commitment to the cause was meritorious in one sense, but counter-productive in another, because, in the end, too many of our players who went on to the field on match day were exhausted before they even got there. They had trained far too hard. Certainly, before the last Test in Auckland, we trained too much the day before. Whose fault was that? I have to say it was Jim's. He had this thing that the players had to be fit. The trouble is, when you're on a tour like that, some guys can take it, others can't. Jim wanted his players to work, work, work. He couldn't ease off. I said to him on that Friday morning that the guys looked tired and probably only needed a short, half-hour workout and then rest before the Test the next day, but Jim couldn't see that. He gave them a hell of a session lasting over an hour and a half. So when they went out the next day, they looked and played like they were shattered. Our team was exhausted. They had nothing to give and we lost, 38–6, a crushing defeat. It meant we had been white-washed in the Test series – my worst nightmare. It was 1966 once more, something I had never wanted to be a part of ever again.

Of course, as was always the case then, the authorities in the four home unions had accepted a ridiculous playing itinerary. We warmed up for the crucial third Test by playing Canterbury, almost invariably the toughest provincial team of the lot. We had played the mighty Auckland in only our second game of the tour, losing 13–12, which was the sort of early setback the New Zealand rugby authorities had doubtless hoped we would experience. Like our own media, our rugby authorities played into their hands. When it comes to planning Lions tours and looking at aspects like playing schedules, you really need people who understand all these things, otherwise the locals will ride roughshod over you every time.

I found the whole tour a very frustrating exercise personally. I learned a lot of things from it, but I didn't enjoy the role I had been given. On most of my other Lions tours, I had been a key player and therefore a voice to be heard. I could propose ideas and pass on views. But as manager, I felt detached from that playing process. I didn't feel it was my role to interfere very much with the policy of the coach or captain. They had to be left to run the tour as best they saw fit. That was how it had been in 1971 when Carwyn James and John Dawes were in harness as coach and captain; likewise, Syd Millar and myself in 1974 in South Africa. Doug Smith and Alan Thomas, the managers of those two tours, did not interfere and, as a player, I had applauded that policy. Now, I could hardly throw everything I had believed in out of the window by seizing control of playing matters. I had to virtually sit and watch it all unfold, which I did not enjoy.

So, in a sense, my life with the Lions had come full circle. I knew it was the end of my involvement with one of the great institutions of British sport. It had been twenty-one years from the time I went to South Africa in 1962 as a twenty-two-year-old, hoping against hope to earn a place in the Test team. That had been followed by the disappointment of 1966, the fun of 1968 and the success of 1971, culminating in the great triumph of 1974. Then, lastly, there had been 1983, which sadly was a huge disappointment. Nevertheless, when I looked back on those years of association with the Lions, I felt thrilled and privileged to have been involved. I have always regarded it as a wonderful part of my life.

CHAPTER 13

The Old Soldier Who Shouldn't Have Gone Back

am sometimes asked my definition of an Ulsterman. I would say he is a guy who has principles that he cherishes and holds onto from his childhood to the grave. I am a very proud Ulsterman, but my roots and ancestors were Scottish, from the Borders region. They came to Northern Ireland during the Ulster Plantation and the old McBride home is a place called Mottram House at Moneyglass. That is where the original McBrides of my connection were and they were carpenters, which explains my proficiency at matters of a DIY nature! Moneyglass, by the way, is near Toomebridge, which is where I was brought up. It is ten miles on the south side of Ballymena. There would be a lot of the Ulster Plantation folk, or at least their offspring, around Ballymena. They were thrifty, well-to-do people.

Doubtless you have heard all the stories about the dour Ulsterman who is never beaten and will always rise again. Well, I don't know about the dour part, but I do know that I have qualities of determination in my blood. That time in New Zealand proved it, when Canterbury punched and kicked the living daylights out of me. There were days when you came off the rugby field with such aches and pains that you didn't know whether to sit down, stand up or stand on your head. Knees, elbows, fists, feet, everything went on the rugby field, but as far as I was concerned, I would never bow the knee to any assailant or opponent. That's not to say I never respected an opponent, because I did. But I was never prepared to give second best to him, and I'm sure that is a trait of a true Ulsterman.

Another trait of an Ulsterman is that he is always prepared to accept a challenge. Thus, after I had got back from the 1983 Lions tour, I felt I still had a lot of rugby left in me from the point of view of coaching and other aspects. I was ready for another challenge. I thoroughly enjoyed my time as coach and then chairman of selectors for Ulster. Rugby had been so good to me and I felt that I was at last giving something back to the game. But then I was asked whether I would be prepared to let my name go forward as possible coach of Ireland and, stupidly, I agreed. It was to lead to some of the unhappiest times I had ever known during my long association with Irish rugby. To this day, I still scratch my head in amazement that it turned out that way.

Trouble started immediately, because I was elected to the job by only a single vote. The fact was that, deep in my mind, I think I knew I really wasn't ready for it. I had only coached Ulster for two years by that time and felt you needed more time in the role to become a national coach. The way I saw it, Ireland asked me and I felt I couldn't and wouldn't let them down. However, if I'd sat down and thought it through I should have known that someone of greater coaching experience was required at that time, because after the successful 1982 and 1983 seasons, Ireland's national side was in transition.

So now, as the 1983–4 season began, an era was ending. Good, valuable men such as Duggan, Slattery, Keane and Lenihan were finishing. Inevitably, the road ahead would have a good few potholes in it. Quite quickly, I found that the selectors would not back me a hundred per cent in my choice of certain players. I wanted to bring in new players, like Keith Crossan and Nigel Carr, but was out-voted in committee. The selectors would not bite the bullet on personnel. Slattery was ill that season, but they kept holding open a place for him, saying let's wait, he may recover. In fact, he only played one game, against France. Ginger McLoughlin was not fit, either, but they didn't want to admit it. The same applied to Duggan, yet he played the whole Five Nations Championship. You could see he wasn't training properly and was terribly unfit, so it all became very frustrating for me.

Then one day, half-way through the season, one of the selectors who had voted for me, Jimmy Donaldson, took me aside and told me he wanted to resign. He'd had enough of it. I said, 'For God's sake don't do that, Jimmy, because it will cause even more problems than we already have.' He stayed, but the situation didn't improve. In fact, it got worse, because if you don't have a selection committee that is united, there is absolutely no way you are going to have a common approach and find harmony. There must be accord in the selection process. Without that, you descend into the kind of mess we slowly succumbed to that year. We lost every game in the Five Nations Championship.

I was appointed near the start of the 1983–4 season, which meant there was very little preparation time available. I put in place the concept of having a few training weekends, meeting up on a Saturday evening and working together through the Sunday, but it created all sorts of frustrations. Players would phone up on Saturday evenings and say they weren't coming, because they'd picked up an injury playing for their club or province that day. However, they forgot one thing. I was an old rugby soldier who had tramped through more trenches than they'd had hot dinners. I knew the ruses and the saw the situation as clearly as writing on a wall. They'd played for Ireland for several years, represented the Lions in many cases and played countless numbers of times for their provinces. The idea of slogging up to Dublin on a Saturday night in winter for more training the next day was anathema. They'd suddenly acquire a hamstring strain and that kept them in their warm beds the next morning. But it gave us enormous problems, because having gone all the way to Dublin we might find that two or three members of our intended front row had pulled out. So how on earth could you practise scrummaging properly without such key personnel?

One thing I wanted to do before we got started was bring in a backs coach. I knew I could organise the forwards, but felt the need to have a specialist backs coach, working alongside me. I saw it as the future for international rugby squads and I don't think time has proved me wrong. I talked to Johnny Moloney, with whom I'd toured South Africa as a 1974 British Lion, and he was enthusiastic, but when I went to the Irish Rugby Football Union about it there was a completely opposite attitude, because officialdom in Dublin frowned on too many people getting involved.

I smile to myself when I look at a current programme for an Irish home game and see job titles such as director of referee development, referee development officer, rugby development officers (twelve of them), national coach development manager, elite player development manager, director of rugby development and rugby administrator. There seems to me to be a hell of a lot of developing going on in Irish rugby these days. What it will lead to, and perhaps more pertinently what it is all costing, are other questions.

I was left very much on my own within the corridors of power of the IRFU. There wasn't really anyone I could go and talk to, openly and honestly, about the situation. The reason for that was the background to my original selection, so you could never be sure whether the person you were talking to was for or against you. I was aware of that the whole time and it was a sad year. The following story encapsulates what went on at that time.

During the season, I asked one of our national selectors if he would go and watch a certain player with a view to international selection and report back at our next meeting. When the time came for the meeting, he sat in front of everyone and gave us his report about the player and the game. It was full of information and opinions. The only trouble was, the player had never played in this game and what the national selector was telling us all was completely inaccurate. He clearly didn't know I was someone who did my homework and had contacts. I knew immediately after the game that the player in question hadn't played, but the selector told us the player hadn't done well and was not, in his view, an international in the making. I just sat and looked at him. I couldn't believe what I was hearing, but it confirmed for me that my position was fast becoming hopeless. If a fellow selector is prepared to lie to you, then you have no chance. Nor does the national team.

After that meeting I drove home with Jimmy Donaldson and the two of us were absolutely stunned by what had happened. I believed that they just wanted to get rid of me as national coach. It seemed far more important to these people than seeing Ireland winning rugby internationals. I found that sad. It was a terrible indictment of jealousy, petty rivalry and getting your priorities totally wrong.

I was ill equipped to handle any of this stuff. I hadn't coached enough and was also insufficiently experienced to handle the political side of affairs, which you invariably get in these national rugby unions. I needed more time to prepare myself for such a role, but the trouble was I didn't have more time to give in my life. It was either going to be then or never as far as I was concerned, because my increasingly senior role as a bank manager required a great deal of my time. Then, as well as that, there were my wife and children. When you consider that I was driving up and down to Dublin every time there was a meeting or the national squad got together, and that the round-trip was between 250 and 300 miles could take anything up to seven or eight hours, you will understand my problem.

Not least of my difficulties was the distinct impression which I got at several stages during that season that certain players who were loyal to Mick Doyle, my beaten rival, were reporting back to him on what we had done and my plans for the season. That was a horrible feeling for a national coach to have. Some of the players lacked proper commitment.

However, the reason we were whitewashed in that 1984 Five Nations season was not all due to what was going on in the corridors of selection, bad as that was. Some of the players lacked proper commitment, too. You could tell they didn't have their hearts and souls in it, but they weren't prepared to call it a day and walk away, when it was apparent that they should have. It was blindingly obvious to me that we needed to change the team, to install traditional Irish fighting qualities of guts, determination and fierce commitment. We might not have produced a team of world-beaters but, by God, we'd have had men cheerfully prepared to go out and die for the cause.

The problem was that, by the mid-1980s, standards were being cracked up quite significantly in terms of preparation, fitness and attitude. You couldn't mess around any more and expect to get by when you were maybe 70 per cent fit. But the players the committee settled on were not all prepared to front up and be honest. That, I regret to say, led to conflict between them and myself.

The sides I had to accept, in conjunction with my selection committee, never once had the right qualities. All that happened was that results on the field reflected the discord off it. We got thrashed 32–9 by Scotland in Dublin, lost to Wales also at Lansdowne Road and went down to France, in Paris and to England at Twickenham, although England only squeezed home 12–9. There was no getting away from the fact, though, that we were a poor side and badly prepared. The players lacked time, preparation and interest. Perhaps you could say motivation, too, and for that I must hold up my hands. No coach is ever blameless when things go wrong on the field, but what angered me was that I never once saw the Irish team I personally would have selected run onto the field. Had that been the case and had we still lost every game, then I would have been the first to walk the gangplank. I would have had my chance and accepted I had got it wrong, but it's very hard taking the blame when you have not been allowed to select the side you want in the first place.

There was one other problem. With hindsight, I believe I was just too close to that generation of players. I had played for some years with people like Moss Keane, Willie Duggan and Fergus Slattery, so when I came in as coach, I wasn't sufficiently remote. If I tried to crack the whip, they probably saw me as one of their old touring buddies and perhaps resented it. If it had been a new generation of players, there may have been more respect in time, once I had demonstrated my qualities to them. What I should have had was three more years of coaching at provincial level. Long enough to give me greater expertise, but also to see the natural end of that era of players with whom I'd played.

So at the end of the day, I have to say it was the wrong decision on my part to allow my name to go forward as a contender for the job. I should have had a better realisation of my own limitations, and my own commitments in other fields, and rejected the suggestion. But although I will always concede this, I will equally always remember the disunity among some of my fellow selectors. I can honestly tell you that, even now all these years later, to realise that was the case was a real blow to me. I like to think I am one of those people who can take knocks and get on with my life and, of course, I did when Ireland sacked me after a single season in charge. Equally, though, I don't deny that the memory of those twelve months as national coach is still painful.

My only reason for getting involved all along was to put something back into Irish rugby. I was never desperate to become coach of Ireland's national rugby team – I didn't lie awake dreaming that one day the selectors would raise their finger seductively and I would go running. I was never like that and, besides, I'd had a whole career of fulfilment in rugby football. The only thing I was desperate to do was to say 'thank you' to the game, in as many ways as possible, for the wonderful times it had given me. If that was a sin, then so be it, I was a sinner, but it was my sole reason for getting involved.

Again with hindsight, that marvellous, three-dimensional trait which proves so elusive to us human beings when we need it, I believe that some people saw me as a threat when I was appointed national coach. I know that sounds absurd, but you have to understand that within these national unions, and the IRFU is by no means alone in this respect, there are all sorts of people who are empire building. For most of them, their whole reason to exist is to climb the ladder and one day become president of their national union. They fantasise about wearing the Irish blazer with the shamrock and taking tea in swanky rooms with other officials from around the world.

Perhaps when I walked through the door, a very familiar face within those circles and someone who had enjoyed so much success with the British Lions, some people thought to themselves, 'Oh no, he's bound to get above me in the pecking order.' Speaking quite frankly, this is the way so many of those people think in rugby union circles.

It wasn't just in Ireland that you came across these silly jealousies. Wales was another obvious example. How on earth was it, for instance, that one of the greatest coaches in the history of world rugby never got to coach his own country? By hook or by crook, those in power within the Welsh Rugby Union somehow made sure that the great Carwyn James never became coach of Wales. The reason? Petty jealousy. He had been acclaimed, and rightly so, after his wonderful achievements with the 1971 British Lions. It seemed absolutely inevitable that when a vacancy next occurred for the

Welsh job, Carwyn would walk into it, but it was the same old story. Some people felt threatened and doubtless feared they might lose their positions of influence if Carwyn got involved, so they managed to get together and keep him out.

The same is true, incidentally, of all manner of highly intelligent, impressive men of rugby in Wales, who could have done so much good for the game in that country had they been allowed to take positions of influence and perform to the best of their abilities. Gerald Davies was an obvious candidate in this category, but I am sure he was like me in that I never wanted to be president of the IRFU. I am not cut out for the politicking that goes with that sort of role and it certainly isn't my idea of fun to hang around for hours at cocktail parties or official dinners. I would far rather spend the evening at home with my wife beside the fire You see, people like Gerald and myself have been at the top as players and nothing can ever surpass that experience. There's no substitute for playing the game, so anything we did after that was bound to come a distant second.

I mention Carwyn James and I want to say there was one big difference between him and me. He was a great coach and a masterful motivator. I was probably never even cut out to be a coach. I certainly went into it too quickly after playing, but whatever the differences between us, we were, in my opinion, both victims of officialdom and it's ways.

Be successful today, be known as a winner and an achiever, stand tall and proud above others for where your efforts have taken you, and you stick out like a sore thumb. People immediately want to knock you down. I see this in all walks of life today and it disturbs me greatly. Why should we want to denigrate those who have succeeded? What is wrong with success if a person has achieved it through decent, proper methods? I don't expect anyone to stand up and applaud a bank robber who has made millions, but so many people in society today trouble me, because they seem to despise those who have achieved more by their own immense efforts and sense of adventure. It is silly and pathetic and I don't understand the motives of people who spend their entire lives being envious of others who have made something of themselves.

When it all ended for me as national coach, a newspaper ran a headline saying 'McBride sacked'. Doubtless in some places champagne corks were popping, but sitting in our lounge at home was a young girl with tears in her eyes. My daughter Amanda said, 'But Daddy travelled all that way down to Dublin all those times and now he's being sacked. It just isn't fair.' How do you explain that life is never 'fair' to your children?

I told her that I had not been paid a penny for the job, so I couldn't be sacked. They could throw me out, which is what had happened, but they couldn't sack me. Frankly, when it did end, I quickly realised that there was an enormous advantage to my departure. What really mattered to me was my family and I would be able to spend so much more time with them. Very quickly, I once again became part of them, rather than just an interested outsider who was hardly ever with them. I think anybody involved with rugby at that level was bound to neglect their family. It went with the territory, if you like. At one stage during that season, I hadn't seen my son, who was by then fourteen and at boarding school in Coleraine, for a month. Those were some of the things you gave up for rugby.

I was always very aware of my family. Amanda had been born in 1968, Paul in 1970, both while I was living and working up in Coleraine. Amanda was a month premature, which was a bit of a shock, but Paul arrived two months early, an even bigger surprise and one that nearly turned to tragedy. One lunchtime I went home from work and found Penny collapsed on the floor. I rushed her to hospital and Paul was nearly born in the car. He weighed just four pounds at birth and was placed in an incubator, although he never needed oxygen. Today, he's still a little weakling. He weighs only seventeen stone!

They were good children. Mind you, Penny was a superb mother who knew the right balance between love and discipline. We always tried to encourage the children and motivate them. They both attended the local primary school in Ballyclare and Amanda did quite well, passing her 11-plus and going off to the grammar school, Ballyclare High School. She got eight O levels easily, no problem, but then she came home one day and said, 'I'm not going back to school. I've had enough.' She could have got A levels and gone to university, she had the ability, but she said she wanted to do hairdressing and beauty and went to college in Belfast to get her City & Guilds certificates instead.

When Amanda was nineteen going on twenty, she went to South Africa for about five years. She ended up as manager of a styling salon in Cape Town. She got married while she was out there and now has two delightful girls, or young ladies perhaps I should say for the sake of family harmony. Shannon is ten and Kerry is eight. Amanda now works at a hairdresser in Ballyclare and is doing well. Most important of all, she is happy.

Paul went to Coleraine Academical Institution, a boarding school. Making the decision to send him there wasn't easy, but I was still heavily involved in rugby football and then there were the problems for bank managers in Northern Ireland at that time, so in a lot of ways it was healthier for him. He was no more than average academically, but the school developed his abilities and interests and he made friends there who are still like brothers to him now.

After Paul left school, he went to Botswana for about fifteen months to learn about civil engineering. When he got home, he studied the subject at Nottingham Trent University. Paul became keen on sport and played lock forward for Ballymena at one stage, but he found he couldn't compete when the game turned professional, because he had a full-time job. Today he is planning to build a house on a patch of land in Ballyclare right next door to us, which suggests that we must have got something right during his childhood.

When you have disappointments in rugby, as everyone does at some stage, there is always a welcome for you back at your club. That is one of the reasons why rugby men of my day, and indeed of generations before me, regarded their clubs in so warm a light. Not very long after the events described above, and despite all my thoughts on the role of president, I agreed to become president of Ballymena. This was not because I wanted to spend all evening back at the bar and be the head honcho at club dinners, but because I wanted to help. Mind you, the desire began to wear a bit thin after nine years in the job. I told them so, but soothing words reluctantly persuaded me to stay another two seasons after that. I suppose I wasn't strong enough to say no. In the end, I wrote formally to the secretary of the committee, informing him that I would be stepping down in three months' time. I was becoming stale, I was fed up with listening to myself and a fresh face was needed, a different voice with a new image.

Some people will always emerge to carry the torch forward and that is just what happened at Ballymena. I'm afraid that, yet again with hindsight, I stayed as president too long, but you know, this is what is wrong with rugby football. The longer you stay in there, hanging on to high office, the longer you are denying much needed change. You have got to have a continual turnover of new people offering a fresh impetus. Rugby clubs are like governments; they become stale if they remain in office too long. New ideas are needed from others. It has been one of the great failings of rugby football down the years that the national unions have been filled with people with the sole ambition of becoming president. To achieve that, they have had to become yes men, agreeing with almost everything put before them.

In the case of the national unions, when you finally reach the top of the ladder and they call you president, you are only in for one year and you want it to be a nice twelve months. So your attitude is, don't rock the boat, say yes to everything and you'll have a most pleasant year and people will always remember you as a thoroughly nice chap. But what this means is that the game suffers because it doesn't change or go forward. Perhaps it is a good thing that now, in the modern day, the unions have professional staff to run their businesses and the president is largely a figurehead with virtually no real powers. Others, like chief executives, decide policy. That is better as long as that person doesn't forget or ignore the ethos of the game. But until professionalism arrived and forced national unions to involve people with proper business backgrounds, the system operated as I have described. It certainly had its failings.

After my involvement with the Lions and Ireland in the first half of the 1980s, there came one final act for me to play, near the end of the decade. In 1989, I was asked if I would manage a World XV which had been invited to South Africa to celebrate their centenary. There had been a bad history of rebel tours going to South Africa for much of the 1980s. That rugby-mad nation had welcomed visits by just about any serious touring party, but the tours, none of which were sanctioned by the IRB, the sport's governing body, had almost certainly involved some sort of remuneration to players. It was an indication of the South Africans' desperation to see some top overseas players on their soil; something that had been denied them by the world sports boycott of the country due to apartheid.

But this time, I was told that the IRB had authorised an official tour, consisting of four matches. I had always been a supporter of South African rugby and especially Danie Craven. He was the guru of the game out there, a man who had done some amazing things for the sport, sometimes even against the prevailing political system. Besides, I always believed in maintaining contacts, because I felt they were healthier than isolation, but I made it clear I supported this particular concept only if the IRFU agreed it was an official visit. They confirmed that was the case. They also said that if this official tour did not take place, they felt sure another rebel tour would be arranged and if that were to happen, their information was that South Africa would be expelled from the International Board. So my name went forward and I was accepted as manager.

This unleashed the hounds from hell, with my scent firmly in their nostrils. South Africa was not exactly the number one news item around at that time, because the Berlin Wall was about to come down and communism was starting to collapse all across Eastern Europe. What a lot of people didn't realise, but I had an inkling of, because of what I had been told by South Africans in influential positions, was that if communism collapsed, it would be only a brief period of time before Nelson Mandela would be released from prison. The fact was that the South African government was terrified of communism spreading into their country and Mandela was perhaps seen as someone who might foment that.

So, as soon as my name was made public as the manager of this tour, which was scheduled to take place in August 1989, just after the Lions returned home from Australia, the anti-apartheid movement, or rent-a-mob as we should perhaps call it, once again crawled out of the woodwork. They put immense pressure on the rugby-playing Catholic schools in the Republic of Ireland. Really, some of these people were in my view the most despicable, bigoted individuals you could ever have the misfortune to encounter. I was perfectly willing to listen to their point of view and hear them out, but they were nowhere near as keen to hear my reasons for deciding to go. Once they had spouted their propaganda, that was it in their minds. The matter was closed and their view must prevail. Well, I didn't buy that attitude.

I had seen enough dogmatism in Northern Ireland over the previous thirty years not to take kindly to this kind of pressure. Indeed, the tactics employed by the anti-apartheid movement in the weeks before our departure were akin to those already in use throughout my province. I am talking about creating fear and stress. Intimidation of this kind is another form of terrorism, but they had badly miscalculated, because it just made me even more determined to go.

The media weren't a whole lot better. They camped outside my bank and also my home for a brief period, waiting to talk to anyone who might have a view and put the slant they had already decided upon into the report. I did not receive any verbal threats, but there are subtler ways of threatening people. To convey a threat, you do not need to stand in front of someone and utter it from your lips. Instead, the pressure from anti-apartheid demonstrators and the media, an ugly combination at the best of times, was sickening. It went on, day in, day out, for weeks.

At one point the local paper had a picture of me in it every single night for weeks. This builds up a terrible pressure on a target and his family, a point they well understood. I was a bank manager trying hard to concentrate on my work and I found it terribly hard to do that and live under such pressure. The newspapers said a lot of things about me, much of which I did not even recognise, despite the years of service I had given to Ulster and Irish rugby. I put up with it all, ignoring it and refusing to sully my name and reputation by becoming involved. But then a Northern Ireland newspaper called me a mercenary in print and I went straight to my solicitor.

That was the straw that broke the camel's back. I wasn't prepared to accept that kind of damaging slur, which had no basis whatsoever in fact. Remember that a mercenary is, according to the dictionary, a person motivated by greed or desire for gain. Remember, too, that I was a bank manager and also an amateur rugby union man. I had never taken a single penny for my involvement in the game, in whatever capacity. This was a serious attack on my good name and professional character. I sued and they settled out of court, agreeing a handsome sum for the damages. They looked long and hard for even the merest shred of evidence to suggest that I, too, had been paid for playing at some stage of my career, but I knew they were wasting their time and that they wouldn't find anything. I had never taken a penny for playing rugby.

While the papers were writing this stuff, dipping their pens in vitriol each day, I am delighted to say that I received wonderful support from the majority of people in this province. I had endless letters of support and that stiffened my resistance no end. Here was I, having made a personal decision about going to South Africa, virtually under siege at my work and at home because a group of others happened to disagree with my views. They were perfectly entitled to disagree, but equally, was I not entitled to make my own judgement and act accordingly? Their way, it seemed to me, was the way of the police state that they claimed so much to despise. They were saying, 'If you don't agree with us, you're wrong and we'll make your life hell,' but they couldn't see how they were compromising their own views.

One day, a local farmer came to the bank. Outside the front door he was accosted by the anti-apartheid people. They told him he shouldn't go in, because I was in charge there and should be shunned by the local community. Now this guy was physically big and after listening to this stuff he turned to them and said, 'I'll tell you this. I'm going in there to cash a cheque and if I find you people out here in the street when I get out, I'll break your bloody necks.' When he got back out, they had gone. Now I don't believe in answering one threat with another, but that shows you how people issuing threats cause widespread trouble, dragging normally law-abiding citizens into the contretemps.

I had to refuse to do recorded interviews after a while, because I discovered that by the time they had been mixed back at the studio, I appeared to be saying something that I hadn't meant at all. I felt abused when I heard these tapes and the way they had changed them around, so the only way to speak to the media was at live press conferences.

When I talked to the anti-apartheid people, it was quite obvious they simply didn't know what they were talking about, because almost all of them had never been to South Africa. Thus, they had no idea of the situation out there apart from what they had been able to read in the papers. And surely no one could claim they knew more about a country from reading newspapers than a person who had visited the place more than half a dozen times and spent months and months living and travelling there?

I always had in the back of my mind the example we had shown on our own doorsteps in Northern Ireland. We men of rugby, north and south of the border, had continued to mix, continued playing fixtures with and against each other. The threats had not been sufficient to stop us and I was fiercely determined that any threats from anti-apartheid people would not prevent me from maintaining my contacts with rugby people in South Africa.

That is what happened. We flew out there for our tour. Mind you, I was utterly amazed when I got there to see so many representatives not just from the Irish Rugby Football Union but administrators from unions all around the world. They were also attending the centenary celebrations in the lovely South African sunshine and they were to be there for three weeks, at the host union's expense. I was the guy who had been taking all the publicity and weathering the storm from the protesters, while all these guys were quietly packing their own bags, unknown to most, for the same trip. I felt I had been used.

When we got to South Africa, there was another unpleasant incident to endure. Bishop Desmond Tutu, the Roman Catholic Archbishop of Cape Town, was reported to have said, 'This man Willie John McBride should be ostracised and shunned in his own community back home.' I thought to myself, 'My God, that's not the Christian way I was brought up.' This man's Christianity and mine were poles apart. I hope that perhaps during his years as head of the Reconciliation and Truth Commission, Bishop Tutu has reflected on those harsh words and come to realise they were cruel and wrong. Of course, a group of international cricketers had gone to South Africa before us in the 1980s and played a tour. I don't know whether the good bishop had similar words for them.

Anyway, the tour happened and we all had great fun, especially the rugby administrators and their wives, who were along for the free ride. Everyone in the outside world said the players were all being paid, but I had no evidence to suggest that. Nor has anything ever been uncovered since – and I know that a lot of people have spent a lot of time looking for evidence. What I do know is that I went on that tour, had my travel, accommodation and food provided, and have a wooden clock hanging on my wall at home as my sole gift from the trip. I estimate that clock was worth about £15 when new. And this was fifteen years ago now.

So we had a wonderful time for almost three weeks and, what's more, we were now playing teams that had coloured players. That was the real progress we were seeing in South African rugby and Dr Danie Craven was the man chiefly responsible for this. The players, who had their wives and girlfriends with them, still worked hard and played some super rugby. We played games in Durban, Johannesburg, Port Elizabeth and Cape Town. I was delighted for Danie Craven, because he didn't have long to live. He had done so much for rugby in South Africa, and he was the grandfather of the game out there. For sure, Craven was never the warmest of men, and I had my differences with him, but I always admired him; on this occasion, when we got there he came up to me, threw his arms around me and said, 'Thank you for bringing this team to South Africa. This is a day I thought would never happen.' He had tears in his eyes.

My greatest sorrow about that tour was not the fact that I went. No, my greatest sorrow came after we had got home and the Irish Rugby Football Union, having accepted wonderful hospitality for three weeks at the South Africans' expense, meekly apologised to the anti-apartheid movement for going to South Africa. That act left me totally isolated and it sickened me. It also brought the media back to my doorstep with the inevitable question, 'Are you going to apologise, too, now they have?' My reply was, 'No, I have nothing to apologise for. My principles are the same today as they were yesterday and the day before that. They will be the same tomorrow.'

What I did, I believed to be right, but in terms of the game in general I believe that it was the sporting isolation of South Africa that hastened the advent of professionalism in rugby football. There seems little doubt that players had been paid on many of those rebel tours, and that sowed the seed of payment for playing in the minds of rugby men the world over, but especially in the southern hemisphere, which was the driving force for professionalism. By the time that tour had ended in autumn 1989, it was very obvious to me that professionalism was going to come, in some shape or another, at some point in the not too distant future.

Over subsequent years, I have thought a lot about that tour and about South Africa as a whole. I have been back often to that wonderful land. I have made some great friends there, too, like Choet Visser, who was liaison manager for the Lions in 1974. Choet is one of those excellent men whom you meet rarely in life and a few years ago Penny and I went out to stay with him for a few weeks. Choet ran a carpet business, while his wife was in charge of a florist. One night, they held a big party and a lot of their friends were invited. It was a super evening and Choet and I finished it, relaxing in his lounge with a night-cap, just chatting about the old days.

When I got up the next morning, Choet and his wife had gone to work. That was fine because I didn't feel very bright after a glass too many the previous night. So I thought I'd go and have a quiet cup of tea downstairs and sit somewhere in a dark corner. Enter Lutea, Choet's housemaid. Now this larger-than-life lady was ninety if she was a day. There was something else about her, too. She was no more than four feet six inches tall. So in she came, and said, 'Good morning,' to which I managed a reply, before pouring myself

Above: Now these boys could play a bit in their time! Photographed at a dinner in Dublin for Irish Lions captains are, from left: Robin Thompson (1955 Lions), myself (1974), Ronnie Dawson (1959), Tom Kiernan (1968) and Karl Mullen (1950). Jack Kyle, extreme right, toured with the 1950 Lions and was guest speaker.

Below: A proud family. My sister Sadie and I flank our mother, as we show the MBEs we had both been awarded for services in our respective fields.

Above: **Penny and I meeting HRH Prince Charles at the opening of Newtownabbey Council offices. I am very proud to be a Freeman of the Borough of Newtownabbey.**

Below: **Coming into Dublin after joining Ian and Kathy Botham for part of their charity walk across Ireland. I only did 40 miles over 2 days but that night I went out to dinner in carpet slippers, my feet were in such a terrible state!**

Feeding the late, great Australian Bob Templeton one of the local Borewoers sausages in Port Elizabeth, during centenary celebrations for the South African Rugby Board. 'Tempo' was a lovely man.

Above: **Penny and me enjoying ourselves well away from rugby football. I'm glad she's never had to make that long walk back to Malahide!**

Left: **Take me home! I saw this sign whilst visiting friends in the Kalahari on one of my trips.**

Above: I was given the Pipe Smoker of the Year award at London's Savoy hotel in 1999.

lots of fresh orange juice. Lutea then disappeared and I sat down quietly. The next thing was she returned, carrying a plate so wide that she had almost disappeared behind it. On this platter was a feast fit for a king: steak, eggs, liver, bacon, mushrooms, tomatoes . . . everything. Now I'd tackled a few fearsome prospects on the rugby field in my time, but I took one look at this and thought, 'That's the last thing on earth I can face this morning.' The mere sight of it was making me feel queasy.

So I said, 'Lutea, I'm sorry, but I couldn't touch that.' However, she'd obviously had instructions to provide an enormous South African breakfast and was not going to be put off. She put the heavy plate on the table, stood there with her arms folded across her front and, from her tiny frame, looked at me and said, 'I made it. You eat it.' And I can tell you, this former rugby man did as he was bloody well told. Or at least I picked through it for half an hour and pushed it around the plate. How could I have dared to refuse?

Through Choet, I got a tremendous feel for South Africa, away from just the world of rugby football, hotels and official receptions. I saw the way apartheid worked. I met his friends, met his black employees, saw how both sides handled situations, saw how they coped. I never once saw anything cruel or nasty towards black people, although of course I wasn't so naive as to think that indignities and cruelties did not occur elsewhere in the country.

Choet had about twenty men working for him, laying carpets, driving vans, working in the store. I remember asking him, 'How much does the average man earn here?' and he when he told me, I was shocked. I said, 'But Choet, that's not a lot of money,' but he said, 'That's not all. Every Friday I take the trailer to the local market and pick up a load of fresh vegetables and fruit for their families. I distribute that to them, because if I didn't, those families would never get that food. That's because in those days the first thing many Africans did when they got their salaries was go and buy drink. At least if I give them a good pile of fresh vegetables I know the families are being looked after.' When I came home and tried to explain some of these things, people probably just saw me as some apologist for apartheid. I want to say that I'm no naive idiot who hasn't got any knowledge about the ways of the real world. I've travelled, talked and listened to people, and seen things and regimes I know are fundamentally wrong.

Apartheid was far from a sensitive method of dealing with human beings, but I feared the worse when I heard that it was going to be dismantled overnight. What I felt would have been better for South Africans, black and white, was to have a partial dismantling of the system, but with the whites working in partnership with the blacks for the first twenty years or so. The whites had the expertise in running the country. Might not that experience have been utilised for the benefit of all South Africans? I had hoped South Africans might go forward together, for the benefit of all sections of the community.

But what has happened has been sad. Yes, all South Africans are free now, but free to suffer what? Murder, muggings and robberies – most of the victims, incidentally, being black people. They have their freedom, too, in Zimbabwe; or at least they did until the tyrant Mugabe gained control of the place. The white man was ousted and everything was set fair for a wonderful future. You see the reality of that fantasy today. The country is run down and ruined, with starvation rampant. It is tragic.

Today, the level of crime in the townships in South Africa is frightening. And there has been a huge brain-drain away from the country, because under the present government, led by Thabo Mbeki, there is great difficulty finding work if you are a white, middle class young person. Go to Warrington or to Wiltshire in England, go to Sydney in Australia and you will find numerous young white South Africans, virtually in exile from their own country, forced out because they had no prospect whatever of employment under their current government. Now I can see the problem from both sides. I understand the government saying that black people have had no chances for fifty years and now it's their turn. But I see, too, the dilemma of young whites who want to contribute to their own country, but find their path blocked. Such a situation can hardly be propitious for the country as a whole.

My viewpoint is straightforward. I love South Africa and I wish it only well. I want to see greater investment from overseas, so that standards of living for everyone can be raised. But I question certain policies of a government that seems to be happily holding open the exit door for so many of its white citizens. Can that lead to a better, a more prosperous, a fairer society of the future? I somehow doubt it.

CHAPTER 14

The Circular That Changed My Life

f I had to live my life all over again, there isn't a great deal I would change. OK, Ireland would have won a good few Grand Slams, and as for those early Lions tours of 1962 and 1966 – well, we'd have murdered them. But seriously, it has been a good life and I have been lucky enough to meet so many good people in it. Certainly, I have made mistakes, but if you are smart enough to learn from them, then you can always put them down to valuable experience.

I have known great elation and immense sadness during my life, but have always managed to keep on what I believe has been a fairly even keel. I have always kept going. I feel that I have packed an awful lot into my life. I still do. I travel a fair amount, speak at quite a lot of dinners and talk to many people. I enjoy that; to me, communicating with people, having a chat, hearing about their lives and discussing their views and yours is always a pleasure. I certainly never get bored.

As for rugby, I have absolutely no bitterness about anything from my own playing days. Yes, there have been downs at times, some of which I have outlined in previous chapters, but there have been more ups than most men could expect from a lifetime's involvement in a great sport. If you never have the downs, you don't

252

enjoy the good times so much, because you have nothing to judge them against. So when I look back, despite occasional difficult times, I cannot really feel anything but warmth and pleasure at my long association with the game. I feel, too, that I achieved my purpose: I put something back into rugby football in various roles, albeit with varying degrees of success.

On a couple of occasions, and I am sure it was done as an acknowledgement to the game itself rather than just to myself, Penny and I were invited to meet Her Majesty the Queen. Once was when the royal yacht *Britannia*, which had been anchored off Belfast Lough, sailed around the Antrim coast to Portrush. Security required that we had to be at the harbour three hours before the departure of the launch that was to ferry guests out to *Britannia*, which was anchored a mile or so offshore.

It just so happened that this day was in the midst of something very unusual in Northern Ireland. A heatwave. We all duly trooped up to the embarkation point, cleared about three separate sets of security checks and waited, out in the sun, for the appointed hour to arrive. It was blazing hot, no shade and pretty miserable. We couldn't go anywhere or do anything but wait. A few other rugby people had been invited, like Syd Millar and his wife Enid. Now, I am something of a people watcher; I enjoy studying folk, trying to piece together little bits of information about them which I think their behaviour reveals. On this particular day, there was this woman present who was wearing a huge hat. While we waited, and it must have been for a good couple of hours, she kept getting her mirror out of her handbag and looking at herself. She'd adjust her hat, check her make-up, brush her hair a few times . . . that sort of thing. She was by herself, a little apart from most of the others, and I came to the conclusion that she regarded herself as a little bit better than the rest of us.

Anyway, it transpired that several others had come to this conclusion, because when eventually the launches began to sail across from *Britannia* to collect us, they were accompanied by a flock of seagulls. One of them, diving like a German Stuka bomber, came over us and unloaded everything right on top of this woman. Upon her shriek of alarm, everyone turned around to look and a great cry of 'Yeaaaaaaahhhhh' went up. The mess was dripping down the side of this woman's hat, and had even managed to splatter her coat. It was a sight to see. God help the poor woman but I think everyone felt, well, perhaps she deserved it. Then, halfway out to the royal yacht on a sea that was really like a millpond, another woman became violently ill, poor thing. They didn't even help her off the launch when we tied up alongside the yacht; she returned to the port and missed her big day.

The other time we met the Queen was when Penny and I were invited to Buckingham Palace for a Jubilee ball. I was working in the bank and did not have a lot of money, so we had to make ours go a long way. Flying to London and finding overnight accommodation in the capital is not cheap, so we decided to stay at Gatwick airport and catch the train to Victoria station. We took a room at a guest house near the airport, but of course had to change there. The ball was inevitably black tie for the gentlemen and ball gowns for the ladies, so Penny and I marched on to the platform at Gatwick airport and got on the London train dressed to the nines. We knew we would not be back until late so Penny, knowing she would be cold, had to wear a mac over her ball gown. The gown stuck out underneath it, and we both had a good laugh at how we looked.

We were in good time when we got to London so we went and had a coffee. I can remember to this day the expression on the face of the scruffy guy in the cafe as he poured two coffees for these two people, who were dressed up in dinner jacket and black ball gown. What a sight we must have looked, sitting there on those cheap, plastic seats in a filthy cafe waiting for the time to go to the palace. It was hilarious and we were in fits of laughter. The best bit was still to come, however.

Eventually, we got outside and hailed a cab. 'The palace, please,' I said to the driver, who turned out to be Irish himself. 'Buckingham Palace?' he said, clearly taken aback. 'Yes, Buckingham Palace, please.' And then he said, 'Are you sure?' 'Yes, I'm sure,' I said. So we drive on a bit further and he says, 'Er, do we go in the servants' entrance or the main gates?' 'The main gates, of course,' I reply. 'Well, er, how do we get in the main gates?' he says. 'Don't you worry. We'll get in the main gates,' I say. And all the while he is studying me in his rear-view mirror, as though my pockets are stuffed with dynamite and he's likely to read that the whole place has been blown to bits the next morning. Anyway, when we got inside, I directed him towards the main door. This unsettled him still further. 'Er, up to the front door?' he said. 'Yes, that's fine. The front door.' He'd lived in London long enough to qualify as a cab driver, but he'd never been inside Buckingham Palace before and the idea of an Irish cabbie transporting an Irish couple there was clearly causing him great concern.

Anyway, we had a wonderful evening, even though we were collared by Lord Longford. Penny thought we'd never get away and meet anyone else. Andre Previn was there, Cliff Richard and plenty of others. We danced – no, that's a bit of an exaggeration in my case – to Joe Loss and his band and several members of the Royal Family did likewise. It was a most pleasant occasion. When we came out, we had to walk across the palace courtyard, for there was no limousine to pick us up, but we saw Frank Longford and his wife ahead of us, so clearly we weren't the only ones using shanks's pony. Well, we walked down to Victoria, and boarded the last train to Gatwick. Just before it left, around midnight, in clambered two of the waiters who had been serving us at the palace that evening!

I attribute my qualities of determination, hard graft and practicality to my mother. I think her influence shone through in all of us. For example, my sister Sadie always had that strong desire to get on in life and achieve things and I think I have been much the same. Sadie was determined to do nursing and she succeeded. I had the same attitude in whatever I did. Mother was almost ninety-two when she died. Sadly, she had had three or four tough years before she passed away, because she got dementia, that horrible illness which robs an elderly person of his or her own memories and reality. The greatest sadness was that Mum did not know some of her own children when they visited her at times. She ended up in a home, because she needed twenty-four-hour care and attention, but I would go and see her regularly. All of us got there whenever we could. That was the type of family she brought up and the kind of values she instilled in each of us.

But in those last few, difficult years, many was the time when I came out with tears in my eyes. I had to take big, deep breaths and tell myself that I owed it to my mother and her memory to get on with life and not to buckle. She taught us those qualities; now it was our turn to show her, although she could no longer understand, that we too had become strong, like her. I found it hard seeing what that illness gradually did to her. She was a woman who taught me almost all the values that have underpinned my life. She had been strong, resourceful and possessed of a fierce will. Now, this condition had reduced her in so many ways, which I found desperately hard to accept.

One of the saddest things of all was that she did not really realise that two of the children she had brought up almost single-handedly after the premature death of her husband – my sister and myself – had been awarded the MBE. Now for any humble family to see one of its own go out into the world and do well enough to win the MBE is a great achievement. For two members of a single family to be honoured in such a way was something else and I know we all felt immense pride when it happened. My award was for services to rugby football; Sadie's, for services to nursing, but my mother, although she was still with us, hardly understood because the dementia was fast advancing. Even to this day, I find it painful to remember how she was robbed of so much pleasure, but that is what can occur in life. As she taught us, you have to be strong, carry on and continue to do the best you can in whichever field you are working or living.

Mother was a role model for me in so many ways. She used to go and talk to people; she always made time for those visits. But then, busy people always make time for others. I have done likewise because I, too, like to go and see people and have a chat with them. I am honoured to have inherited this trait from her, because I believe that talking to your fellow human beings is one of life's greatest pleasures. It is a simple activity, but one that gives me enormous delight.

I think that was why, when I went into banking, I always liked to involve myself with my clients. Talking to them was never a chore for me. If a client had problems, I wanted to help them, but I could only do so by talking. As one commercial advertisement of recent years put it, rather appropriately you may think, 'It's good to talk'. I was in banking for thirty-six years and enjoyed a special relationship with a lot of people. Frankly, they enriched my life, because without them and those on-going relationships, my working life would have been extremely dull. Instead, it was filled with people and challenges, busy times that gave me the chance to make something better, for the bank and myself, and also for our customers.

My retirement was a strange business. I went to work as normal one morning with not the slightest idea in my head of retiring. I assumed I would go on until I was sixty-five and then bow out. Certainly, the bank had said nothing to suggest otherwise. In our branch, the deputy manager went through the post each morning and put on my desk the mail with which I had to deal. Among my post on this particular morning was a circular from head office. It was to change my entire life.

Circulars from head office were as common as mushrooms in autumn. They seemed to sprout up everywhere. But this particular one caught my eye because it had a bold headline on the top. It said:

'An offer of voluntary retirement to over-fifties'. I looked at it and began to read the small print. What it turned out to be was an offer to anyone past fifty to cash in their chips, as it were. It suddenly hit me that I was over fifty and this applied to me. So I started to read it carefully and began to work out what it would mean to me. When I had done so and had an approximate settlement figure in front of me, I sat bolt upright in my office chair and thought to myself, 'Good God, why am I sitting here?'

I had endless other things that I could be doing, which I enjoyed. I thought to myself that I didn't need this daily hassle and that it would be mad to refuse an offer like this. That was particularly true because I was already spending ever more time doing daily reports, typing up stuff and going through forms and sheets in minute detail, as opposed to the work I really enjoyed. The offer from head office was a lump sum, tax free, with a healthy pension, too. I had thirty-six years of service behind me and the more I thought about it, the more I wanted to do it. I phoned up Penny and told her, very bluntly, 'I've got some news for you. I'm retiring.' There was a brief pause on the other end of the line. 'Are you mad, or just ill?' was the reply. 'Neither, but I'll tell you more about it when I get home.'

When I went through it all with her that evening, she agreed I would be crazy to turn down the offer. Most people had to work until they were sixty-five, but I was in a fortunate position. I owed nothing to anyone. Amanda was married and Paul was doing his finals. There really was no decision to make. The next day, I telephoned a couple of my business pals in other branches, managers like me, and asked them if they'd had the circular, too. 'Oh yes, we've seen it, but we're not having that,' they told me. 'They won't be getting us out.' I didn't say a lot, but I thought to myself, you're mad, you don't know what you're missing. I told them all, 'I'm away. That's me gone, out of here.' So I sent back the form and within twenty-four hours the office of John Wright, the bank's big chief in

Belfast, called. John would like to pop in the next day, see the bank and have a chat, we were told. I knew what it was really about.

John Wright was a man I could work for. I liked and respected him. When he arrived, he sat down and said, 'Now look. That offer wasn't really designed for people like you. We'd want to keep the likes of you until you retire.' I pulled out a copy of the sums I had done and asked plainly, 'Have you got anything better than this for me?' He said, well, banking was changing and the high-tech world would revolutionise the industry, so there could be no promises. That was enough for me. I knew I'd made the right decision and I said just one thing to him: 'Please don't block it.' He looked at me with a somewhat pained expression and said, 'But will you be all right?' 'John,' I replied, 'you have a lot on your plate. Don't be worrying about people like me. I'll get through because I have a thousand and one things to do.'

That day became the last day of my last life. When I finally left the bank, roughly five months later, the first day of my new life began. I can tell you, it has been a wonderful new life. I have had breakfast almost every morning with my delightful wife, most mornings I have not had to rush off anywhere and, best of all, Penny and I can suit ourselves. We arrange our lives as we wish, not at the behest of an employer. I have never regretted that decision for one minute. I grabbed the deal and ran. The fact is, I never really had any serious money until I retired, but I was lucky because I was used to being prudent with it.

Once the details of my severance package had been confirmed, a weird thing happened. I had agreed to stay a final six months, to give them time to find my successor, but within four weeks I had to ring head office and say, 'Look, I'm sorry, but just get me out of here. I've retired already in my mind. I never thought this would happen to me, but every file that I lift and every client that I speak to, I will never be dealing with again. So I'm not really giving it the attention I should be.'

I told them this was no good for the bank or for me. As it turned out, I managed to stumble on through the rest of the winter, to May. Then one evening I turned the key in that door and walked away. I never looked back. After thirty-six years in the business, banking was never again a part of my life. It ended there and then in every sense. I never even woke up once at night, wondering what on earth I had done. So I would like to say, here and now, that I hope all those who may be reading these words enjoy as peaceful and happy a retirement from their work after their own long years of service as I already have.

Banks today do not receive a good press. Why? Well, where should I begin? The fact is, banks only reflect life and life has changed so much today. The world has become more profit orientated. I retired in 1994 at the age of fifty-four and in my working life I saw enormous changes. But since I retired, the pace of change has simply taken off, sweeping over most things we know in life and have come to regard as our roots, like some tidal wave. I retired early because by then they were doing away with bank managers and my job was being replaced by computers and other high-tech machines. These facilities have totally transformed the face of banking, as they have so many other businesses, professions and aspects of everyday life. But this change came at a cost. The primary one, I would suggest, is that we have gone away from people. This is true now in most of life.

You pick up the telephone to call someone and ask a simple question and you are connected to an automatic voice-answering machine. That gives you instructions to press numbers for whichever query you have. Now this may all be very efficient from a business point of view, and doubtless saves companies many millions of pounds over a period of years through getting rid of real people and their jobs. But this creed has become widespread in modern life. It is that people have become less and less important. They have been subjugated in the relentless drive for maximum profit. It is exactly the same in banking. It is all about profit and less about people.

In Northern Ireland, I believe the sense of loss at this move to an impersonal world is especially acute, because what the province has always needed is for ordinary people to communicate, to meet and to chat. I was from a Protestant family but, of course, I would go and visit people from both sides of the religious divide. Thank God, there were no barriers thrown in front of me when it came to dealing with my clients. No one threw me out or showed me the door because they thought I might come from a different religious background from themselves. Northern Ireland has always needed that contact between people of different backgrounds. Denied it, we have seen the cost of the isolation and the entrenchment of views.

So today, banking is like so many things in life; unrecognisable from thirty years ago. It is very impersonal, all done in the name of progress, but progress in what? Chiefly in making more money for big companies, I suspect. So I wouldn't want to be a part of the world of banking today, no thank you – not in a world that has so lost touch with people, because that was the part of the job that I most enjoyed.

So, once retired I began to get myself organised in other ways. I could indulge myself in all sorts of things, tasks that I had either wanted to do for years and never had the time, or things that badly needed my attention. Now you couldn't accuse me of being Mr Handyman (I hear shouts of 'You're not wrong there' from the kitchen!) but on the other hand, I am not a fool with a workman's tool in my hand. I positively love having a good-quality garden spade in my hands, to turn the earth and plant my vegetables for the new season. That gives me a particular pleasure, because I love gardening. I cut the grass, trim the hedges and grow all our vegetables. Within my modestly sized plot you will find tomatoes, courgettes, carrots, potatoes, leeks, onions, radishes and lettuce. I like nothing more than spending a few hours on my vegetable patch, digging, preparing new soil, picking out weeds, harvesting the produce when the time comes or whatever task needs my attention.

Then there is the DIY. One day, I set to with the intention of constructing an outside toilet attached to the house at our home. Now building was something that always interested me and I got down to it with great enthusiasm. I had a bit of help from a local friend, but when it came to the plastering, I said I'd be fine with that. I wanted to try plastering, because it was always something that had intrigued me. You see the experts do it and it looks as easy as taking candy from a baby.

So there I stood, loading great dollops of the mixed up plaster on to my builder's trowel and then dragging it across the wall. Mixed up? You could say it was the workman who was in that state because, like a lot of amateur workmen, I quickly came to realise that this job was nowhere near as simple as the experts made it appear. I just couldn't get the ultra-smooth surface on my work that they seemed to do with their eyes shut. I spent an entire day on that particular job and at one stage was actually holding the wretched stuff on with my two hands. Whenever I put it on, it would fall off. At least by the evening it was sticking to the wall, but there again if you'd run your hand across it when it had dried, you would have torn off most of the skin, it was so rough.

Well, I finished it eventually and thought it wasn't too bad. Not long afterwards, an old friend of mine who used to be a builder happened to come by and I said, 'Tom, come and have a look at the outside toilet I've built.' He wandered inside, put the light on and peered suspiciously at it all. He reserved his closest scrutiny for the plasterwork. After a while that seemed like an infinity, I asked cheerfully, 'Well, Tom, what do you think?' 'Aye,' he said, rubbing his chin, 'I'd say yer best idea would be to leave the light off!'

I couldn't believe my luck at retiring so young, but the reality was, I didn't retire. I just changed direction. I'm not even retired today; I'm too busy. I soon found that the telephone was ringing and people were asking if I would go and speak at so-and-so club's dinner. Then came requests for more formal events, often overseas. I have spoken at countless numbers of sportsmen's dinners. These events are popular, especially with corporate people who bring along guests. I tell a few stories and what I can't remember I make up. I enjoy them because you get a bit of a buzz from these things.

Then the BBC in Northern Ireland made contact one day and asked me if I would be interested in discussing a new radio series with them. I went along and loved the idea. The concept was that I should go out into the country of Northern Ireland and meet all sorts of people involved in old-fashioned jobs or pursuits. So one day I might be chatting with a man thatching a roof or training greyhounds and the next with a guy building stone walls, racing pigeons or shooting rabbits for the pot. We have forgotten about so many of these things that went on and, consequently, many are dying out.

One day, I went and met a guy who was digging peat out in the country. Well, I have never laughed so much in my life. There can be few places lonelier than a peat bog and yet it is wonderful to be there, as I told you earlier. You would dig the peat in early May. You had to dig it where you could get it dried, off the ground, and then get it home. If you left it until much later in the year it would break up, get wet and mulch, and wouldn't be worth picking up. The grass grows through, as well. You cut it, shred it on the bog top and then lift it up and lean it against something. This is called footing and stacking it. That is the final drying part of it and then you bring it home. Much depends on the sunshine and the wind as to how long it needs to dry – it certainly takes between two and three weeks to dry it properly. Some years you may lose it due to adverse weather conditions; it may break up and crumble and that is no good.

I simply adore a peat fire. For me, there are few greater pleasures than sitting down for tea beside one. The smell of it is divine. It takes me back to those early years on my family's farm, when life was simple. Sure, we never had all the modern-day work tools and implements that are supposed to have been designed to make life easier. Nevertheless, sometimes I yearn for those good, simple days.

Sitting around a peat fire, enjoying the smell and having a chat with people, is wonderful. It is so relaxing. You can stretch out and feel your body and mind completely winding down. All there is to do is share the pleasure of your friends' company and watch the fire glowing and smoking. Then I'll light up my pipe and suddenly there doesn't seem to be very much wrong with the modern world. I suppose for young people, having a peat fire may not be very practical today. It can be too much trouble and too expensive. But for me, it is an essential part of our winter lives. It brings back those memories of nice times, in the bosom of my family. Happy days, shared experiences and emotions.

The BBC series, which was called *McBride's Country*, was exactly my kind of job, because it involved what I love doing most: chatting with people. I'd ask them questions about their work, which I knew I would find interesting, and just hoped that the listeners would, too. From the response I had, I felt sure they were enjoying it as much as I was. It was broadcast from 1997 to 2000. I was out in the air, doing this work. and it gave me another new interest, but when the BBC asked me to take the series on to TV, I refused. I knew that would mean an awful lot more hassle, and would take away the simplicity of the idea.

With just a microphone to hold, it was very easy, relaxed and pleasurable. Best of all, the people I was talking to were completely natural. They would be dressed the way they always were and they'd talk the way they always did. For me, that was the essence of the whole programme. But television obliterates all that. With TV lights, make-up people, producers and directors all wanting to get involved, I knew that the humble little series I had so enjoyed would become unrecognisable. People would not be themselves any more. I think, too, that people can use their imagination far more with radio. They can build up a picture in their minds of the guy being interviewed and what he is like. But TV takes away the need to think in that way. Worst of all, I feared it might become a chore and I never wanted that to happen. So I turned down their approach and walked away from it.

I've done lots of other things since my departure from banking. One day I had a phone call from a senior executive at Rolls Royce called Peter Somerfield, asking me if I would go over to their headquarters at Derby, in England, to speak to their management about motivation. In the United States, 11 September had occurred not long before and the media was full of stories that aircraft were being laid up because no one wanted to fly anymore. There were fears that a great British company like Rolls Royce, which is of course famous partly for making engines for jet aircraft, was facing years of decline. It seemed a gloomy picture and this man seemed to think I might be able to help them raise morale.

I agreed to do it, but I don't think it was until I was on the aeroplane going over to the English Midlands that the situation really hit me. I thought to myself, 'Here am I, a retired bank manager and a guy who played rugby football, God knows how many years ago, going to address countless numbers of senior management executives at one of the blue riband companies of British industry. I cannot fob off such people with generalisations. I can't talk tripe. These are highly intelligent business people. They will see through any nonsense immediately. What on earth am I going to say to them?' When we landed at East Midlands airport, I wouldn't quite say I felt like staying on the plane for the return trip to Belfast, but it certainly set me thinking about ways of motivating management.

When I stood up to speak the following day, I followed my usual habit of talking without notes. I ad lib because I have found I cannot read notes while I am speaking. I like to cast my eyes wide around a room, to look at individual faces and talk to them for a moment or two so that people really do think what I am saying affects them. For me, there is nothing worse than a speaker who never veers from his prepared text and rarely focuses on individuals in his audience. It is too impersonal, that way of speaking, in my opinion.

I stood up and kept it simple. I said, 'Most of you won't even know who I am. My name is Willie John McBride. I used to play rugby football.' I begged their indulgence to give them a little of my background and told them where I was from, about my upbringing and about life in Northern Ireland. I said, 'Britain has had its problems in the last 100 years or so. Indeed, compared to some of the things that have happened, 9/11 was not the worst thing that ever occurred in the world, horrible as it undoubtedly was. Take the first day of the Battle of the Somme, for example, during which 59,000 Allied soldiers were killed, wounded or went missing.'

I went on, 'You know, the British Army still got through 1 July 1916. Northern Ireland is still there – we have got through thirty years that have been pretty grim at times. We have wonderful people, great management and we have held our heads high and gone forward.' I told them that one thing they should always remember was that we were living in a very small world. 'Why do we live in a small world? It is simply because of aeroplanes. Can anyone seriously tell me that within a period of time, and it would not be that long, there would not be an even bigger demand for aeroplanes and, consequently, aircraft engines?' I continued on that theme. I told them what the name Rolls Royce meant to the wider world – reliability, quality, all the good work that you could think of. I told them it would always mean that. It was up to them, the management of this great company, to keep the standards high for the next layer of management coming along.

I could see all these faces looking at me, listening intently, and I just hoped that I had struck a chord within them. It was not a fancy speech, particularly high-brow or based on financial acumen. It was a plain and simple assessment of where we were, what we had been through and how I felt they could go forward once the world recovered from the immediate shock of 9/11. Whether a single businessman in that room thought it was of any help to him or a positive hindrance, I do not know. But I am pleased that Rolls Royce have twice invited me back to speak to other members of their staff. Peter Somerfield rang me recently and asked me to go over again to speak. I said, 'But Peter, I am no more use to you. I have nothing new to say.' However, he replied, 'Ah, but they're all different people and I want them to hear this message.'

One of the things I have always been clear about in retirement is never to get involved in routine. My routine days are gone and now I never have a clue what I am going to be doing the next day. That is how I like it. I am always busy, but never tied to a routine. Two things are very important to me – friends and humour. You must laugh. I remember one day I'd had a bloody awful time at work and as I was coming out I was behind this girl. She was going down the stairs, singing to herself.

I remember sitting back in my chair when I got home and thinking to myself, 'Isn't that great? At the end of a terrible day you come out and hear someone who is so happy that she is singing to herself.' Somehow, that seemed to ease the memory of my bad day. I believe that if you can sing or laugh each day, then life is certainly worthwhile. I am a great believer that twenty-four hours can heal a hell of a lot of problems. When I was presented with a particularly difficult piece of paper at work, I would often say, 'Oh, I'll look at that again tomorrow.' One day, one of my staff said to me, 'Manager, why do you always leave it until tomorrow?' I said to him, 'Well, twenty-four hours can change a hell of a lot of things.' The whole world can have changed in twenty-four hours, making everything seem so different.

It is my view that you have got to work at life. You must keep at things, keep yourself busy, keep going out and meeting people, keep challenging yourself. I have never been scared to go out and do the little things. For years, I used to go and speak to the local Rotary Club or the Women's Institute, or present the prizes at the local school or boys' club if I was asked to do so. I did these things voluntarily and enjoyed them. I was always meeting new people and seeing a fresh slant on life. Better still, it created for me a huge number of friends, well-wishers and people with whom I could just have a chat.

In Northern Ireland, Mary Peters, the former Great Britain Olympic athlete, and I have been very fortunate in that, politically speaking, we have been able to go anywhere and have been accepted by everyone. At least I hope that is the case. We have kept that thing through sport that means we have been greeted in all communities. Believe me, that is something I really treasure.

I enjoy my golf, too. Now I wouldn't want anyone to run away with the idea that the real class act in this part of the world isn't Darren Clarke, but yours truly. I have my days, but I have many I'd prefer not to mention. I play off 16 nowadays . . . sometimes. But I was in Bermuda last year for the Classic Barbarians, a tournament for former players. We go out there for a week and have a marvellous time. Some play a bit of rugby, we go around the golf course, meet up with many old friends and generally enjoy ourselves. I can think of worse ways to spend a week.

Well, the last time I was there, I hit a purple patch on the golf course. No, it wasn't a clump of heather a few yards from the tee. In fact, I had to shake my head sometimes to see how well I was striking the ball. Every time I hit it, it went on the green and every time I struck a putt, it went in the hole. 'Now I know what Tiger Woods feels like.' I thought to myself. There was one price to pay for such superlative form. I announced my retirement that very night for the logical reason that anything I did on the golf course after that was bound to be worse. I had finished 4-under my handicap, which made me the winner. So I am world champion. I have beaten the representatives of all those countries that were there. Sadly, like an idiot, I didn't keep to my promise regarding retirement and, yes, you've guessed it, I have got worse.

But seriously, I am very lucky really because I am not addicted to anything. Some people have to go out and play golf every couple of days, but not me. I don't need that sort of sporting fix. I'll enjoy a round with friends, but I'd die of boredom if I were out there playing much more than once a week. It is like a lot of things in my life: I can do something and then walk away and do something else. I never get tied to just one thing.

All manner of things interest me, especially food and how it is produced. For example, I have a local butcher who makes special sausages for me from a recipe I once brought home from South Africa. They are boerewors sausages and anyone who has ever visited South Africa will know how good they are. But my local butcher produces such good ones that when friends come from South Africa and taste them, they cannot tell the difference between these and the genuine South African version. They are made with prime Ulster beef.

The great debate on food interests me hugely. I get our lamb from my brother on his farm and the quality is exceptional, but intense farming has altered the small farming ways of Ireland almost completely. Now there have obviously been scares concerning beef, but since then, rigorous safety checks have been put in place and so I will eat beef, especially if it comes from our local butcher and we know the origins of the animal. I'm like most men of Ulster: I love a good, hearty steak. Something else I enjoy very much are our own free-range eggs. We keep a good flock of hens and they lay splendid eggs. You can taste the difference, too, so we never buy eggs from the supermarket anymore.

Penny bakes a sponge cake with our free-range eggs, but when I taste other people's cakes, they seem anaemic. Ours are strong and vibrant, full of colour and health. I suspect it is because our chickens are scratching the ground and running around everywhere. That is the natural way it should be. I'm sorry if I offend supermarkets, but I firmly believe we would be much healthier if we ignored all the fast food that is piled high on supermarket shelves and bought produce mainly from smaller suppliers. I mean things like fresh bread from the local baker (or better still, baked at home), fresh vegetables from a local shop that has almost certainly got its supplies from local farms, proper meat that really tastes of something from a good local butcher. In many areas now you can find a local farmer's market once a week, selling produce that has literally come straight off the farm. It is fresh, wholesome and altogether different in taste to the kind of stuff you will find in a supermarket.

One of the dishes special to this part of the world is an 'Ulster fry'. If you're feeling down or hungry as an ox, then there's nothing like a plate filled with an Ulster fry. Bacon, sausages, pancake, eggs, tomato. In our town, you'll pay around £2.95 for it. I saw it somewhere recently for £1.75 and thought to myself, 'I bet they're stinting on the wheaten farl and soda farl! My mother used to bake that every day of her life. And a pint of buttermilk to go with it.

I live in an area full of history and that, too, interests me. Occasionally, Penny and I will take the time to join one of the local walking tours of the area, which provide you with a great deal of information on what went on in your area hundreds of years ago. They are run by the local historical group. I call them hysterical walks, not historical ones, for the craic is always good. It is amazing, the history around here. Close to where we live they were building a bungalow and discovered a Stone Age factory. They dug up all these old spears and things and it is now known as the Ballyclare hoard. It is in the Ulster Museum.

Getting out with the members of the historical society provides a good chance to have a chat with a few people and enjoy the fresh air, both of which have always given me pleasure. Our village is close to a river, similar to most villages in Ireland. Near to us, you can see some of the old mill cottages where the workers lived at the time when the linen trade was at its peak. This was around the 1860s, 1870s. Ulster linen was a huge thing worldwide but, sadly, that has gone now. The village of Ballycorr is also near to us, but much of it is falling down nowadays. Just off the little, twisting lanes that run through and around the village, old mill houses, now derelict and deserted, lie around, most of them in a state of disrepair. It is very sad to see, and all a result of the collapsed linen trade.

Another little village near where I live is called Ballyeaston. It was a small satellite village of Ballyclare and I assume it would have had some connection with the linen trade. It is a beautiful little village, which won a best-kept village award a few years ago. It is quiet, peaceful and well kept by its inhabitants. HRH Prince Charles visited this area a year or two back and he went to a small village named Broughshane, near Ballymena. He went into the local pub, the Thatch, and had a pint of Guinness. One guy looked at him, turned to his pal and said, 'Would yer look at him? He never even offered to pay.'

The biggest thing in Ballyclare is still the livestock market, but with EU restrictions, this may see the end of its days in the near future. You have all these butter mountains, beef mountains and God knows what. There is massive over-production and yet they still haven't produced the sort of stuff people want nowadays. To my mind, Europe has all but killed farming. However, the May fair still has animals and it takes place in the town square. You can see horses, donkeys and ponies with traps being paraded around for prospective buyers. Years ago, there was a big horse and trading fair where you hired your farm helps and maids and things for the next year. Now it has developed into a May fair, but I have to say, each year it diminishes a little and one of these years it will die. That is sad because it is part of our tradition.

Tradition – in rugby football and in life: I'll tell you what, I rather like the notion. Quite honestly, I am disturbed by the carelessness with which we in modern-day society give away our traditions. I believe traditions provide a community with its true roots. But life today is too fast and we seem unable to sit down and treasure those things that have been handed down to us. Sometimes when I see people rushing about and the pressures they are under, I think to myself, for what? As a bank manager, I saw millionaires rushing all over the world and then they'd have a sudden heart attack and die. I would think, what for? Why? I believe there is a balance you must keep.

We lose respect so often and get completely carried away by this rushing. That is why I think it is so important not to become addicted to anything. It might help society a little, too, to remember a simple maxim: that the best things in life cannot be bought. Health, love, friendship – where do you purchase those things? Not at any shops I know. Sadly, too, people lose sight of what is important until it is too late. How often do you get people who say, 'I wish I had listened to what you told me ten years ago'? Sometimes gaining experience can be very expensive and that is why it is so important to listen to people who have been through it. The older generation knows about these things.

I attribute so much of my happiness to the loving relationship I have enjoyed all these years with my wife Penny. She was the girl I tossed a coin for that Dublin evening, all those years ago, back in 1961. We have a laugh about it, because I say to her, if I hadn't won that toss, what would she be doing now? I keep saying I saved her. (But maybe, just maybe, I was really the one who was saved by meeting such a great person.) Penny has been incredibly supportive. She never moaned or complained when I kept going away on rugby tours, which happened for so many years of our marriage. She also brought up two fine children in the right way, for she was always there for them.

I was not around for so much of our children's formative years, as a normal father would have been. Trying to pursue a career and play rugby at the top level was not easy. Sometimes I felt like a circus performer, desperately juggling two or three things and trying to keep them all going at the same time. I'd rush home from work, collect my kit and go training. When I got home, a pile of washing needed to be done. Then at weekends, I'd be away or certainly out for most of every Saturday. But it helped make Penny strong, because she had to act for herself and our family, making her own decisions. She had no choice, with me not being there.

As I said right at the start of this book, I am never happier than when I am in and around my home or my home town, surrounded by my family and friends from the area. I am a Freeman of this Borough now, an award with which I was presented a few years ago, which was nice. It doesn't mean a lot in practical terms, but it was special because it is the highest honour a Borough can bestow upon a citizen.

I would not want to live anywhere other than this part of the world. I feel that I fit into it as snugly as a hand into a glove. I have been most fortunate in that I have travelled around the world. I maybe don't know Europe as well as I should, but I've been all over the southern hemisphere. It is lovely there, but it's even nicer to come home to my part of Northern Ireland. This might seem a strange thing to say when you consider the image Northern Ireland gets through the media, but to my way of thinking there is nobody like the people of Ulster. The friendliness here is exceptional and people always talk to you. If you are in a bit of trouble, there is always someone you can ring up and ask for help or advice. Without exception, he or she will say, 'How can I help? What can I do?' I wonder if there are many places left in the world like that.

I first came to Ballyclare in 1971. I used to shoot duck off the river here. The town did not even have traffic lights or pedestrian crossings then. During the Troubles we had one bomb left here but, thankfully, it failed to go off. We were lucky because there didn't seem to be people stirring up trouble in our community, yet we have people from both sides of the religious divide, living side by side.

They get along fine, which shows it can be done. The problem is, all you need is one idiot and he destroys it all. I have to say I don't know why it is always Northern Ireland that gets the brickbats. There are probably more murders committed in London and Birmingham, but you don't see the intense focus given to those places. I wish people could see the good things in life, rather than focus entirely on the bad things and give prominence to the bad people. The media are especially guilty of this.

You cannot completely ignore incidents of great evil. No one is suggesting that. But there are many good things that you can find in society if you want to look for them. For example, there are a heck of a lot of good kids around today. Yes, even in Northern Ireland. Especially in Northern Ireland. They are all quietly going about building their lives, achieving things and helping others, but you rarely hear of them. Those kids never get the acknowledgement they deserve for their efforts. They're rarely mentioned; it's the bad ones you hear about all the time.

We would do well to remember that there are problems all over the world. The part of the world I inhabit is not so bad after all. In fact, I think it has a huge amount to commend it. The people are wonderful, the food produced locally is superb, the scenery is magnificent and the strong sense of community is all you could want. I'll never be dragged away from it.

CHAPTER 15

A Game That Went Backwards

When I played, we were not allowed to receive a thing. There was no Man of the Match award, nothing at all, because it was total amateurism. Or so we were told . . . Not that it bothered me. I made friends all over the world by playing the game; I got so much out of it; by the time I retired it was as though I had a bounty chest full of treasure. The friendships I made were worth far more to me than a pay packet at the end of a rugby game, but then I was never one to collect material things. Yes, if I was given an award when I retired I was very pleased and it has a place in my home today, but with other things, I gave them away as fast as I could.

For instance, I don't have a single rugby jersey left in my cupboard from my playing career. Ballymena, Ulster, Ireland, the Barbarians, the British Lions – not a single one. I gave them all away to charity or to various clubs. I am an Honorary Member of a few clubs like Coleraine, Trinity College, Dublin, Ballyclare, Larne; they all have jerseys of mine now. I knew that they would only be lying in my attic, rotting, years later. So if money could be raised for good causes from them, far rather that than having the vicarious pleasure of thinking they were somewhere in a cupboard.

What of my rugby blazers? They are long gone. I grew out of them. The ties? You can imagine how many of those I collected down the years, but there is a funny story about them. A friend of ours is a bank manager and his wife, Joan Hayes, has always been very talented with her hands; knitting, sewing, all that sort of thing. One day when she was here, she asked me if I had any old ties that I didn't want. I told her she was the person I had been waiting for, because I had faithfully kept all the ties I had ever been given. I went out to the garage and got a big plastic bag. In our bedroom I opened the cupboard and filled the entire bag full of the things. There must have been hundreds of them. I went downstairs and said, 'There you are. I wish you'd asked me years ago.' The woman nearly passed out with surprise at seeing so many ties. Penny nearly passed out with shock, too, because she'd been on at me to get rid of them for years. Anyway, I never thought any more of it and, frankly, I was glad of the space I had created in the cupboard.

Two or three months later, we bumped into Joan somewhere and she said, 'You must come and see what I've done with your ties.' I had completely forgotten about them. When we got to her home, she brought out this wonderful quilt spread. It was about six feet square. She had cut the ends off the ties, and stitched all the broad pieces together into a colourful design. It was unbelievable. She had embroidered the letters 'Willie John' across the front of the quilt and also embroidered a pipe. It was made as a wall hanging, but could just as well have served as a bedspread.

She said to me, 'There you are, you take it and do whatever you want with it.' My heart sank. I'd got rid of the ties and now they were threatening to come back into my life. So I said, 'Look, I don't want it, but if you don't, why don't you take it to some charity shop or maybe raffle it. You might get a few pounds for a good cause.' Which is what she did. There was a big raffle coming up at that time at the Culloden Hotel, just outside Belfast, and they put it into that. And do you know what? Someone paid an astonishing amount of money for it – £2,500. I could not believe my ears when I heard. Joan also made a couple of huge cushions from the ends of the ties and they too were superb. I was delighted a charity had benefited to such an extent, but it was all because of Joan's wonderful work.

So all the detritus from a lifetime's association with the game has gone, but not the things that really matter to me, because the point is, people have always meant the most to me, not baubles. Friendships are the essence of my life, not goods. The one item I treasure most from my playing days is a simple, silver-plate water jug of no great value, which sits on the ledge in my sitting room at home. Why is it special? Because the inscription on it reads, 'To Willie John, it was great to travel with you. British Isles Rugby Union Team, 1974'. That means everything to me, because it reminds me not so much of winning a Lions Test series, but of the friendships we created throughout that tour. Those were friendships that have lasted ever since and that is why that one jug is so important in my mind.

So at the end of it all, what has the game given me? Well, it has been so much a part of my life. It took me out of a very small, inward background and helped me develop as a person. I was fortunate to have the breaks I got so early in my life. Not only did it give me those broader horizons in life, but also it taught me an awful lot about people; how we are all so different; how we need to live with each other. It taught me that you can't go through life fighting with each other, because life is very short. I'm sixty-four now and it is like a flick of your hand. I remember when I was in my teens and people would talk about a hundred years ago. I would think to myself, that's another world away it's so long ago, but today it's nothing.

What I learned most of all was that you only go this way once, so make the most of it. Luckily, I have been one of those people who, when opportunity has knocked, has grabbed it. I keep saying that to young people today – when a chance arises, snatch it, seize the moment, because it may not come up again.

I used to feel that I learned more on a rugby tour than in thirty years of banking, but I brought all those things from the rugby field into my banking career. I never forgot that you are only as good collectively as the weakest man in your team, whether it be in sport or business. So you have to learn how to cover the weaknesses, how to encourage others to cover them, but also to find and use the best of the abilities of the most weakest man, so that he too can feel important. We can all live together and there is a place for us all, but we are different in so many ways. Some people have to be kicked on the backside to get them going, others need a gentle pat on the head to encourage them. It is knowing how to get the best out of all these different types of people that makes it such a fascinating challenge.

Rugby has given me all that. The lessons I learned from it helped me not only in my own life, but also in my career and all the things with which I have been involved. That is one of the things that worries me about professionalism in rugby football. The late Vernon Pugh talked of the way forward for the sport, but I ask now, 'Have we gone forward?' It seems to me that in so many ways the game has gone backwards. For example, have we forgotten why we played this game for over a hundred years?

I certainly fear that so many of the great qualities the game espoused for young men have now gone. I am talking about the ethos of the game, about the development of young men, about teamwork, about tolerance, about building character . . . all the good things you try to teach men. These are values that you could take from the rugby field into your day at work, because it was the same thing. It was about the setting of standards, about bringing human beings together for a common cause, a fine purpose. It was part of life and that was the way it was. However, I fear so much of that has gone today, because we do seem to have forgotten why we played this game for so long. It certainly wasn't for money, but unfortunately, everything today is about profit. Yet that is incompatible with the whole raison d'etre of rugby football.

I have been going to Ballymena Rugby Club for over forty years and you don't do that without having a deep love for what it offered. I played on that ground, supported them, helped out on the administrative side. I played my guts out and lost blood on that ground, for that club. You cannot walk away from all that without feeling something very close to you. So today, when I see those young guys who are now wearing the famous jersey of Ballymena, I just hope they have the same feelings that I had when I was out there representing the club. I felt a pride in wearing that jersey, a pride in being a part of all that it stood for. I am delighted to see this carrying on, still vibrant despite the difficulties that professionalism has laid in its path.

I have always been proud of the management of our club. Unlike some, we have had a sensible approach to life. We never got carried away through the change to professionalism. We handled it very well and ensured that we cut our coat according to our cloth. The fact is, we are still there; we have survived, unlike some others who have been forced to merge or have just died.

I have been out of it now for three years, but last year, the club showed a surplus and that is very difficult to achieve nowadays. It was proof that good men are continuing to run our club, sensible people who are fine custodians of the club's future. I just wish I could say the same thing about all the clubs of Northern Ireland and, indeed, of so many other parts of the British Isles and Ireland. For the fact is, professionalism has been a painful experience for so many simple rugby clubs in this part of the world.

I remember going to a meeting of clubs in Dublin after professionalism had been thrown at us and standing up and speaking about the decision. It had been thrown at us because the decision had been made in complete haste. Nothing had been planned about it. One day the game was strictly amateur, the next totally open and professional. I said it was total rubbish to make it an open game and tell everyone they could be professional. I said then that everyone under the level of provincial rugby should remain amateur. I said that if there was even a question about money being paid to players below that level in Ireland, then I thought they should be dealt with in a disciplinary manner. I still believe that firmly today.

Look at the cost of professionalism to the structure of our game. Some of the finest clubs have gone. The club that produced the great Jackie Kyle and Mike Gibson, North of Ireland Football Club, is one of them. They couldn't cope with professionalism, so they had to amalgamate, which is very sad. There are many others that have declined, too, throughout the British Isles and France, clubs that were once household names, such as Pontypool, Pontypridd and Aberavon in South Wales, Coventry and Blackheath in England, Lourdes and Dax in France. Even clubs in my area, like Ballymena and Dungannon, hardly ever have their best players playing for them because they are with the provincial sides run by the IRFU.

I believe there must be players in the modern game who are totally frustrated by it. Take a guy like Brian O'Driscoll, the Ireland and 2001 British Lions centre. If he had played in my day, Brian would not only have been a world star, but would have had the time of his life in terms of enjoyment and giving full rein to his attacking ambitions. That's because it was those little passes, the little flashes of skill and inspiration, that made world stars, but the modern game does not permit those things, except on very rare occasions.

Perhaps the aspect that bewilders me most is how the issue was able to pass an entire committee and become part of the whole game. I understood before that fateful meeting in Paris in August 1995 that there was a majority against the notion of professionalism. Yes, the southern hemisphere countries may have accepted a huge sum from Rupert Murdoch, but that did not mean the entire northern hemisphere had to rush to sign up to the notion. The influence of the late Vernon Pugh troubles me, because here was a man who came from a country where the game was already an absolute shambles and had been for the better part of fifteen years. Yet he was the guy who presided over its arrival, without even so much as a vote taking place. I find that extraordinary.

Professionalism arrived in a sport completely overwhelmed by the notion. Nobody was in the remotest sense prepared for it. Thus, as in life generally, what you do in haste, you repent at leisure. I have to say that, if that had been a board of governors running a school, given the subsequent mess and chaos, the guy at the top who had presided over it all would have been sacked. Yet the man at the top of world rugby was able to survive, despite forcing the game into a quantum leap from which it still shows little sign of really recovering and allowing 100 years of history to disappear overnight.

I believe Pugh was weak in his chairmanship. He allowed this to happen. The representatives of the game who sat at that table in Paris were also weak, because they should have insisted on a vote being taken. The representatives from our home unions went to the meeting with the instruction that we were not ready for professionalism. They should have said, 'We have to plan for it.' This is one of the problems of rugby football – no one is ever accountable. It is still the same today. The game has paid the price for that weak leadership ever since.

These were men whom the game at large had put in the position of controlling and administering rugby football, yet they abandoned their responsibility to the sport that day and all we have had ever since is crisis management. Over the years, the IRB has not directed the game, taking it forward in a logical, sensible way, but I have to say I am heartened by the fact that a man who understands the game, Syd Millar, is now at the top of the IRB. With Syd's background in the sport, he is very aware that the ethos of the game has been damaged. Let us hope that he can recover some of the things that have been lost.

The only way the game can now survive, what is left of it anyway, is for a firm line to be drawn under which nobody can pay anyone anything for participation in the sport. To have players running around the world of junior clubs earning a grubby £50 or £100 a week or match, and then clearing off to join another club the minute the first one looks as though it has financial troubles, is an utter nonsense.

Some have said the die is cast and nothing can be done, but to accept that and say we can't do anything about it is to give in. I am not prepared to do that. Today, you have kids coming out of school and going around clubs asking what sort of package they have for them. These kids haven't proved anything when they leave school. They haven't earned any respect either as rugby players or young people, but they're demanding and often receiving top dollar because the clubs accept this sort of nonsense. I find that absolutely horrendous.

Rugby shouldn't be throwing away that role of upholding standards and I'll tell you why – because our game is dying. In Ulster last year there were dozens less teams playing the game than the year before. Some clubs who were turning out six teams each week are now struggling to fill a couple. It is just the same in England and Wales, to mention just two other countries. Yes, even England, despite their World Cup win. There is something dreadfully wrong when that is happening and I believe it is a widespread disillusionment with the game and what it has become.

Because of professionalism, people regard rugby today chiefly as a money-making business and fewer and fewer people at the lower levels feel an affinity with that kind of organisation. OK, they'll go and watch a big international match here and there, but they are actively participating, either on or off the field, in fewer and fewer numbers. That is why I say the game is dying and I fear professionalism will prove to have been the stake through its heart. There will always be some form of rugby played, but if you are judging it against the vibrant, healthy sport that I knew some years ago, then it is hard to avoid the conclusions I have reached.

No one hears the word 'loyalty' mentioned in conjunction with rugby football any more. That, too, is a cause for great sadness. You play now where you get offered the top pay packet and if someone else offers you more, you go there. This is the reality of professional football and professional rugby is merely following it down that unappealing path.

I like to think my club, Ballymena, has stuck very closely with the ethos of the game. I'd also like to think I played a part in that. We don't pay our players. The only ones who are paid are the Ulster players who are funded by the IRFU. What we do is provide them with the best coaching possible. I personally flew to South Africa a few years ago to recruit the former Springbok Neelie Smith as our new coach and I then got three local businessmen to cover the costs, because the club couldn't afford to do it. They felt the town had been very good to them in business and they happily accepted my suggestion that they could put something back, if you like, in this particular way.

At Ballymena, we feel we have a vibrant club. We won the All Ireland League title in 2003 under our Australian coach Tony D'Arcy, a man who understands the meaning of involving the whole community in club affairs. Never forget, if you don't have the people behind you, you won't have a club. Another good thing is that Ballymena are still turning out six teams every week, which is what we always used to do. Yet even we are confronting immense difficulties. The sixth team struggles to get fixtures, which means we may have to give it up. You cannot escape the outside influences that are occurring in the game at large. But this malaise affects all of Ireland, not just the north. As I say, there is a similar story to be heard in the other home unions.

The conclusion to all this is that you cannot run professional-ism and amateurism together. A lot of clubs have already said they wish to return to amateurism and end this absurdity of having to pay some players from money that would otherwise go into the club for the greater benefit of everyone, not just a single, greedy indi-vidual. The sooner ninety-eight per cent of the game returns to the concept of amateurism, the better. What is needed is a new amateur administration to look after amateur rugby in Ireland. Rugby is a very small game in this country anyway and if it is going to survive in the next ten years, then we need a governing body that is going to be solely focused on picking up the game, looking after it and making it strong again.

There is a clear and obvious danger to Irish rugby here. If the club scene that nurtures the stars of tomorrow is allowed to decay and die, then where are we going to get the players who are going to grow up to be the internationals of the future? Ireland, not to mention Wales and Scotland, cannot go running all over the world for very much longer for its future team members. Anyway, there won't be any interest left in the sport in this country if it is allowed to contract so significantly.

Or are the authorities now so preoccupied with the professional game that they don't really care what happens to the junior game and all those clubs that were once the bedrock of the entire sport? Are they planning simply to have a series of professional academies from which future international players can be groomed? If that happens is it not like some American sports, where the game is played at school and college, but then there is a great vacuum before you reach the professional ranks? Is that the bleak future rugby is facing? I sincerely hope not, because if it is, then our generation will stand charged with abandoning and deserting a once great sport that was played with enthusiasm at every level.

I will say here and now that if rugby union does not get this separate amateur administration in Ireland, the game will die.

Hundreds, if not thousands, of people whom the game badly needed have already walked away from it. This is a huge blow to the sport, because it was developed by volunteers; people giving their free time to make the teas, cut the grass, wash the kit, serve in the bars and sweep the dressing rooms clean. All those jobs that have to be done by someone. So many of those people are no longer there today because if you make a game professional, who do you not pay and why? A lot of these good people have walked away in disgust.

I talked of a ten-year time scale to save the game and I meant it. That was no hypothetical figure plucked out of the air for no good reason. Time is short because society is changing with alarming speed. We live in a different world and young people are already finding other things to do with their time. Many have already drifted away from the sport, pursuing other interests. Now maybe a country like England, with its huge playing numbers, is better able to withstand the loss of certain numbers of participants. But a country like Ireland can't; it doesn't have a sufficiently large playing base to begin with. Rugby football is only the fourth most popular sport in winter here and there is no way it can afford to suffer a similar loss of support.

What also depresses me about professionalism is that it snatched away all the assets that had been established over a century of tradition in the game. The great grounds like Lansdowne Road, Murrayfield, Cardiff and Twickenham were taken under the professional umbrella, hijacked like some security van crammed full of money. Yet volunteers who had given long hours, indeed years, of service had helped create the money that established those grounds. If those individuals had not worked on behalf of the game, then they had supported it with their hard-earned money. That was what made the rugby unions individually worthwhile in a financial sense. But suddenly, all that was professional and lost to the amateur side. Which was very clever. Because only very rarely nowadays does the average club player get the opportunity to play on those grounds. That's another sad loss.

But these days, of course, under professionalism, England has all the money, all the players and all the support of business in London. And that is taking those assets away from the other countries in the home unions. England will rule the roost in the years to come, as I see it, not only in the Six Nations, but world-wide. Their victory in the 2003 World Cup was probably just the start of this process.

Another down side to the professional game is that, because it has a voracious appetite for money, in financial terms the game has been taken beyond the reach of so many average club members. Asking a father who wants to take his son to an international match to pay around £200 for a single day out is obscene. How do I arrive at such a figure? Most match tickets at the international grounds now cost around £50 or more. Then add on the expense of travel from your home in another part of the country, parking, a programme, some lunch and perhaps a souvenir and you might be lucky to keep it to £200. To see one game of rugby lasting eighty minutes? I cannot believe I am the only person who thinks such an amount is ridiculous.

All these prices have done is drive away from the game the ordinary club supporter, with the corporate world taking more tickets. The people who now attend may know nothing about the game, but they have the money to be there. That seems to be the sole criterion as far as the home unions are concerned nowadays, because they are so desperate to make money at every turn. Even if ordinary supporters want to splash out that amount of money, their chances of getting tickets are increasingly slim, because so many go to the big corporate sponsors.

This, therefore, is not the game I grew up with and came to love. You can make excuses for rugby by saying that society has altered so much and rugby is no different. But I don't believe the game can excuse itself by hiding behind society's failings, because rugby used to be about setting standards, not tamely following the worst elements of society. At one time, it stood above the rest, showing a better way, better standards and principles. But no longer. It is now reduced to the level of any other professional sport; scrabbling around to try and snare the punter's pound – or euro. The standards that persuaded people to say, 'Let's go and play this game because it sets standards for life, about life,' are gone.

I am not saying the sport can isolate itself from all reality and the outside world. What I am saying is that professionalism can go and do its own thing and, if it is prepared to, reflect modern-day society with its declining standards and disappointments. My point is that the amateur game should be continuing to offer young people an environment where they can learn and understand about values, for where it exists this game should still be part of the local communities. Clubs need to focus on their communities because that is where they will find their future players and officials. But they won't find those people if they are tied to a professional game that bears little relation to all the good things for which the sport was once renowned. The game has lost its way, but it shouldn't have done so. I want to see the amateur side of it recover its health and, if possible, its prosperity.

There are encouraging signs that, in Ireland anyway, these matters are slowly being faced up to. It is clear the IRFU are also worried about the way the game has gone, because they have lost huge amounts of money this year and you can't go on like that. Also, a lot of people are extremely angry that so much money has been squandered on a bunch of players who simply were not worth the money they received. That money could have been used for the greater good of the game.

You see, you don't get improved facilities, more work in the community, healthier junior clubs or anything like that through professionalism. All that happens is that players earn ridiculous sums of money and are able to afford equally absurd motor cars to run around in. Prop forwards driving Porsches means that someone is paying them a large amount of money. Too much, in my opinion. Professional soccer demonstrates this.

Nor is it only the players squandering money. There is a huge gravy train rolling around all the national rugby unions of the world. Officials are living a life of which they can only have ever dreamed; first-class travel all the way, five-star hotels, the best meals, the finest wines, the best of everything. But someone has to pay for it all. That vehicle, I believe, is being abused. Consequently, we are not getting the administration the game needs and we are not seeing accountability.

Administration was a common failing even in the old world of rugby football and I don't think we can blame professionalism for the failings of the sport in that direction. I'll give you an example of what I mean. At one time when I was involved with the Ulster Rugby Union, the committee was asked to agree a new design for its letterhead. It seemed to me, as I sat at that table, that this was just a rubber-stamp job. I looked at the new design and thought it was fine.

But the old committee members reacted as though we had decided to relocate the Ravenhill ground to London's Isle of Dogs. Hours and hours were spent arguing over this new-style design on more than one evening. Some people said, 'We've had this since the Ulster branch was formed, why should we change it now?' The arguments dragged on until I said, 'For God's sake, all we're trying to do is modernise the letterhead.' I was in charge of the public relations and marketing, but it was as though I'd proposed something completely imbecilic. In the end, I had to keep going back to this committee, but facing me were guys with hearing aids, saying 'We can't see the need for change. It looks all right to us.'

Perhaps that was a microcosm of those people who ended up in charge of rugby football. People in blazers and club ties who meant well but, in reality, stood in the way of progress in the game. Is it any wonder, I find myself asking, that with those people in charge, we ended up with an almighty split through which professionalism marched in. Might not we have avoided so cataclysmic an event if some reality had been shown in previous years and some manoeuvrability had been allowed when the debate about payment for time spent away on tours raged? I suspect the game could have held together if that had been allowed. As it was, we had the authorities saying, 'No, no, no – a thousand times, no,' to any request by the players. In the end, all that happened was that the dam burst and the whole game as we knew it drowned. But that's rugby football for you. At times, you feel great pride in a sport you have known all your life. But on other occasions, you just think to yourself, 'Oh God.'

In 1994, for instance, we had a twentieth-anniversary reunion of the 1974 British Lions in Northern Ireland. It was held in Belfast at the Culloden Hotel and was organised by Newtownards Round Table. All proceeds were to go to local charities. That weekend, the Ulster Cup final was on at Ravenhill and it was tremendous for Syd Millar and myself to have the 1974 Lions in Ulster and to attend the Cup final which, at that time, was one of the most important fixtures at Ravenhill.

I felt all the city would feel it an enormous privilege to have the Lions there and, indeed, it seemed a great opportunity for the Ulster branch of the IRFU to host a unique gathering. I was on the Ulster committee at the time and I told them we should get a photographer to take a picture of the squad and put it up on the wall at Ravenhill, to remind people of the day the most successful Lions ever came to Belfast. Please don't misunderstand me – it wasn't so that I could bask in any reflected glory. I just wanted Ulster to make a fuss of the boys and show them what great Northern Ireland hospitality was about.

Well, the crowd made a great fuss of us when we went out on to the field before the match, but afterwards, when we went into the committee rooms, we just hung around, had a beer or two and no one said a thing. There was no one making a little welcoming speech, saying how honoured and delighted the people of Ulster were to have this great Lions squad there. Players had come from all corners of the United Kingdom, but there was nothing like that and they'd even forgotten, or not bothered, to get a photographer. I writhed in embarrassment. So in the end, we climbed into the coach and drove away and I, as a proud Ulsterman, thought to myself, 'Why the hell did we even bother coming here?' It saddened me no end.

The reason it was like that? I don't think the people in charge had a clue as to how to go about organising anything. I'm sure they didn't mean to be discourteous. Believe me, no true Ulsterman needs to have the meaning of the word hospitality explained to him. But having said that, there was this awful empty feeling as we drove away. There are times when you feel very let down by this game, great as it undoubtedly has been.

I can say with hand on heart that I wouldn't want to be a professional sportsman today, because you have to do as you're told. You become owned the minute you sign a contract for financial reward. In my day, anything I did, I did voluntarily. If I didn't want to play, I didn't. It was as simple as that. Today you sign your contract and you are at the whim and mercy of your employer, usually someone who has no allegiance whatsoever to rugby football. More than likely, he is just someone trying to make as much money out of it as he can. Or as you can. Is it any wonder those values for which the game once used to stand have been blown away, like so many autumn leaves on the winds of early winter? Nor is that so fanciful an analogy as some might think, because I fear we have seen the great summer of rugby football. What will ensue in years to come may prove to be the long, hard winter.

I never took a single penny throughout my career for playing rugby football. No pound notes stuffed into my boots, no plain brown envelopes as I walked out of the dressing room, slipped covertly into my overcoat pocket. Just a cheery wave, a 'well done' or 'bad luck', and invariably a 'see you in the bar'. That was all. But I have absolutely no envy whatsoever for the guys playing rugby for big money. I wouldn't swap my years with them for anything; no, not even the £500,000 to £1 million a year players like England captain Martin Johnson and outside-half Jonny Wilkinson were said to be set to earn when they helped their country win the World Cup in Australia in late 2003. When I look back, I feel I played in a great era. I have wonderful memories, great friends and had a hell of a lot of fun. I don't know where the fun is today in the game and a life just focusing intently on rugby matches and videos of opponents would certainly not have been for me.

While on the subject of the 2003 World Cup, I'm glad that it was a very successful event. I was there from the quarter-finals onwards and saw England's triumph in the final in Sydney. It was well deserved. I watched the early part of the tournament from my armchair at home and, I have to say, I found it irrelevant. It was, by and large, a series of matches between the major countries of the world against those from the emerging nations, but no one learns anything from one-sided contests that end with scores of 80–nil or 100–nil. What else could Namibia feel but demoralised after losing 142–0 to Australia? That wasn't a match, it was a joke.

Mis-matches like this should not be played in a World Cup. You cannot mix amateur and professional within the game, running both together. Run them side by side, certainly, but not together. Golf is a sport that splits amateur and professional successfully. You don't get an amateur club player thrown up against Tiger Woods once every four years. It is ridiculous. Both thrive in their own separate environment.

I am not saying those countries should not be in the World Cup, but they should be playing opponents from their own level. They should be developing their game outside the World Cup, not using it to try and do that. It demeans the game to have such one-sided matches that you can't even call contests. All it does is say to the watching world that this is not a sport of worldwide strength. I believe there should be a competition between the emerging nations with the top two going through into the World Cup proper.

However, in terms of the tournament as a whole, I thought it was superbly run by the Australian Rugby Union and marvellously supported by the people of Australia. They virtually managed to fill the grounds, which was always one of my criticisms of past World Cups. I was most disappointed with France. I thought they were coming good, but they flopped badly in the semi-final against England. Two of the leading southern hemisphere nations, New Zealand and South Africa, also disappointed me. They never really threatened to win the tournament, yet conversely, Australia came through a disappointing beginning to finish on a very high note. I thought the Wallabies gave tremendous performances against New Zealand and England.

Maybe the final was not the greatest game I have ever seen from a technical point of view, but it had tremendous atmosphere and was played in great spirit. I don't think you could write a script for such a final, but it was typical of rugby football that, after all those games, one dropped goal should decide the World Cup. I am delighted England won and were able to bring the World Cup out of the southern hemisphere for the first time. They deserved it, for they were the most consistent team in the whole tournament. Everyone in the northern hemisphere will benefit from this win. Now, everyone wants to beat England and that is good and healthy. Ireland's win over them at Twickenham in March 2004 was a good example of this.

The truth is, England didn't play anywhere near their best rugby in the world cup, but they did the simple things of rugby football that I remember so well. They scrummaged well, had a good, strong line-out, were powerful in the rucks and mauls and their defence was superb. There was something else I liked about England. Their side was filled with Englishmen and they were coached by Englishmen. In my view, Scotland and Wales have suffered in recent years because they have chosen too many foreigners. My advice to them is, fix your game from the bottom up, not from the top down, before it is beyond repair. We have to develop young players from within our own countries, not go off raiding places like Australia and New Zealand for players with tenuous qualifications. In fairness to Ireland, they have not done that very often, but Scotland and Wales have.

The fact that England built their successful campaign on the basics of the game proved that Super 12 rugby in the southern hemisphere does not enhance rugby football. It enhances television coverage, that is all. But New Zealand, South Africa and Australia all suffered because of that. Such a style of rugby will not win World Cups, but it is now proven beyond doubt that there is very little difference between the northern and southern hemispheres. The performance of Ireland in the quarter-final against Australia demonstrated that.

It would have been nice for Ireland to reach the semi-finals, which they would surely have done had they beaten Australia rather than losing to them by a single point in Melbourne. But we in Ireland have lived on dreams for years and, once more, we nearly did it, but not quite. I think we always know our capabilities. It was nice we reached the quarter-final and nice we put up such a performance. France had us well beaten at half-time and it was possibly a game too far for the personnel that we had out there, yet they gave it their all. As for Irish rugby's future now, I believe they have to look at the grass roots of the game, see where the problems are and get to grips with them. The professional game will look after itself in many ways; it is the base that we have to strengthen, because if it keeps going the way it is, the base will disappear and then we won't have a peak to the pyramid.

If England don't build on this success they will be silly, but they have the same problems as we do in Ireland, even though it may not be as obvious in England. Even their Premiership clubs still have a lot of financial worries, but it is the base of the game that most concerns me and needs attention.

As for New Zealand, I was disappointed that they have gone so far away from what I remembered and admired about All Blacks rugby. The game is obviously under a lot of stress in that country at the present time, but I was especially disappointed in their forward play. It seems to me they are depending far too much on island players to fill the All Blacks side and that surely reflects the pressure on the sport in New Zealand itself, where so many young white children are no longer playing the game. That is because they cannot compete physically at younger ages with the tough, powerful island boys who mature so much quicker. The Maoris have contributed some outstanding players to New Zealand rugby down the years – players I knew in my time like Waka Nathan, Mac Herewini, Billy Bush and plenty of others. I enjoyed many good nights with Waka at various times when I visited New Zealand.

However, to see a New Zealand pack struggle like the All Blacks did in the semi-final against Australia was astonishing. I thought back to the days of strong men like the Meads brothers, Whineray, Gray, Tremain, Nathan and Lochore, and it seemed inconceivable that New Zealand rugby had descended so far. Where are the likes of those players today in New Zealand? Where is the current generation of powerful young men? Obviously, players like that are no longer coming through and that has to be a major concern to the New Zealand rugby authorities.

Perhaps the most heartening thing of all at last year's World Cup was the sight of Wales scoring brilliant tries and giving strong countries like England and New Zealand so many difficulties. They played simple, traditional Welsh rugby, which I recognised and remembered. They took on the might of England and frightened the hell out of them. They threw the challenge at England and, for a time, found them wanting. In many ways, they exposed England and could have won the game.

I just hope Wales build on those performances in time for the 2007 World Cup. They must have gained a lot of confidence from that experience but, of course, long before the next World Cup, we shall focus on the 2005 Lions tour to New Zealand. Yet even Lions tours today seem only an extension of the monotonous regime these guys endure day in, day out, through their entire sporting lives. Ye Gods! The fun we had on those tours was legendary, but coaches today who take Lions teams away are being paid, and everyone they are working with is also a professional, so they probably feel they are justified in demanding an intense approach that never falters.

We saw the cost of this intensity during the 2001 British Lions tour of Australia. They were being flogged, mentally and physically, so by the time they came to the last Test, they had nothing left to give. There had been no real switch-off period for the players. The tour had been rushed, squeezed into just a few weeks, and recreation time was virtually nil. No one there had the vision or opportunity in such a manic schedule to say, let's give them three or four days off, right away from a rugby field. Let them climb this mountain or go down to this resort and have a piss-up and a bit of fun. Bring them back on Wednesday morning bright and fresh and they will work hard in preparation for the vital match.

This isn't rocket science, but it alarms me how few coaches today understand that simple precept that you cannot expect human beings to go on and on without a complete break. This is manifested in the amount of top level rugby that is being played today. Frankly, it is obscene, but no one challenges it because it is all designed to make more money for the national unions and because television says it wants to show the matches. So that's all right then – or so most people seem to think.

Vernon Pugh talked of the way forward. Rugby football, in my view, has gone backwards in so many ways. Players are twice the size now physically but are their skills twice as good? Players of smaller stature have all but been excluded from the top level game. For the few improvements there have been, such as the greatly enhanced mobility and ball handling skills of the forwards in the modern game, we have paid a price. Where are the Gareth Edwards, the Mike Gibsons and Barry Johns, the Phil Bennetts, the J.P.R. Williams of today? Let us hope the game will once again evolve towards players of this quality.

I remember someone telling me of a conversation he had had with a former Scottish rugby international a few years ago. The player was entering the twilight of his career when professionalism came in, but managed to have two or three final years earning some reasonable money. Then came the time to finish. 'Was he envious of the money which players of the future would be making from the game?' he was asked. He smiled. 'In the years to come, people will come up to me and say, "You were lucky. You played in the great days of rugby football."' he said. How true I suspect that remark is already proving to be. What we have today in the game is a kind of hybrid version of the sport we once knew. It is not the same game and now never will be – which is one hell of a shame.

I too am delighted that I played my rugby when I did. I loved the great qualities for which the sport was famous, such as honesty, friendship and concern for others and their well-being. Nothing will ever take away my pleasure and pride in having played in one of rugby's great times.

A Hell of a Man

I t seems to be obligatory for former sportsmen writing books to delve into the archives to nominate their best ever XV, the team with which they would like to have played, in some fantasy world. They trawl laboriously through every position, discussing candidates for this team which will never come together, never smell the liniment and never play a single game. That seems to me a bit of a waste of time. I don't mind telling you about a few players I admired hugely during my playing days, but I'll only dally briefly in that arena before finishing by talking about someone for whom I felt a very close affinity and whose early death shattered me.

Of all the opponents I faced in my playing days, none bettered the great All Blacks team of the early 1960s. I would honestly say one of the great combinations in the history of second row pairings was Colin and Stan Meads. It was a wonderful partnership. We know all about Colin, for his reputation crossed the oceans, but Stan was a great player, too; a superb line-out forward who could also get around the field and handle the ball.

Then you had someone like Kel Tremain, who was at the peak of his career at that time. Also in that pack was Ken Gray, one of the greatest prop forwards I ever saw in my life. The same goes for Waka Nathan, in a different position – open side flanker. He was a player who was absolutely everywhere and I've never seen a guy who covered the field like him. Alongside him at No. 8 was the towering presence of Brian Lochore, a genuine ball-handling No. 8 forward. The captain of this team of teams was Wilson Whineray, a real gentleman and a marvellous leader of men. Perhaps it was no surprise they were so good with him in charge but, really, the quality of that New Zealand pack probably made them the best set of eight forwards I ever saw in my life.

I talked earlier about great Irish players and, in my view, I never saw better than Mike Gibson. He was one of the most talented all-round players the game can ever have seen. His maturity and vision on the field, his solid defence and eye for an attacking opportunity made him a player even other internationals envied for his talents. I felt 1971 was his peak, for I always saw him more as a centre than a fly half, and on that year's Lions tour he played in midfield with Barry John and John Dawes. In terms of quality, that was about as good as it gets. Mike wasn't superb only in attack, but also in defence and, like me, he was around for a long, long time.

I have talked about the many French rugby men for whom I held a deep respect. It was similar in Wales. I came to know players like Gareth Edwards and Barry John, Gerald Davies and J.P.R. Williams, J.J. Williams and John Dawes, Phil Bennett, Mervyn Davies, John Taylor and Bobby Windsor, not only during the Five Nations Championship but more especially on those Lions tours. I saw the supreme talents of all those men, and many others, close up during those trips. Suffice to say, I came home more than aware that they had played a fulsome role in our triumphs of 1971 and 1974.

But someone else had played an immense part in what the British Lions achieved in South Africa in 1974. I began this book with the story of our success there, exactly thirty years ago this summer, and it is appropriate that I end this tale with the memory of one of those Lions who will not be at our thirtieth reunion this year. His name was Gordon Brown and he was one hell of a man. I first came across G.L. Brown of the West of Scotland club at Lansdowne Road, Dublin, on 28 February 1970. I'd been around a bit by then. In fact, that day I was winning my thirty-fourth cap. Brown, by contrast, was a mere starter, winning just his fourth cap for Scotland in only his second season of international rugby.

At one stage during that game, Ireland looked like running up a cricket score against the Scots. We had scored four tries to nil at one point, but then came what we knew existed deep in Scottish bellies: a fightback of some substance. They scored two late tries and lost only 16–11, when it could have been a rout. Young Brown in the second row was clearly one of those who could raise his game when the need arose, I noted.

Our paths crossed again when he was chosen for the 1971 Lions tour of New Zealand. He was initially regarded as no more than third or fourth choice lock. However, with a spirit that reminded me of what I had set out to do (and achieved) in seizing a Test place on the 1962 Lions tour from a senior player, Gordon Brown forced his way into the side for the third and fourth Tests. He packed down alongside me in both those games, having been selected ahead of Delme Thomas. In fact, Gordon got injured during the final Test and was replaced by Delme, but Scotland had clearly unearthed a rugged gem.

Then, in 1974, he came on tour and won the Test place for the first three Tests, until injury kept him out of the fourth and final international. But by then, having scored a try in both the second and third Tests, he had more than emphasised his enormous value to the side. He and I became very close on that tour. He was thrilled to be a Lion, because that meant he had achieved what he had always set out to do in his sporting life. That gave him no end of pleasure.

Gordon was no perfect performer, though, not on the training ground, anyway. He was the first to admit that. He often needed geeing up and sometimes you had to give him a real verbal kicking to get him going, for he was at heart a lazy bugger. He had the enthusiasm but didn't want to do the work sometimes. However, we got him really fit in 1974 and he was tremendous. Gareth was Gareth, Benny was little Benny, dazzling and delightful, J.J. Williams was a runner of coruscating skills and the front row was superb. Then you had Mervyn Davies, Fergus Slattery and Roger Uttley in the back row, an absolutely champion combination. But if anyone typified the spirit, commitment and never-say-die attitude of that British Lions pack of forwards, it was Gordon Brown. He was immense throughout that tour. He took the punches and returned them with relish; he made his great storming runs in the loose and battled mightily to secure line-out ball. If ever a player was inspirational, it was he.

When he retired, the game banned him, predictably, for writing a book, but he started working on the after-dinner speaking circuit and became most successful. People loved his cheery humour, his lovely open face, which was usually creased with laughter, and his jokes. A few times, he and I did a double act together and we had wonderful nights full of laughter. We laughed and laughed until we ached. At one dinner at London's Grosvenor House Hotel, in front of about 1,500 people, Gordon helped raise the astonishing sum of £65,000 for charity through an auction. But that was Gordon; always laughing, always cheerful, always helping out others.

Then came word that he was ill. It seemed impossible. He had been healthy, strong and fit for almost his entire career. Worse still, it wasn't just an ordinary illness, but a really serious one. Cancer. I spoke to him on the phone every week during that illness and it went on for over a year. He went through the physically draining process of chemotherapy and the news was that he was much better. He was out of hospital and walking a mile or two a day. He seemed genuinely on the road back to health. We decided to plan a celebration dinner in London; Broon of Troon, as he was known widely, was back and in excellent form again. The plans were made and the tickets sold – all for charity, of course.

I rang him about a fortnight before the scheduled dinner in London and said how much I was looking forward to seeing him. He said he'd walked a mile that day and was feeling good. There were laughs and a couple of jokes; it was like old times. But then, just forty-eight hours later, he was on the phone to me this time. When I heard his voice, I had a horrible, sinking feeling in the pit of my stomach. He used to call me Big Man, and said, 'Big Man, I've bad news. This damn thing has taken over again and it is rampant. Instead of a celebration, I have to tell you this will be the last supper. There is no hope.' This was ten days before the dinner. I thought long and hard about it that night. I turned it over in my mind again and again. Why should he be the one who was going to be taken from us? Life is so cruel sometimes, because Gordon had given so much. He loved to laugh, but he also loved people.

Well, I went to the dinner, hardly knowing what to expect. I went up to his room and there he was, exhausted by the journey from Scotland, even though it had been by private jet, with a specialist medical team travelling with him. He was that determined he was going to be there. He said, 'Big Man, I'm not good.' He was obviously in a lot of pain and was on morphine. By then, he was confined to a wheelchair, but he said, 'Tonight is for me and I'm going to walk into this dinner. I want you to come and support me with your shoulder and take me to my chair.' I told him it would be an honour and a pleasure to do that.

In those private moments, you hardly know what to say, still less how to hold in check your emotions. I may be a big man physically who played a tough sport, but I am like all others – moved to immense sadness by such moments as this, my mind a whirl of emotions and thoughts. However, I said to him, 'Gordon, I don't know what the future holds, but there is one thing you must always remember. When you and I were in partnership for the British

Lions, we were never beaten. We were undefeated.' He put his hand on my shoulder and said, 'Big Man, they'll never do it again.'

Those were some of the last words I spoke to him, but he made it to that dinner. He walked in, even though he must have been in hellish pain. By then he was also a shadow of himself. He had once been an eighteen-stone man, but this terrible illness had ravaged him. It was a most moving dinner, but an unreal one for me, because we had so many laughs. But also many tears, although Gordon didn't want that. He even got up and spoke that night; not for long, but he spoke. God knows how – sheer willpower and determination, I suspect. Ten days later he was dead. I was shattered, the tears flowed.

He was buried in his beloved Troon, on Scotland's wild, rugged west coast. I couldn't go to his funeral; it was the weekend of the Hong Kong Sevens and I was in Asia. I was sorry I missed it, but I keep telling myself I spent some of that last year with him, talking to him regularly. We were close right up to the end. I think, I hope, that was the most important thing.

Gordon did so many good things. He raised millions for charity, and I do mean millions. There was so much good in him. He contributed to society and he had so much still to offer the world when he died in 2000 at only fifty-two. Of course, it was far too young. Now, there are two types of people in life, the takers and the givers. Gordon was a giver, but he was taken from us. I confess I find that so unjust, especially when I look at the people today in society who kill, murder and maim innocent people. They survive, but Gordon died. I know not why that is.

Index